Women Shapeshifters

Transforming the Contemporary Novel

THELMA J. SHINN

Contributions in Women's Studies, Number 156

Greenwood Press
Westport, Connecticut • London

Library of Congress Cataloging-in-Publication Data

Shinn, Thelma J.
    Women shapeshifters : transforming the contemporary novel / Thelma
J. Shinn.
        p.   cm.—(Contributions in women's studies, ISSN 0147–104X
; no. 156)
    Includes bibliographical references (p.   ) and index.
    ISBN 0–313–29676–6 (alk. paper)
    1. American fiction—Women authors—History and criticism.
    2. Women and literature—United States—History—20th century.
    3. English fiction—Women authors—History and criticism.
    4. American fiction—20th century—History and criticism.
    5. English fiction—20th century—History and criticism. 6. Women
and literature—History—20th century. 7. Authorship—Sex
differences. 8. Literary form. I. Title. II. Series.
    PS374.W6S56   1996
    813'.5099287—dc20   95–40027

British Library Cataloguing in Publication Data is available.

Library of Congress Catalog Card Number: 95–40027
ISBN: 0–313–29676–6
ISSN: 0147–104X

First published in 1996

Greenwood Press, 88 Post Road West, Westport, CT 06881
An imprint of Greenwood Publishing Group, Inc.

Printed in the United States of America

The paper used in this book complies with the
Permanent Paper Standard issued by the National
Information Standards Organization (Z39.48–1984).

10 9 8 7 6 5 4 3 2

Copyright Acknowledgments

Earlier versions of some of this material have appeared in the following publications:

"Toni Cade Bambara's *The Salt Eaters*" and "A. S. Byatt's *Possession*," in *Masterplots II: Women's Literature* (Pasadena, Calif.: Salem Press, 1995).

"What's in a Word: Possessing A. S. Byatt's Meronymic Novel," *Papers on Language & Literature* (Spring 1995).

"A Pattern of Possibility in Maxine Hong Kingston's *Woman Warrior*," *Explorations in Ethnic Studies* (Spring 1994).

Women Shapeshifters

For our children's children, for whom all these stories have been told—especially in this moment to Clarissa, Jake, Aaron, Caleb, Zakary, Tyler, and Noah.

Contents

Illustrations

Preface

How can we understand each other? Language becomes increasingly necessary as the human race develops and multiplies, yet the meaning of each word of a living language is continually evolving to reflect its current usage. The connotations and weighted meanings that the word ultimately carries can reveal much about the evolution of its social setting; often, however, they can also obscure its original "story." Every word is in itself a poem, the simplest, or "root," word being the first linguistic imaging of its corresponding phenomenon. As Lavoisier has explained in *Traité Elémentaire de Chimie* (1789) in regards to the link between science and language, "To call forth a concept a word is needed; to portray a phenomenon, a concept is needed. All three mirror one and the same reality." Within a single word, therefore, concept and phenomenon, idea and reality, coexist. Words are invented by a human consciousness, which "call[s] forth a concept" by *imag*ining what expression will best communicate that concept to another human consciousness as corresponding with the phenomenon it is meant to represent. The word then can *make sense* to us, because our senses can receive both the word itself and the phenomenon imaged by the word. The concept is *not* sensually apprehendable, however, so the gift of language is that we now share with its creator an abstract idea as well as a concrete sensual experience. We will then apply that word, that linguistic image, to other occurrences of the phenomenon so named, extending and sometimes even expanding the concept as the precision of the word enables us to make and share *sensible* connections and correspondences.

Just as we connect the word with other phenomena, so too we will connect it with other concepts as we learn/create other words, eventually producing what scientists would call a taxonomic group of related terms in a classification. The almost interchangeable terms we use for the taxon that defines words recognized as such mental images are "figurative language" and "imagery," the former reminding us that language serves as an emblem of the phenomenon (a *figure* of speech) and the latter identifying the *imag*inative process that has married concept to phenomenon to produce the image. A word, therefore, is a marriage of mind and matter, of concept and phenomenon, that conveys a specific human perception of Nature. Language by extension contains in itself a culture's ideological definitions of what is real, reminding us that the word *real* means "royal" in Spanish, thus giving authority to that particular perception.

Words themselves can offer complex stories. When a word is formed by internal connections, we are moving into idiomatic language rather than language rooted in the organic principle defined by Lavoisier. We can connect the word *letter*, for instance, with each discrete part of the alphabet that can be sensually apprehended. On the other hand, the word *alphabet* is a compilation of the names given to the first two letters of the Greek alphabet. Even in its original meaning, therefore, this word depends upon the preexisting concept of *letter* and the social context of Greek words for at least two different letters. While *letter* is a literal image, *alphabet* is already idiomatic.

Both *idiomatic* and *idiot* share the Greek root *idios*, which means "one's own" or "private," revealing that even at the level of individual words a language can become *idio*tically exclusive, understood fully only by members of its own group and/or in the context of its cultural moment. Although they draw on idiomatic language to capture the voice of a certain time and place, literary artists must depend primarily upon the root meaning of words as the raw material for an art that seeks to express universal meanings linguistically. When our language becomes too exclusive, it obscures its connection with the organic principle it was created to convey, the meronymic marriage of phenomenon and concept.

From the Greek root word *mero-*, or part, a meronym is an image composed of discrete parts that simultaneously constitute an independent image. Gray, for instance, is composed of both black and white, yet it is distinguishable from either black or white. Meronymic, therefore, implies at least three acknowledged parts interpenetrating and coexisting, while the word itself identifies only the third, apparently single, image. This recognition of the contributing parts as well as the variations of the current image allows the meronym to be simultaneously individual and diverse. Gray is a simple expression of a complex concept: it acknowledges its dependence on the independently existing colors of black and white, while in itself it includes so many possibilities that a recent Hewlett Packard advertisement for a computer scanner can promise to detect "256 shades of gray." Everything coexists independently in this "community" of black and white and the myriad shades between which share the word gray; so too any meronym expands our perception of reality because it encompasses simultaneous realities even when only one concrete image, such as charcoal or platinum, is apparent.

On the other hand, the Greek root *met-* means change, and the metonym and metaphor imply that one thing changes into, or is subsumed in, another thing. A metonym such as the Crown, for instance, subsumes the human being who at any moment happens to be wearing the crown. No third phenomenon is produced; rather, two becomes one. Another linguistic image that encompasses diversity and unity is the metaphor. However, in our primarily English-speaking United States, where perceived reality is defined by a dominant discourse, only one of the two parts of a metaphor is usually considered *real* while the other is subsumed: when a man is "a lion," for instance, we imagine the power of the lion residing in the man; while the opposite image is created when we say a man is "an animal." Either way, one of the two loses identity to the other term, as two discrete parts are metamorphosed into one.

Yet, as Aristotle argues in his *Rhetoric*, the best metaphors are "proportional," or balanced and reversible, and "must always apply reciprocally to either of [their] co-ordinate terms" (174). It is this balancing act, the reciprocity, that makes a metaphor most valuable to the literary artist, as it acknowledges the equality and independence of both terms while it asserts at least a temporary marriage of those terms in the present instance. Metonym and metaphor may in fact be considered to represent the phenomenon and concept that are married in the meronymic thought process. Applying this to the metonymic Crown, we metaphorically accept that the king *thinks* for the country as well as *appears* for it as a symbol of its unity, and reciprocally that the government is a thinking body of which the king is the head.

The dialectical process of reasoning, in which thesis and antithesis are subsumed in a synthesis, can also be expanded into a meronymic thought process. In synthesis, two become one, but generally at the expense of elements belonging to one or both of the original ideas. Contrast this with the marriage of black and white in gray: neither original is diminished; the possibility of gray depends on a greater whole in which the three concepts both interact and continue to exist independently. Inasmuch as dialectic operates, as *Webster's New Collegiate Dictionary* says, "in accordance with the laws of dialectical materialism," which assert "the priority of matter over mind," such reasoning favors things over thoughts. We would reason, for instance, that gray is *only* the synthesis of black and white, and literary precision would encourage us to choose a more specific word such as charcoal. Meronymic reasoning might choose the word gray precisely because it includes the simultaneous existence of each of its parts (black and white) as well as every finite variation of their synthesis. Rather than unspecific, such a word becomes inclusive and allows the reader to broaden or narrow the meaning according to context, involving reader and writer in the creative process.

When dealing with concepts rather than colors, this expanded perception becomes increasingly important. In the United States, with its history of slavery, black and white are significant—and divisive—concepts. A unity of so-called *blacks* and *whites* in the concept of the American is essential if we are to survive, but to subsume one, as in our earlier "melting pot" image of unity, is to lose the rich diversity belonging to each. On the other hand, the meronymic perspective argues that both can interpenetrate and simultaneously maintain independent identity, and the interaction will itself further add to the richness of our ever-expanding reality with yet a third independent concept that coexists with the other two. Linguistic intermarriage enables us to expand our perception of the world continuously. Meronymic reasoning, then, shares with dialectic the dialoguing of seemingly conflicting opposites, resolving that conflict in the apprehension of a greater whole in which the diverse parts coexist and interact.

The exclusivity of a patriarchal language that assumes common definitions by subsuming discrete parts makes it particularly difficult for those members devalued by the patriarchy either to express themselves adequately or to be understood fully by other members of their own society. Feminists have been particularly sensitive to this problem: Monique Wittig challenges "the straight mind," which tends to deny any perspective on reality but its own; Hélène Cixous calls for a reclamation of the "language of the body"; and Diana Fuss focuses our attention on how society acts on the body to show that we need to communicate with all our members by *Essentially Speaking*.

Taken literally, there are at least two important aspects to essential speaking. First, root meanings give us a place to begin reconnecting with the essential, organic principle upon which each word is based. This original meronymic marriage of concept and phenomenon must then be seen in its social context. Once created from such *sensible* words, the concept eventually takes on its own life as an abstract word. Who knows how many contradictory images may be generated in individual imaginations, how many idiomatic meanings evolved in the society, in that process? Lavoisier suggests that "when errors have been thus accumulated there is but one remedy, by which order can be restored to the faculty of thinking; this is, to forget all that we have learned, to turn back our ideas to their source, to follow the train in which they rise, and, as Lord Bacon says, to frame the human understanding anew." He would return us to that sensual observation of the world, the original marriage that creates our language, so that we can once more understand our world and each other. How can we communicate unity when each group creates an idiomatic, exclusive language?

However, when we revisit that simplest image, we may discover differences even there. Then we must examine the ideology that named the phenomenon, the cultural mythos naming its world. "What's in a name?" For Shakespeare's Juliet, it is not Romeo but his membership in an opposing family that his name signifies; to connect with her he is more than willing to abandon the divisive name. The play reveals how destructive and divisive words can become, how far concept can stray from phenomenon. On the other hand, experiencing the phenomenon freshly can reveal its true *name* or character, whatever word is attached to it. When the story of the word is understood, when we can put a phenomenon in our own words, both our differences and the potential for unity can coexist, just as gray can unify the seemingly irresolvable differences of black and white in its many sensual expressions without subsuming either black or white. Shades of gray can show us the way, the middle world in which opposites can be united and alternatives discovered.

Nathaniel Hawthorne images his symbolism as the turning of a diamond so that each facet, each face, can be seen; its meaning will therefore be cumulative, as is the meaning of the scarlet letter in his romance of that title. One of the ways, therefore, that we can share meanings despite the seemingly exclusive face our dominant discourse turns to us is to re-turn them to their organic correspondence and accept its changing faces—its proportional metaphorical meanings—as its cumulative reality.

Who can better help us understand our words today than writers? Who can better explore our whole story than novelists? If our words have become obscure, loaded with ideological conflicts by those empowered to name the world, who can better see those words freshly than the Other writers? My interest in the contemporary American novel as a key to the whole story of my own life has come up against that dominant discourse. So it is that I have turned to Other American novelists for the other parts of our common story. This study of contemporary women novelists celebrates the meronymic perspective that sees the shadow in its double, that knows every boundary to be a threshold. The dynamic marriages of equal and discrete consciousnesses to create human communities, societal and familial histories, and individual relationships constitute their meronymic content. But our real focus will be on the art of the meronymic novel, an art of style and structure that begins to heal the fragmented tradition of the novel and to encompass its seemingly endless labels in a common, maturing form that yet offers seemingly endless variations. Some critics have narrowly defined the novel to exclude even some of the works we will discuss here, so I have added the term meronymic to focus on that artistry that turns any content—biographical, historical, and imaginative—into mythtelling.

Woman is the obscured or shadow meaning of Man in our language, that as an idiomatic social construct reflects the dualistic and exclusive ideology of a patriarchy that has truncated the root word human, or *homo*, to exclude what is "not Man" and added a baggage of "wo" to create its concept of the Woman. Even the isolated term "homo" is used to denigrate otherness. Forced into the position of the Other in a patriarchy, woman must re-vision that world meronymically. She knows herself to be human inasmuch as she is subsumed in the word Man and yet also to be "not Man," a seeming paradox that teaches her to reclaim that part of her self and to seek the root, the organic principle. These women novelists re-turn the word and the world, sometimes even turning themselves inside out to materialize the potentials of the human mind, a process especially useful for those humans whose gender has located them ideologically on the left, as negative, covert, hidden images.

While Lewis Carroll's Alice may have taught us to go through the looking glass, to find the "negative world" of the other that has been subsumed into Man's reflection of himself, these novelists remain inside the looking glass, refusing to be either negated or defined as the Other. To center ourselves, we must first know that we exist. Challenging the confines of the mirror, they push at boundaries from the margins they have been assigned, only to find that what

xvi   Preface

seemed to be a flat surface world is itself a social construct. They re-turn us to the roots of our language, to our roots in the larger universal community from which we are never separated as long as we are alive, to once again make sense of themselves and the human community of which they have always been an integral part. Since they have chosen the art of literature to express their insights, they also reveal the ideological genesis of our societies, shaped by those empowered to name our world. Their stories are in turn shaped by the human imagination freshly imaging its relationship to the universe that surrounds it and, because of the new life they give our common language, their stories also reshape those patterns as our common story continually reshapes itself. As one of the epigrams asserts in Octavia E. Butler's *Parable of the Sower*, "God exists to be shaped. / God is Change" (24).

The myth of the Eternal Return, which has offered hope of renewal to Western society at least since Plato's time, promises us an ever-renewing story line, but for Plato this meant that history as we know it would be followed by history in reverse. This pendulum swing reflects the dualistic and linear biases of Western society; it also suggests the confinement that Annis Pratt calls the Enclosure of the Patriarchy. Nor will it heal the divided self, as C. G. Jung warns in *The Undiscovered Self*: "What then happens is a simple reversal: the underside comes to the top and the shadow takes the place of the light. . . . All this is unavoidable, because the root of the evil is untouched and merely the counterposition has come to light" (94).

When boundaries are confronted and dissolve into thresholds, there is no need to retreat; we can begin again with a renewed understanding. This cyclical story of rebirth Nature has always offered us, this "other" story still emblematically intact in our living language. When the cycle is married to our linear quest for precision, a spiral replaces the decline of entropy so prominent as an expression of contemporary despair with the promise of evolutionary growth, offering yet another moment in which to try to heal the abuses of the past and shape the future.

When we begin with the perspective that has been devalued by patriarchy, its opposite is not subsumed but released from its confinement into an ever-expanding universe with room for everyone. Already encompassed in the word woman is the man, in the word mother is the other to which she offers individual existence by giving birth. That first "letting go" is not a denial of connection; rather, it is the beginning of relationship and communication with an acknowledged Other. "I cannot imagine the world without you in it," I have said to each of my children, because each has expanded my definition of the world simply by existing in it; each has in turn transformed my present and promise to make me a part of a future I may never see.

Read in the organic sense, in the "logic of metaphor," each word is turned around and returned to its beginnings only to be born again into a larger perception of the world it is trying to describe. As Hart Crane defines this "organic principle . . . which antedates our so-called pure logic, and which is the genetic basis of all speech, hence consciousness and thought-extension," words "are selected less for their logical (literal) significance than for their associational meanings" (221).

So too do these writers help us turn our mutual story around, to see it freshly. What seemed to be the edge of a flat world, the boundaries of our society inhabited by "marginal" individuals trapped inside the mirror of Man, shows itself to be a threshold to the other side of our sphere. What is a marginal perspective in the universal subject matter of literature? Just as modern scientists have learned to study the exceptions rather than the typical to discover more inclusive rules that have married classical physics to quantum physics, so too these atypical novelists, in writing what they know from life in the "margins" of society, marry themselves to both sides of the mirror to achieve a balanced perspective.

To appreciate the "whole story" of any word, we must balance its empowered metonymic and/or metaphoric meaning with its subsumed other meaning, by turning it around, even inside out, and by re-turning it to its roots. Imagistic language, if that is not already a tautology, helps us explore both the rational sense of the figure and the associative or organic sense of the reasoning imagination that named that figure for us. It is the marriage of these two logics that opens up the borders between us. Only then does the word—and the world— begin to make sense. As Northrop Frye points out in *Words With Power*, "Ever since Plato, most literary critics have connected the word 'thought' with dialectical and conceptual idioms, and ignored or denied the existence of poetic and imaginative thought" (xvi). It is time to re-turn with Frye to such "words with power."

In our patriarchal society, women constitute the primary Other hidden within or obscured by our language; women's literature that acknowledges and explores our common experiences from that other perspective helps us better understand the "whole story." Society is the "phenomenal" expression of abstracted human concepts inasmuch as it "tells" in idea and act the story of the human community. What contemporary women's literature reflects, however, is that the story of Society has forgotten its generation from the universal community and its own organic principle. It has become indeed the story of "Man and His World" just as old history books claimed, while the other part of the story has been confined to oral tradition, passed down from mother to daughter or ignored because its written expression has been obscured or denied preservation.

Yet that story is reinvented each generation as people use their senses to make sense of life. Many people today hope to recover such insights by turning to societies closer to nature to share their stories. In *Wisdom of the Mythtellers*, Sean Kane warns us, however, that "[no] source can tell us directly what mythtelling meant to those who practiced it and heard it" because "these cultures are not as they were eons ago" (14). He suggests instead that we need "to recreate imaginatively something of the dialogue with nature of the mythtellers" (15) to dialogue with nature today. In our imaginations we can share myths and histories other than our own, but it is in our own ideas and actions that we must ultimately uncover our meronymic truths.

Some people turn to earlier modes of life, moving closer to nature to achieve understanding, but this too can express a denial of the present moment and the contexts in which we live. The dangers of such denial can be seen in Jane Smiley's novella *Good Will* as well as in the movie *Mosquito Coast*; in both stories the children long for the world of their generation, and the patriarchal decision to deny them that world leads to violence. A return to the past is as impossible as a return to innocence or ignorance; we are products of today with all of its complexities and therefore need, as Ralph Waldo Emerson reminds us in "The American Scholar" is true of each generation (1532), to write our own "novel" versions of the common human story.

Novels both record and critique our social story, allowing us to share human experience imaginatively. If we are to be a society and not a collection of individuals babbling in different ideological languages, we need storytellers who offer a meronymic perspective and reclaim our common tongue. We may always tell the same human story; but when that story becomes fragmented, broken apart by oppositions and fear, we need to pull it together again. The meronymic novelist offers a "whole story" to heal us.

In my first book, *Radiant Daughters: Fictional American Women*, I turned to realistic novelists to examine their women characters as a better way of understanding my world. In my latest book, *Worlds Within Women*, I chose to look at what our society would call the left, the sinister, the female side of things, and studied, as the subtitle explains, *Myth and Mythmaking in Fantastic Literature by Women*. Our society has devalued everything in that title: myths are not true, fantasies are not real, literature is not useful in "real" life, and women are not men. Yet I still believe that novelists are artists who help us understand our own humanity. Our society and our selves seem to be out of balance, off center, because of a dualism and a hierarchy that devalue and subsume part of every word, every story, every truth we might have shared. When that ideology narrows the story to what is "right," what is "left" hides behind the shadow in our unconscious unless we bring it out and share it. Maybe my interest in this "marginal world" lies in my own double marginality: I am both a woman and left-handed.

The novelists I include here seek to reveal the connections between those supposedly separate worlds on either side of the mirror and make the mirror disappear. They marry the left hand to the right in a fictional meronymic body that perceives marginality as liminality and turns boundaries into thresholds. They rediscover balance and love, and from the middle they look in every direction to see the world justly. As a result, their vision not only embraces both left and right but also offers a unity of both in the whole story of our social body.

To achieve this perspective in the novel, they heal the division that began with the rise of the Romance novel in the nineteenth century and found its opposing form in the rise of Realism a generation later. They communicate the multiple meanings of words and images; Mikhail Bakhtin's *The Dialogic Imagination* will help us follow the dialogues they establish with myth and history. But they do not stop with dialogues, which run the danger of becoming serial monologues perpetuating our fragmentation. Instead, they offer oral conversations and written correspondences, which interpenetrate to encompass and unite multiple perspectives. Love balances the fear of the quest, a fear that draws us inward until we disappear into the mirror. When we seem to be pulled apart by external conflicts or diminished by internal fears, it helps to read a story by someone who perceives a possible balance and blending of worlds.

To appreciate my role as a critic, I have returned to the moment of that nineteenth-century split to find our common critical language. Margaret Fuller, best known for *Woman in the Nineteenth Century*, explains that role in "A Short Essay on Critics": "Next to invention is the power of interpreting invention, next to beauty the power of appreciating beauty. And of making others appreciate it; for the universe is a scale of infinite gradation, and below the very highest, every step is explanation down to the lowest" (1617). Fuller identifies three types of critics, warning us about becoming "subjective," encouraging us to be both "apprehensive" and "comprehensive." The "subjective" critics she describes as stating "their impressions as they rise, of other men's spoken, written, or acted thoughts. They never dream of going out of themselves to seek the motive, to trace the law of another nature. They never dream that there are statures which cannot be measured from their point of view" (1616). Conversely, "the comprehensive, who must also be apprehensive," can "enter into the nature of another being and judge his work by its own law." Then he must "put that aim in its place, and . . . estimate its relations. And this the critic can only do who perceives the analogies of the universe, and how they are regulated by an absolute, invariable principle" (1617). As a teacher, I have tried to be an "apprehensive" critic, helping my students enter fully into the perspective of the piece of literature. In this study, however, I have tried to be a comprehensive critic, choosing novelists whose artistry reflects that universal order.

When a writer successfully enters into the perspective of the Other, as does Hawthorne when he tells the story of Hester Prynne in *The Scarlet Letter*, then the imaginative marriage of persona and author is meronymic. In a 1990 article, I have discussed another meronymic novel by John Crowley. However, for the purposes of this study I have chosen only women writers who both imagine *and* embody the meronymic perspective; to understand themselves fully, both idea and act must unite in their perspectives on what is real and universal. They explore visible and invisible, geographical and cultural, external and internal boundaries as they balance the individual and communal self in that unbounded realm of the human spirit, the imagination.

I have chosen a focus on the American version of our story not only because this is my area of expertise but also because I agree with Crane that "here are destined to be discovered certain as yet undefined spiritual quantities, perhaps a new hierarchy of faith not to be developed so completely elsewhere" (219). However, I have had to dissolve boundaries to achieve a meronymic perspective on that social story by including a Canadian, a Latin American, and two British novelists whose geographical distancing expands our understanding of American.

Not nature but human society has drawn the boundaries that divide this small planet; not nature but human ideology has given our story this shape. Perhaps we need to tell another story, to transform our society, not to participate in its ideology by demanding our possessions and exacting our revenge. "I don't write out of anger," Eudora Welty tells us in *One Writer's Beginnings*. "For one thing, simply as a fiction writer, I am minus an adversary—except, of course, that of time." Linear history is not our only story; cyclical myths and nature's own story remind us that time only appears to end. Yet the cyclical story alone leads only to repetition and passive acceptance. Boundaries can be thresholds; the past, the present, and the future can all be found in the present moment, in the human consciousness. Hierarchy and dualistic exclusivity could be replaced with dynamic balancing and inclusive diversity. "It isn't easy; it has never been easy," Leslie Marmon Silko reminds us in *Ceremony*. But we are alive and imaginative, and as members of the potentially loving human community we are not alone.

Acknowledgments

I am indebted to Arizona State University for a sabbatical leave during which I was able to complete the initial research for this book, to the Women's Studies Program for a grant to further that research in London, and to the English Department for ongoing secretarial and photocopying support. I would also like to thank my various Women and Literature classes for their input and insights, my Fulbright class in women's literature at the Universidad de Granada in Spain for the multicultural perspective they provided me, and my friends and family for the patience, support, and understanding they always give me.

Introduction

I think aesthetic teaching is the highest of all teaching because it deals
with life in its highest complexity. But if it ceases to be purely
aesthetic—if it lapses anywhere from the picture to the diagram—it
becomes the most offensive of all teaching.

—George Eliot

The first problem we face as writers is the ambiguity of language. What is
a novel? *Webster's* defines it as an "invented prose narrative that is usu. long
and complex and deals esp. with human experience through a usu. connected
sequence of events." We usually define invention as creation or fabrication,
but the Latin root *invenire* means to come upon or discover. This is an important distinction, relating inventiveness to observation and recognition of
already existing phenomena. *Gnarus*, the Latin root of narrative, means "to
know," reminding us that the recitation of details that constitute a story is as
much a teaching process as is the analysis of data that constitute the scientific
process. This ties the novel into the ancient art of storytelling; as contemporary mythmaking, it offers a version of what Mircea Eliade calls the "absolute truth" of a culture (*Myths* 23). He attaches the term myth to stories
that express a cultural cosmology and/or value system, a way of knowing the
universe around us and of which we are a part. Fiction has been defined as
"one of the chief devices by which man communicates his vision of the
nature of reality in concrete terms" (Thrall 202).

Myths preserve at least remnants of the science, the religion, and often the
history of a culture. When the details or characters can be found as well in other
sources, we call the story a legend. Folktales are even less verifiable because of

all the changes that have been incorporated over years and often centuries of storytellers transforming the stories. Western society rejects the reality of these "unverifiable" stories, although repetition of patterns and particulars from culture to culture verify their claim to truth for many. The myths of a different culture are usually treated as lies or fantasies; yet our own myths are accorded a religious respect.

The definition of the novel will help us reconsider the value of myth if we focus on the experience and the *mythos*, the "connected sequence of events," which are common to both. The "absolute truth" of myth, the term I will use for the entire heritage of ancient storytelling, is that of pattern and process. The Greek word *mythos* means the plot, or pattern, of a story. Pattern of actions or relationships in an individual story are recognized as archetypal when our *ratio*nal ways of knowing can count many repetitions in our cultural history; such a pattern is then considered verified. Sigmund Freud, for instance, defines for us the Oedipus and Electra complexes by borrowing from myth to explain the workings of the human mind. This marriage of two "ways of knowing," the rational mind counting inductively the observable occurrences of phenomena and patterns and the mythic mind re-counting the details of human life in a recognizable repetition, allows us to explain and comprehend a shared vision of what is real and thus to tell the cultural "whole story."

Whether or not the explanations provided by a myth carry any weight for the contemporary reader, its pattern preserves its claim to "absolute truth." The contemporary novel presents such patterns as well, while the informational content reflects our time and place. These patterns reveal that truth, the universal understanding that *stands under* our diverse actions, as perceived by the novelist. When novels echo the shared patterns we have "verified" from Aristotle and Greek myths, they earn critical praise; if not, they are considered "flawed."

The *mythos* that has shaped our critical expectations may not always apply, however; Greece has not provided the only myths shared by Western cultures. In today's world, cultures do not remain discrete either geographically or ideologically. These women writers have known, with each of us, multicultural human experiences; the "absolute truth" of one culture has often merged or conflicted with that of other cultures that share our United States, whose very name suggests its diversity as well as its claim to unity. By reading these novels for the patterns of character and action they offer, we can experience the ongoing mythmaking process. By comparing the patterns that emerge with our wide legacy of mythic and literary patterns that other sources make available to us, we can expand our own understanding of the nature of reality. Finally, by identifying the conscious choices made by the author and her characters, we can re-affirm our human power of naming and ordering the world.

The truth of storytelling is a truth of human pattern and process, but that pattern must be expressed in the language of the storyteller. In oral literature, the pattern of "absolute truth" is always being translated by the storyteller into the continuously evolving spoken language and adapted to the details of an immediate situation. Written literature, on the other hand, is fixed in the language and details of its time and place. Literary prose depends on rhetorical patterns. Aristotle's *Rhetoric* recognizes the rhythm of prose style and establishes common ground with poetry: "Prose-writers must, however, pay specially careful attention to metaphor, because their other resources are scantier than those of poets. Metaphor, moreover, gives style clearness, charm, and distinction as nothing else can" (168). Distinct from either poetry or prosaic, everyday speech, such prose might best be identified by the term poetic narrative to remind us that novels belong to art, not history.

Poetry immediately reveals its dependence on pattern to the reader. Its imagistic process is inclusive, as Frye explains: "Poetry faces, in one direction, the world of *praxis* or action, a world of events occurring in time. In the opposite direction, it faces the world of *theoria*, or images and ideas, the conceptual or visualizable world spread out in space, or mental space" ("New Directions from Old" 119). The poet balances these worlds metaphorically and sensually.

The fiction writer must also provide information, which is conveyed by the accumulation of metonymic images and rational arguments as well as by the sequential order chosen. Characters are defined by the things with which they are associated. Since the novel tells its stories in prose rather than poetry, it runs the risk of being read as nonfictional information. This is particularly true of the realistic novel, which hides its art beneath a carefully created recognizable surface.

What makes the novel ancient is its connection to archetypal patterns; what must make it perpetually novel is its art, its conscious use of the metaphors and symbols, rhythms and patterns, of poetic narrative to convey more than just information. Each novelist must have a poet's love of language to rediscover in contemporary diction the original marriages of phenomenon and concept that shape the words themselves. In her 1856 essay on "The Natural History of German Life," George Eliot discusses the evolutionary aspects of language: "Language must be left to grow in precision, completeness, and unity, as minds grow in clearness, comprehensiveness, and sympathy. And there is an analogous relation between the moral tendencies of men and the social conditions they have inherited" (128).

Both poetic narrative and a mythically validated *mythos*, then, enrich these novels, although both may contrast sharply with the language and patterns of the dominant discourse. Nor can a novel perspective easily be achieved if they are confined in a predefined form that itself is an ideological social construct. Just as Walt Whitman felt the necessity to free verse from inherited traditions to allow the evolution of a uniquely American poetry, so too the contemporary novelist recognizes a need for the American novel to shape itself to this society. Women and other marginalized novelists have felt particularly confined in canonical forms.

Thrall and Hibbard explain the novel as the marriage of the traditions of the Italian novella to the medieval European romance. The form of the novel is itself paradoxical: "the conflict between the imaginative and poetic recreation of experience implied in *roman* and the realistic representation of the soiled world of common men and action implied in the *novel* has been present in the form from its beginning, and it accounted for a distinction often made in the 18th and 19th centuries between the ROMANCE and the *novel*" (318). Today's novel must again unite the "soiled world" to "the imaginative and poetic recreation," which blossoms in the human consciousness and imbues that world with value and meaning. Can an elitist literature be the appropriate, empowered artistic expression of a democracy?

The meronym acknowledges the verbal marriage of concept and phenomenon, thereby legitimizing its offspring, the mestiza/mulatto/half-breed concept that reflects its genetic parents in a unique balance of their traits while simultaneously asserting its independent existence. The sensually apprehendable surface of human experience neither negates nor limits its metaphoric possibilities. Each helps us understand the other as perceived, because it is the human mind that "knows" the metaphoric meaning of any figure and can "see" its invisible correlation with another figure. The meronymic is a "both/and" perspective, inclusive rather than dualistic; additionally, it evolves a third alternative, thus actualizing even more possibilities.

The meronym is inclusive literally as well as figuratively, because its sensually apprehendable surface varies. Gray can range from a preponderance of white to nearly black. Any shade, any immediate expression, of gray contains in itself a specific balance of black and white. We, too, are meronymic: as our right brain reasons by "counting the correspondences" in our rational analysis, our left brain anticipates the ways in which the relationship will be manifested, "imaging" the correspondences in our imagination. Both the ideological and concrete offsprings of this mental marriage can be seen in our social structures.

The image that enables the writer to connect visible historical and invisible conceptual realities as perceived by both the reason and the imagination of the human consciousness is the symbol. "Symbolism," Eliade asserts, "*adds* a new value to an object or an act, without thereby violating its immediate or 'historical' validity. . . . Seen in this light the universe is no longer sealed off . . . : everything is linked by a system of correspondences and assimilations" (xiv). The story itself then can be seen as archetypal patterns of action and character motivated (put into motion) by ideological patterns. In Hawthorne's *The Scarlet Letter*, we begin with the ideological perception of the "A" for adulterer as the metonymic image of Hester Prynne's guilt and punishment. As Hester transforms the letter through her embroidery art, the reader begins to balance social and personal meanings; when the child Pearl emerges as a living emblem of the letter, the reader is in effect allowed the "other" side of the story—the future asserting its own possibilities that have resulted from Hester's transformation of the present and her society's dogged demands of the past as they culminate in the moment of the novel. In order to balance its two languages, the informational prose and the poetic narrative, the novel offers imagistic and structural symbolism that both comprehends and explains its ideas while shaping its story.

"A masterpiece of art has in the mind a fixed place in the chain of being, as much as a plant or a crystal," Emerson argues in his essay "Art" in *Society and Solitude*. Science, however, countered this artistic vision of organic unity with such giants as Freud, Darwin, and William James, so that by the end of the nineteenth century, art itself as Realism seemed to limit reality to the sensually apprehendable universe in which the human members are governed by rational and scientifically predictable patterns of behavior. Naturalism went so far as to rob humanity even of its claim to rationality. As the twentieth century opened, both art and science offered a world seemingly devoid of divinity, with humanity only questionably in possession of its own reason.

The birth of the novel is often traced to the Renaissance and attributed to Shakespeare's contemporary Miguel de Cervantes. *Don Quixote*, despite its episodic structure, is still considered by some as "not only the first novel in point of time, but the greatest novel of all time" (Wagenknecht 697). Its title hero admirably balances his contemporary reality, in all its depressing and graphic details, with a faith in the potential of human beings, which continually transforms that reality, as is reflected in the twentieth-century musical *Man of La Mancha* based on the novel. Here the individual still dreams "the impossible dream" and directs his life at realizing that dream in the real world, undeterred by the discouraging appearances of reality. The assumption of an orderly universe, of a Great Chain of Being that promises that justice and virtue will triumph, supports the actions of this heroic, if apparently ridiculous, faith. Cervantes' appreciation of the human comedy offers graphic pictures of human shortcomings and social inequities and at the same time asserts intangible values that motivate his hero's faith and action. Seldom is this balance found again, as novels choose either a realistic study of social realities or a romantic celebration of heroic individuals.

Hawthorne explains the Romance in "The Custom House," his introduction to *The Scarlet Letter*. Moonlight, his metaphor for the imagination, transforms a "familiar room" into "a neutral territory, somewhere between the real world and fairy-land, where the Actual and the Imaginary may meet, and each imbue itself with the nature of the other." But this is not sufficient alone for the Romance writer; the appeal to human warmth, to love, must also be present. Hawthorne adds this metaphorically with the light of a coal fire: "The warmer light mingles itself with the cold spirituality of the moonbeams, and communicates, as it were, a heart and sensibilities of human tenderness to the forms which fancy summons up" (2197). Imagination and emotion are the essential ingredients for the Romance writer.

The Romance is written in a poetic narrative that clearly depends on the emotional aspects of poetry as well as its ability to speak simultaneously of the actual and the imaginative, which together constitute the reality of the Romancer. Hawthorne remains in the actual "familiar room" as the Romancer's perceptions of that room are expanded by moonlight and enhanced by firelight; symbolically speaking, to the evidence provided by the actual room is added the mental images conjured by the Romancer's imagination and lit by his spirit, the warmth of his heart. This is why we can read *The Scarlet Letter* symbolically and still feel that we have learned much of the historical Puritan New England in which it is set. Hawthorne was careful to keep historical details accurate while distancing the story in time to allow linguistic transformation of its surface.

The Romance apprehends a greater than human reality, often expressed in Neoplatonic terms, a larger context in which admitting to our inevitable human imperfections is constructive and striving for the "impossible dream" of the intuitive, atypical individual is applauded. Its potential weakness lies in the tenuousness of its ties to the historical surface, and when those ties are broken romances become escapist and stereotypical rather than intuitive and archetypal. Yet Hawthorne did not feel comfortable writing what he felt "would have been something new in literature." As he explains,

The wiser effort would have been to diffuse thought and imagination through the opaque substance of to-day, and thus to make it a bright transparency; to spiritualize the burden that began to weigh so heavily; to seek, resolutely, the true and indestructible value that lay hidden in the petty and wearisome incidents, and ordinary characters, with which I was now conversant. The fault was mine. The page of life that was spread out before me seemed dull and commonplace, only because I had not fathomed its deeper import. (2198)

The Realism that followed the Romantics would aim at realizing Hawthorne's desire to "diffuse thought and imagination through the opaque substance of to-day," but seldom did this version of the novel reveal that "true and indestructible value that lay hidden." Art rather than information is the greatest demand on the novelist. Henry James assures the reader in his preface to *The American* of his own meronymic balancing act:

The real represents to my perception the things we cannot possibly not know, sooner or later, in one way or another; it being but one of the accidents of our hampered state, and one of the incidents of their quantity and number, that particular instances have not yet come our way. The romantic stands, on the other hand, for things that, with all the facilities in the world, all the wealth and all the courage and all the wit and all the adventure, we never can directly know, the things that can reach us only through the beautiful circuit and subterfuge of our thought and our desire. (*The Art of the Novel* 31–32)

The successes of Hawthorne's "symbolic romances" and James' "symbolic realism" emphasize the meronymic perspective each was able to achieve despite the limitations of the fragmented genre. Realism, however, often loses touch with what "we never *can* directly know." Learning from the emphasis in science on observation and logical assumptions, it seeks to identify the typical, predictable, and consequently representative aspects of human experience. To achieve this aim, the knowable past must necessarily provide the information upon which the literary present of the novel is based. Consequently, this form of the novel emphasizes past over either present or future. We learn from this perspective the ways in which we behave like our immediate predecessors, and the conclusion we draw is that our future will reflect that past. However, the past it reflects is the apparent past, which is reported to us as information. Often neglected in Realism is the atypical past, the possible but improbable dream and invisible past values, precisely because they cannot be apprehended sensually or explained by logic or reason. Not surprisingly, therefore, the twentieth century soon found itself announcing the deaths of the hero, of God—both "past ideas"—and the death of the novel as well.

The linear pattern of the realistic novel argues a logical sequence of human events, borrowing its typical plotline from Greek tragedy with its rising actions of conflict and tension, its climax or recognition scene, and falling action of inevitable loss and isolation. Chronology offers a typical timeframe from which shifts are measured and within which they are understood. This Greek *mythos* also focuses on the individual hero, always supposing an antagonist; I was taught that the four major themes of the novel each began with "man against" and included self, other, society, and the universe as his opponents. Since the form strives to represent reality, the characters and their circumstances are said to reflect typical cultural roles.

However, what is apparently typical must be weighted by other available data. Since American society is a complex balance of diverse lifestyles, it soon became apparent that the typical American character of canonical novels reflected instead an empowered white male, typical only of the dominant culture. Consequently, Realism was soon challenged by Naturalism, which quarreled with the identification of even the middle class as ordinary characters and examined instead the lower classes. Naturalism also demanded a greater attention be paid to the element of chance and the less apparent irrational forces on the individual, which frequently disrupted the predictability of the plotline. The climactic pattern of individual action was often replaced with the cumulative pattern that evolved into mass action when irrationally triggered by a seemingly unimportant event. Even more likely was the repetition of individual failure and mechanical replacement of one worker with another doomed to the same endless cycle, which revealed the dehumanization of familiar social processes. Metonymic images negated the characters and asserted the power of *things*, biological and social, as the motive for human actions.

Another challenge to Realism came from Modernism, which agreed with the Naturalist shift of attention to internal, often irrational, forces, but which concentrated less on sociological and more on psychological influences on individual perceptions. This movement inward, even while it refocused attention on motivation by invisible forces that had to be conveyed metaphorically, encouraged monologic explorations of the self.

While each of these forms expanded the possible focus of the realistic novel to include a greater range of character types, associative as well as logical reasoning, and less dependence upon linearity, each also remained within the perspective of its monologic cultural reality. Naturalism still proved the rule by the irrationality of its exception, as in Theodore Dreiser's *Sister Carrie*, questioning the possibility of human rationality. While the Modernists replaced supposedly objective observation with admittedly subjective perceptions, if we were locked into someone's nightmares we were allowed to sift the observable details for evidence of remnants of the "real world" transformed by those fantasies. Metaphor served only to reinforce these connections with external objects or recorded information that were themselves a part of or explained by the material world. Freud's *Interpretation of Dreams*, for instance, became a key to identifying the meaning of each image as it related to events and people in the dreamer's life. The seemingly incomprehensible was explained by what was already culturally defined as real.

Fragmentation of the novelistic tradition continued not just within Realism but also among the descendants of the Romance. "All novels are representations in fictional narrative of life or experience but the form is itself as protean as life and experience themselves have proved to be," Thrall and Hibbard argued; certainly the flexibility of language and form must follow the flexibility of character and action if the novel is to communicate effectively its author's "vision of the nature of reality in concrete terms" (202). But if it is to critique the "nature" of that reality, it must dialogue with other "visions" as Bakhtin will remind us; without such dialogue the novel becomes as eccentric and idiosyncratic as its author.

Romantic speculation would seem the best way to explore alternatives, but only if those alternatives clearly correspond with the observable reality of the reader can the dialogue begin. Instead, most speculative fiction was escapist: romances and adventures that obscured the complexities of human character, gothic novels that emphasized the atypical and irrational, or utopian and science fiction modes that escaped the present in alternative times and places. Seldom did these capture the attention of literary critics, until the various descendants of Realism seemed unanimously hopeless, offering little beyond the probability of social, human, even environmental extinction.

If science had helped fragment the novel by leading us away from appreciation of our own humanity and the divinity implicit in creation, it would also bring us back full circle to that holistic view. A unified nature—the wholeness implicit in the word universe—encompasses all possibilities of mind and imagination. Within that universe, it is natural to affirm the simultaneous existence of visible and invisible realities. Science internalizes its search for truth in the twentieth century to explore the infinitely small world of the subatomic, reminding us that infinity lies before us in whatever direction we might choose and that in the infinite even the paradoxical is comprehended. Quantum physics discovers in the microcosm of the atom a reality of pattern and probability rather than discrete particles. Matter becomes energy becomes matter as probabilities shape themselves to the expectations of the observer.

To a century out of balance, a century limited by the realities of time and space so brilliantly measured by classical physics, new scientific questions began to provide new directions for the questing human consciousness. In literature, these will first be explored, not in the mainstream descendants of Realism, but in the stubbornly speculative children of the Romantics, from fantasy to hard-core science fiction. A greater unity within which seeming contradictions between the visible and invisible worlds can be encompassed is easily expressed through the language of mathematics. To translate such a perception into the logical positivistic language of Realism seemed impossible. Speculative fiction offers views of possible futures, mythical pasts, and alternate realities, settings that had kept it clearly separated from Realism but that began to be considered metaphorically as fresh perspectives on a shared reality.

Just as scientists continued their quest for truth beyond the obvious, even beyond the accessible, to posit a greater whole, so too have novelists expanded the perceptions of the novel by reuniting the richness of metaphor from the Romance with the precision of metonymy from Realism in novels that more easily encompass the "whole story" of our experience. Magic Realism is one such marriage, and Christopher Nash's study of *The Anti-Realist Revolt* identifies others as well. However, "anti-Realism" suggests still that a choice must be made; these contemporary experiments depend as much on Realism as on the Romance. An acceptance of the truth of metaphor as well as the discernible truth of the metonym places the individual "at the center," demanding that human consciousness balance the visible and invisible worlds that surround us. Perhaps we must accept that we humans are limited in "our ways of apprehending things," as Nash argues (69), trapped as *things* are by time and space. The human consciousness, however, that spirit so admired by the Renaissance writers, may be limitless in its "ways of apprehending" the possibilities that shape those things, the energy that may itself determine the form it will take as matter at any measurable moment. If we assert, as does the new physics, that these invisible realities are not fantasies, we rediscover the Great Chain of Being of the Renaissance.

The meronymic perspective celebrates our ability to re-create reality within each moment as we perform the balancing act for which we are famous—the flesh and the spirit, the world we see and the world we intuit—and testifies by extension to the balance and wholeness of the universe itself. As far as we know, only the human consciousness is capable of such expansion within the realities of time and space, for within that consciousness, as St. Augustine explained, "(t)he present of things past is the memory; the present of present things is direct perception; and the present of future things is expectation" (269).

Stylistically, realism is wedded to the historical past and to the typical, predictable present. For most women novelists, while this form adequately addressed the "Female Problem," it left little room for the "Feminist Alternative." The realistic novel reflected its culture's definitions of what and who were representative of human experience, and as feminist literature would so clearly demonstrate, the basis of those definitions came from male experience in most cultures, empowered white male in Western society. Ursula LeGuin is one of the many writers who recognized that women, even in speculative fiction, were "the Other" and were defined by their relationships with men or were feared for that otherness ("SF and the Other"). Women share this otherness with oppressed ethnicities within a culture as well, as seen in speculative treatments of the "alien." The monologue of the dominant male speaking of and to himself as definitively human limited the content of the realistic novel even more than its fragmented form limited it stylistically. Any unknown not responsive to its attempts at explanation that Realism did encounter was identified as a "horror," a "heart of darkness" that demanded rejection or denial of some form. Homi K. Bhabha discusses dependence on the dominant culture for our definitions of "real experience" in "Articulating the Archaic"; the "Other" is frightening and incomprehensible, left beyond the scope of the novel's perspective. Bhabha argues that such fear reflects "the alienation between the transformational myth of culture as a language of universality and social generalization, and its tropic function as a repeated 'translation' of incommensurable levels of living and meaning" (205).

Marginal writers who are centered in their own traditions, who have the strange habit of perceiving themselves and others like them as representatively human, presented our common story from decidedly different angles. As in Ralph Ellison's *The Invisible Man*, readers from the dominant culture not only confronted otherness but also learned that the Other shares our humanity. We saw our society freshly by being introduced to part of it with which we had been unfamiliar but that had existed coterminously with the part we knew.

The modernist style also proved valuable to some writers, especially women with "double marginality," who showed us along with social revelations unique internal perspectives that reminded us that each human is a balance of traits that have been culturally identified as masculine or feminine. Even recognizing the literary community as that part of the human family who serve as storytellers opened novelists to a dialogue among themselves, if not always within a single work. Writers purposely established such a dialogue with literary tradition itself, as does Welty when she dialogues specifically with W. B. Yeats' poetry (Cf. Patricia Yeager's article) and generally with classical and Celtic myth in *The Golden Apples*.

These women examined their own human experiences, and men started paying more attention to the lives of women in their novels (See Shinn, *Radiant Daughters*). Other writers chose speculative forms, as I have discussed in *Worlds Within Women*. More recently, however, novels by women discover their "other worlds" in contemporary society. Some remain closer in style to Romance than to Realism: Butler's Patternist series explains American ghettoes from an African perspective by backing up three hundred years in *Wild Seed* and then passing through our contemporary moment and beyond it in *Mind of My Mind*. Doris Lessing's *Canopus in Argos* "space fiction" series offers a map of human consciousness spread across the macrocosm of space. The balancing of language needed to tell the whole story is examined in Antonia Susan Byatt's *Possession: A Romance*, which finds history and myth actively intruding into the present moment. Margaret Atwood defines the future by its past and present heritages of history and myth in *The Handmaid's Tale*. These "marginal writers" see within their social context the promises as well as the limitations of human experience. The borders to which a dominant culture would assign them begin to be understood as thresholds rather than boundaries; the margins are themselves already a large part of what is.

In "Circles," Emerson credits St. Augustine with describing "God as a circle whose centre was everywhere, and its circumference nowhere" (1528). He sees valor as "self-recovery," the ability of the individual to re-center as new truths are discovered. "In the thought of tomorrow there is a power to upheave all thy creed, all the creeds, all the literatures of the nations, and marshal thee to a heaven which no epic dream has yet depicted," he promises (1530). The circle of American society is in such a process of expansion, making us aware that what we once called American literature seems arrogantly narrow, a United States literature that inwardly as well as outwardly denies many of its alternative voices. Such half truths as can be offered must be married to those silenced voices before the whole truth of America can begin to be told.

Some of these novelists began to widen the perspective within their novels by defining themselves "at the center"—by being centered in their own traditions, as Toni Cade Bambara will explain in *The Salt Eaters*. Especially for "doubly marginal" women writers, the ancient storytelling of their families and cultures offers fresh details of the human story and varies the patterns of novels to make them new again. Writers drawing on their ethnic traditions find symbolism that provides new structures. Spider Woman offers Silko in *Ceremony* a spider web of connections that help her protagonist Tayo find his way to sanity and health, while a pottery kiln defines the centering among her circles of community and consciousness that unites Velma's African and American heritages in Bambara's *The Salt Eaters*. Maxine Hong Kingston ties a complex knot of historic, mythic, and biological maternal relationships among Chinese women in *The Woman Warrior*. Isabel Allende literally houses the complex heritages of Latin American culture in *The House of the Spirits*, reminding us that the body "houses" the spirit and echoing Poe's gothic insights in "The Fall of the House of Usher" into the familial and genetic heritages of such a house.

These stylistic transformations challenge the fragmentation of the genre and the reduction of fiction to fabrication. Literary art lies in the expression and patterns by which writers communicate and structure their stories rather than in the sources of its information. Fiction is an inclusive genre:

Sometimes authors weave fictional episodes about historical characters, epochs, and settings and thus make "historical *fiction*." Sometimes authors use imaginative elaborations of incidents and qualities of a real person in a BIOGRAPHY, resulting in . . . the "fictional BIOGRAPHY." Sometimes the actual events of the author's life are presented under the guise of imaginative creations, resulting in "autobiographical *fiction*." Sometimes actual persons and events are presented under the guise of *fiction*, resulting in the ROMAN A CLEF. (Thrall 202)

Yet Kingston was given a "nonfiction" book award for *The Woman Warrior* simply on the basis of the autobiographical source of some of the details and information, while Allende's *The House of the Spirits*, which is just as clearly based on her family, was accepted as a novel immediately. Critics need to return to the inclusive definition, which concludes with a reminder that "*fiction* is a subject matter rather than a type of literature" (202), to recognize today's art of the novel.

Finally, these women challenge the *mythos* in which the mainstream novel in America has been written, rediscovering the balance of the comedy and tragedy of human existence that Cervantes maintains in *Don Quixote*. Early American women novelists seemed much more conscious of the literary techniques connected to the comic mode than are recent writers. Louis D. Rubin, Jr. has argued that "American literary imagination has from its earliest days been at least as much comic in nature as tragic" (3), yet "it is remarkable how comparatively little attention has been paid to American humor, and to the comic imagination in general, by those who have chronicled and interpreted American literature" (4). Similarly, Regina Barreca has explained that "[o]ften women's humor deals with those subjects traditionally reserved for tragedy: life and death, love and hate, connection and abandonment" (31).

Many of these early novels were labeled comedy of manners and dismissed by attitudes that even today see manners only as ritualistic or habitual social behavior. They were also labeled as didactic, dismissed again by attitudes that would separate the arts from our "practical education" as if learning to be human were a luxurious addendum to living life seriously. Novels of manners are teaching stories, but if their aesthetics are appreciated rather than ignored, many easily escape the criticism of being didactic. They hope to make us think before we act, to be as concerned about our motivation as we are about our manners. George Eliot explains the importance of the types being explored, not to perpetuate manners but to reveal motives:

It is not so very serious that we should have false ideas about evanescent fashions—about the manners and conversations of beaux and duchesses; but it *is* serious that our sympathy with the perennial joys and struggles, the toil, the tragedy, and the humour in the life of our more heavily-laden fellow-men, should be perverted. . . . The thing for mankind to know is, not what are the motives and influences which the moralist thinks *ought* to act on the labourer or the artisan, but what are the motives and influences which *do* act on him. We want to be taught to feel, not for the heroic artisan, or the sentimental peasant, but for the peasant in all his coarse apathy, and the artisan in all his suspicious selfishness. (110–11)

Being "taught to feel" goes beyond dialectic: "Appeals founded on generalizations and statistics require a sympathy ready-made, a moral sentiment already in activity" (110). That Society has robbed itself of its fullest moral development by limiting women is suggested as well in her essay on Madame de Sablé: "Let the whole field of reality be laid open to woman as well as to man, and then that which is peculiar in her mental modification, instead of being, as it is now, a source of discord and repulsion between the sexes, will be found to be a necessary complement to the truth and beauty of life" (37).

Balancing the comedy and tragedy of life, as the cyclical human community absorbs the linear despair of individual death, enabled early Americans to tell the stories that reveal how we as a human community can survive. Their characters did not offer answers; they, like us, were simply imperfect individuals attempting to understand and connect with the inner self, the Other, society, and the universe. Emphasis is placed on the patterns, the type each comes to represent, and on the steps in their education, for which nature serves as the ideal model. The story explores individual instances that reveal the pattern of that larger home so that the human community within its borders can know its manners in order to survive literally and its motives in order to make conscious choices and survive as fully human. The author is the balancing third perspective, writing a "teaching story" or "exemplum" by presenting characters and situations true to our society from which we can learn.

Even then these techniques, which derive from rhetoric rather than drama, seldom earned critical praise. Despite that, many women embraced them as more appropriate for conveying the story of the human community and the cyclical pattern of new beginnings, which allows us to see even the darkest events in life as integral parts of the human comedy. Dialectical argument may convince us that we are human and therefore we die, but the associative logic of common beliefs argues that we live on as long as memory and community survive.

The dialectic arguments of Realism only appear to give "objective truths," ignoring the selectivity of the examples upon which the arguments have been based. All novels are subjective, reflecting their creators; the novel that introduces its reader to that creator is no more or less didactic than the novel that creates a persona to mask the puppeteer manipulating character and action. Similarly, Bertoldt Brecht contrasts epic and drama and chooses the epic mode that acknowledges the art and artificiality of theater; he wants to encourage his audience to think as he instructs and entertains them simultaneously.

The meronymic novel explores the potential inclusivity of the human perspective: the individual *is* communal; the self *needs* the Other; and in this world, the world of the literary present, the body *is* coterminous with the soul. Without this "both/and" perspective, we exist in Flatland, a linear reality condemned to entropy. This fresh perspective helps us perceive as well the cyclical reality in which all lines are curved, and the point at which we find ourselves determines our relationships to all other points. This recognition of the simultaneity of linear and cyclical truth puts us back on the globe: that road before us only looks like a straight line because we had lost perspective.

But the novel demands equally that we see the road clearly; it has learned from Realism that we must keep our eyes open and our minds working if we are to encompass multicultural diversity. Gender and cultural blindness does not mean that we see instead the purely universal truths, because any truths must be realized in this moment. Only through a sequential pattern of human experience can we tell the whole story. The evolution of the meronymic novel is the artistic maturation of the genre; it is an attempt to fit the form to the content just as was Whitman's experiments in free verse. We know that free verse takes as many forms as there are poets and poems whose ideas determine the shape; so too does and will the meronymic novel take as many forms as can marry the polarities of Romance and Realism to capture the many truths of human experience.

While women are not alone in experimenting with this marriage of form and content, their participation has helped us see the futility in marginalizing the otherness that is already a part of us. The members of the human family are as essential to each other as the members of the human body, and it is our inter-dependence that defines us as well as our diversity. I have chosen select contemporary novels by women to exemplify the evolution of the meronymic novel, dividing them into three chapters depending on their stylistic balance. The first group of writers expands Realism to concretize the mental images that have shaped our world; the second group chooses speculative forms of Romance to materialize the spirit of Love; the third group centers itself in its ethnic traditions to embody the balance of self and other, form and content, internal and external, and visible and invisible human truths.

The whole story of the mind, spirit, and body of humanity thus becomes accessible through the incredible flexibility of this English language we share with its roots in the dead languages of Greece and Rome and in the living languages from which it is continually borrowing. In the denotations and con-notations of individual words, in the stories imaged in figurative language, and in the ideas conveyed by linguistic structures and literary patterns, simultaneous messages from self and other, individual and society, humanity and the universe can be conveyed and understood with surprising ease. When we cross the thresh-old that appeared to be a boundary between worlds, we realize that there has always been only one world that we must share, one story that defines our hu-manity, one body of which we are all essential, if diverse, members.

Women in patriarchal society are taught to limit themselves to the definitions they share with men, accepting patronymic, diminutive names and supportive and protected roles as daughters, wives, and mothers. Only within such roles, as long as the patriarchy is itself intact, are women offered socially human status. How-ever, the wars of the twentieth century have unravelled our social fabric, nor have we been able to pick up the threads of our communal lives in the cold war years. Hoping to weave a stronger cloth from the severed threads by the protests and riots since the sixties, we succeeded only in rending the fabric into a collection of disparate scraps.

Decades may still be needed before our nation can expand its perspective enough to weave an inclusive new pattern that fully realizes its democratic ideals. Art, however, can already offer a patchwork quilt, a multicultural egalitarian inclusivity that re-visions a united American reality. The construction of that metaphorical quilt is chronicled in our contemporary novels, and the novels themselves help us understand the expanded perception by reflecting it back to us in their looking-glass role. Seeing reality freshly from our socially constructed margins, these women novelists can teach us aesthetically without lapsing "from the picture to the diagram," however much this study tries to peel layer from layer to reveal their artistic processes.

The women writers I have chosen to discuss express in themselves the composite reality that we subsume in the word American. Within the geographical borders of the United States can be found the regional wisdom of Eudora Welty, the Amerasian heritage of Maxine Hong Kingston, the Mexican, Euro American, and Laguna Indian Southwest of Leslie Marmon Silko, and African American perspectives from the Georgian setting of Toni Cade Bambara and the Northeast urban ghetto of Gloria Naylor to the vast panorama from Africa to California past and future provided by Octavia E. Butler. Helping us to understand the expanded geographical realities of American literature are the Canadian Margaret Atwood and the Chilean Isabel Allende. Helping us better understand the continuing cultural domination of British ideology that keeps our literature housed in English departments are Doris Lessing and Antonia Susan Byatt.

Only selected novels by these women will be discussed. If we are to have a truly representative canon of American literature, we need to shift our attention from the author to the text. My university offers four courses in Shakespeare, for instance; when in their brief college career will most students have time to learn about any Other? Striving to be a comprehensive critic as Fuller has defined it, I have made difficult choices, neglecting books I admire greatly, because choices must be made. These novels best exemplify the transformative power of the meronymic novel.

My conclusion will pay tribute to that transformative power of these women novelists, who turn boundaries into thresholds to offer us fresh perspectives on our contemporary malaise and alternative possibilities within our own time and place. The meronymic novel is an art form, but it is also a social document, the melding of myth and history, of the personal and communal, of possibility and probability in the eternal present that allows us to begin to heal our fragmented past and recapture St. Augustine's promise of future expectations. The incomprehensible horrors realized in the twentieth century led us to believe in—even to consider the advisability of—our own extinction. The meronymic novel reminds us once more that *we* are valuable as the storytellers; it is the gift as well as the task of human consciousness to vision, and re-vision, reality. As myth-tellers, a term Kane would confine to archaic humanity but that is deserved by the meronymic novelist, we reinvent the world, discovering in the marriage of the individual and communal selves the motive force of love, which embraces the world around us. What Kane defines as "a dialogue with nature that "was—and still is—an affectionate counterpoint to the earth's voices, with no ambition to direct them or force them to give up their meanings" (14), is achieved by the meronymic novelist. These stories correspond with the story of nature, reestablishing the purpose of cultural myth through the consciously constructed cultural self. For those of us who believe that Nature is always evolving, un-folding, she must be read freshly by each generation if we are to stay in harmony with her universal story. We have neither a future nor a past without such con-sciousness; without our stories through which we share that consciousness, "There is only the eternal present, and biology," as Kingston tells her mother in *The Woman Warrior*. The novel's realistic, metonymic sequence of events de-fines the journey of our lives; its romantic, metaphoric symbolism comprehends its human meaning. As Smoky Barnable concludes at the end of Crowley's *Little, Big*, "The Tale was behind them. And it was to there they journeyed. One step would take them there; they were there already" (532).

Part I

Re-Visioning Reality

Literature must encompass *theoria* and *praxis*, and in a world in which both seem to be controlled by men, women writers still manage to communicate the "other" motivations of their women characters. In *The Madwoman in the Attic*, Sandra Gilbert and Susan Gubar note ways in which women writers encode their works with feminist ideas that implicitly challenge the actions and apparent motives, while Ellen Moers' *Literary Women* offers a feminist reading of Mary Shelley's *Frankenstein* that explores its origins in birth traumas rather than science. Such encoding and uncovering of "other" motivations behind the *praxis* of women's fiction suggests an otherness of *theoria* that shapes the world as it is perceived, and the literature as it is written, by these women. Re-visioning our reality through the senses and words of women will not change the recognizable surface, but it may change the weight we give appearances, the way we apprehend that reality. Challenging the ideas rather than the actions, the social constructs rather than individuals, lets us "begin to work together for an understanding of literature that is truly universal, and for a criticism that accepts contradictions and limitations, but that does not make them an excuse to avoid working for social change" (Showalter 199).

Coming to women's novels with preconceptions about the appropriate form, language, and content limits us from learning what shape is appropriate to the ideas being expressed. The tragic *mythos* of Greek drama transfers easily to the heroic structure of climax and resolution in novels, but novels offer more complex stories than do plays. A novel seldom reduces to the story of any individual; its narrative impetus is found more in epic than in tragic poetry. Ideology can remain hidden, although individuals must reduce *theoria* to *praxis*, even Hamlet.

For these novelists, often the communal story takes precedence over individuals, whose actions are simultaneously unique and part of a larger pattern. That pattern can be suggested by allusions and by cumulative connections established on the historical level. We are encouraged to stretch our imaginations to encompass the whole story, cyclical and linear, communal and individual, and to focus on the interdependence of each part. The larger *theoria*, ideology, both encompasses and is affected by individual consciousness.

The novelists focus on ideology, although each creates realistic surfaces. While a reader can find linear climactic scenes in the novels and can follow the story's chronology, consciously cyclical patterns stress community over individual and life over death. We will examine each novelist's experiments in language, structure, and content as she expands our choices by varying the possible patterns within which literary—and by extension social—order can be achieved. It is by telling the whole story that literature becomes an agent of social change, by helping us see in its historical accuracy what the problems are and reminding us in its mythic dimensions what human perspective shaped society that way. If our stories shape the world, "novel" stories can begin to re-shape it as well.

In a patriarchal society, women provide the perspective that has been obscured. The present study offers novelists who must balance seemingly oxymoronic polarities to define the self. They cannot settle for male or female, social or theoretical, definitions; they must live in a world that fears or ignores their differences from what has become accepted as probable and typical. When a novel can balance those polarities, the meronymic perspective achieved can expand reality for each of us, while the "novel" pattern can offer alternative social structures, new possibilities for ordering our communal lives.

1

The Wheel of Life:
Eudora Welty and Gloria Naylor

After a fifty-year career (*A Curtain of Green* was published in 1941), Eudora Welty received the National Book Foundation 1991 Distinguished Contribution to American Letters Award. This well-deserved award reflects the critical esteem she has earned, primarily as a regionalist. However, from the beginning of that career, myth has transformed her language and expanded her perspective. It unites the seven stories of her novel *The Golden Apples* and raises the small Mississippi town in which it is set to a timeless realm so that we can better see the multicultural influences that have shaped Welty's—and our—America.

The short story has become a significant art form in America since the mid-nineteenth century, fragmenting the novel formally just as Romance and Realism fragmented it stylistically. American Realism began as regional fiction, reflecting our geographical and cultural fragmentation. Yet if the short story divided the whole story like a jigsaw puzzle, allowing a writer to concentrate on one piece at a time, Welty's interest in myth revealed her potential for fitting those pieces together. Nor does the social confinement of her characters in Morgana limit their ability to represent the human family; it simply defines the historical and geographical details of their lives.

What their perspective does obscure, however, are the stories of an integral part of Morgana: its African American population. To balance this myopia of Southern whites of both genders, I have juxtaposed Welty's vision of reality with Gloria Naylor's Northern black ghetto in *The Women of Brewster Place*. More than three decades separate these novels, but a shared concern for the female community and consciousness of the literary, mythic, and historical contexts in which they wrote enable us to parallel their seemingly irreconcilable visions of America and see better the common threads weaving us together.

The earliest writer we will be discussing, Welty has often been compared with Faulkner in her ability to capture the realities of their shared region. M. H. Abrams identifies "setting, speech and social structure and conditions of a particular locality . . . as important conditions affecting the temperament of the characters and their ways of thinking, feeling, and interacting" in such regional novels (121), and Welty's language in particular has been frequently praised for capturing the nuances of Southern speech. Just as the "mythical Morgana relates consistently to the historical world, outside in time, in the details of its chronicle" (Isaacs 36–37), so too do its residents speak and behave precisely as we would expect of their time and place. Her realism provides Welty's literary construct of Morgana with "a local habitation and a name."

Simultaneously, however, Welty marries that moment to myth by her multimythic allusions and the communal roles of the women who keep myth alive in Morgana. The opening chapter, "Shower of Gold," is written in realistic oral discourse, which helps us realize that the speaker, Katie Rainey, is a mythic storyteller, filling her tales with allusions that establish connections to both patriarchal and Goddess/old wives' tales discredited by the prevailing social myth but remembered within the community.

Structure as well as language transforms the realistic style of the novel. The short story cycle balances the linear quests of individuals, especially that of Virgie Rainey. A baby who has survived swallowing a button while Katie visits Snowdie MacLain in the first chapter, Virgie will circle back to Morgana until Katie dies in the final chapter and she is finally freed from communal responsibilities to pursue her own dreams.

If Virgie's dream has been deferred, she has plenty of company among Naylor's women on Brewster Place. Naylor in fact prefaces the novel with the Langston Hughes poem that asks about such dreams. Discussing her writing with Naomi Epel, Naylor says, "If certain dreams plague us they're probably things that plague us in our waking life, so writing—by going to that same level where dreams live, wherever that may be—helps to clean that out" (177). Both women balance realistic depictions of their known worlds with the dream, the mythic promise of other possibilities. "Despite Gloria Naylor's shrewd and lyrical portrayal of many of the realities of black life," Anne Gottlieb recognized in an early review, *Women* "isn't realistic fiction—it is mythic" (25). Both women focus on American "peasants," on what Eliot called "our more heavily-laden fellow-men," in order to teach us as she recommends "to feel . . . for the peasant in all his coarse apathy, and the artisan in all his suspicious selfishness" (110–11). Only then can we see what ideas "stand under" their actions and what possibilities shape their dreams.

Shakespeare is Naylor's literary source for dialoguing on dreams, and both novels can best be compared imagistically and formally by paralleling the passages in their structural cycles of life to his description of our "acts being seven ages" in *As You Like It* (II, vii). First, however, we need to share a common meronymic language with the writers to understand the mythic and historical complexities of their versions of our story.

The title itself provides the first imagistic clue to Welty's novel, and scarcely a name is without some degree of symbolism. As a physical image, the ripe fruit represents the cyclical rebirths of the natural world, of which human fertility is an integral part. As a mythic image, they unite Greek, Celtic, and Norse European myths, pre-patriarchal goddess myths, and even the American folklore of Johnny Appleseed. Welty dialogues with literary tradition by recalling W. B. Yeats as well as Shakespeare. Yeats was as enamored with myth as is Welty, and his poem "The Song of the Wandering Aengus" ends with a reference to "The golden apples of the sun." The wanderer of his poem connects with an Irish myth about a trout who turns into a girl, the knowledge she possesses, and the quest to find her again. The wanderers throughout Welty's novel follow similar quests, and other lines from the poem will be echoed as the dialogue continues, while Yeats' poem "Leda and the Swan" will be transformed into "Sir Rabbit" (perceptive feminist analyses of Welty's dialoguing with each poem are given in the critical essay by Patricia Yeager).

Welty's dialoguing expands rather than attacks our literary traditions. In *One Writer's Beginnings*, she credits Yeats with introducing her to passion and adds that "the poem that smote me first was 'The Song of the Wandering Aengus'; it was the poem that turned up, fifteen years or so later, in my stories of *The Golden Apples* and runs all through that book" (88). She widens the vision already provided by Yeats to include the female perspective; her wanderer Virgie Rainey is female, and his "fire . . . in my head" description of passion is identified with at least three women characters. Cassie Morrison quotes the poem and Miss Eckhart starts such a fire in "June Recital," while in "The Wanderers" we learn that Katie Rainey was known as Katie Blazes for setting fire to her stockings: "She had the neighborhood scared she'd go up in flames at an early age." Thus gender does not determine who will be haunted by the passionate questions that make us wander from our Morganas. When Welty transforms the "fire . . . in my head" to a fire in Miss Eckhart's hair or on Katie Rainey's stockinged legs, we recognize simultaneously the humor—and the horror—of human passions.

The known stories from literature and myth are being brought into balance with neglected female insights by this dialogue, which helps dissolve the gender exclusivity of patriarchal myths and social stereotyping. The "goddesses" of Morgana—Lizzie and Jinny Love Stark, Snowdie MacLain, Katie and Virgie Rainey, Cassie Morrison—are assigned diminutive nicknames that obscure their mythic importance (goddesses diminished to fairies), indicating that they have accepted their subsumed position as part of the patriarchal pantheon; but outside the Olympus of Morgana, Mattie Will Sojourner in "Sir Rabbit" represents our ability to "Will" our "Matter" and discover the goddess in ourselves, while Easter in "Moon Lake" offers the possibility of rebirth. Maideen Sumrall, however, represents the vulnerability of the outsider, lured by the attractions of belonging to such apparent beauty.

Welty draws our attention to the mental images conveyed by myth, the ideological perceptions it embodies, through multimythic allusions that interpenetrate and dialogue with each other simultaneously. "Shower of Gold" refers to Zeus' impregnation of Danae with Perseus, for instance, establishing the individual struggle to balance love and separateness as expressed in the struggle between Perseus and the Medusa, to which Virgie will refer in the final chapter. This struggle, paralleled in a painting of Siegfried and the Dragon, helps Virgie connect the myths with each other and with her present struggle, a multicultural perspective offering a balancing third element:

Because Virgie saw things in their time, like hearing them—and perhaps because she must believe in the Medusa equally with the Perseus—she saw the stroke of the sword in three moments, not one. In the three was the damnation—no, only the secret, unhurting because not caring in itself—beyond beauty and the sword's stroke and the terror lay their existence in time—far out and endless, a constellation which the heart could read over many a night.

The mythic allusions are not simple clues to a contemporary version of a cultural absolute truth. Welty forces us to look through the sequential events to the *mythos*, to see "things in [our] time" and understand what stands under and motivates our actions. Her language undermines our desire to solve the puzzle by tracing individual myths, as might be done in the Greek parallels of John Updike's *The Centaur*, for instance. As Sir James Frazer collated cultural myths to record the recurring patterns in his monumental study, *The Golden Bough*, so too Welty traces the Greek Olympus back to its Goddess origins and forward to its Celtic transformations to understand what reaches America. This is particularly important to center us in the traditions of the WASP Americans who inhabit Morgana, because their Anglo-Saxon Protestantism is a product of many European traditions.

The golden apples introduce a variety of myths to center the characters. Classical myth offers the golden apples of the Hesperides, guarded in a western garden by the three daughters of Night, a wedding gift from Gaia to Hera. The Goddess gives the gifts of nature (*Pan-dora* in Greek), reflected in the natural beauty that surrounds and fills Morgana, and reappears herself as the "Virgins" Virgie and Jinny Love. The apples are taken from the garden by Hercules with the help of Atlas, but Welty's version in "Music from Spain" re-visions this heroic theft. The apples are returned later by Athena because they are "too holy" to be anywhere else, which suggests their connections with the golden apples of immortality held by the Norse Idun and the apple in the Judaic-Christian Garden of Eden, other symbols of our passionate quest for knowledge and the answers out of our reach.

Apples crop up again in the myth of Atalanta, distracted from her race by three golden apples tossed by her opponent Melanian that allow him to win the race and claim her as his bride. This myth is mentioned in "Music from Spain," and Atalanta is also connected with Virgie as virgin goddess. Yet again a golden apple shows up in the Judgment of Paris, to be given to the fairest of three goddesses. Consider in this context the three goddesses of "Moon Lake"—Easter/Esther, Nina, and Jinny Love—linguistic parallels to Hera, Athena, and the love goddess Aphrodite. Paris chooses Aphrodite because she promises him the fairest woman—Helen of Troy—in exchange, which leads to the Trojan War, but Welty's Paris—Loch Morrison—will save Easter and be reborn free from Morgana to wander East. However, since Helen is the daughter of Leda by Zeus, the myths interlock with Yeats' poetry and the MacLain family.

The Old Testament story of Queen Esther and the New Testament Easter resurrection further define the queen and sacrificial orphan of "Moon Lake." Celtic myth and "the silver apples of the moon" are equally important here, attesting to the ongoing influence and evolution of storytelling, which culminates with Katie Rainey's rendition of the Morgana myth within Welty's own mythtelling.

Welty very carefully names her world of Morgana. Her list of "Main Families" begins with King and Snowdie (Hudson) MacLain. It is easy to see King's role as Morgana's Zeus, while his Celtic surname, son of Lain, recalls Cuchulain, the greatest Irish hero. He may be treated like a god, not confined to the social morality by which others in the community must live, but his final return to Morgana and his aging reveal his humanity. The swan-like Snowdie twists the Leda myth as well. Yeats' own explanation of his poem "Leda and the Swan" in *A Vision*, prefigures Virgin Mary:

I imagine the annunciation that founded Greece as made to Leda, remembering that they showed in a Spartan temple, strung up to the roof as a holy relic, an unhatched egg of hers, and that from one of her eggs came Love and from the other War. But all things are from antithesis, and when in my ignorance I try to imagine that annunciation rejected I can but see bird and woman blotting out some corner of the Babylonian mathematical starlight. (268)

Yeats saw the classical cycle replacing the Earth Goddess cycle of Babylon and itself being replaced by the Christian cycle. Welty adds her female perspective to his vision by staying at home with Snowdie and the twin boys Ran and Eugene, parallels to the "Love" egg of the mythic Castor and Pollux, rather than following the wandering god or retelling the more familiar "War" stories of their sisters Helen and Clytemnestra. When the mortal Castor dies, Pollux refuses immortality from Zeus, who then places them both among the stars as the constellation of the Twins. Robert Graves connects them as well with the pear tree (*The Greek Myths* 249–52), a link to yet other "golden apples."

Since we are back to apples, we must admit that Nature has been a wicked stepmother to Snowdie. An albino with weak eyes, this Snow White must avoid the sun. If she seems to sleep until her returning royal lover wakens her, she also connects to Arienrhod, the Celtic Snow Queen. Arienrhod also has twin boys, which Graves in *The White Goddess* connects to the co-king pattern behind the classical myths of the waxing and waning year.

In Celtic myth, as in this novel, the images associated with the twins are fire and water. Snowdie, as fixed/frozen water, balances Katie "Blazes" Rainey, for communities shelter their own diversity even while they exclude foreigners. Water may wander, as does the river by which King leaves his hat and in which Virgie swims before each wanders, or it too may be fixed in Moon Lake which reflects our faces as it reflects the moonlight of our dreams but which also threatens to drown us. Easter's resurrection depends on a heroic revival process, but Virgie, who "saw things in their time," is her own hero—has fulfilled her obligations and is old enough to take the plunge.

Fire can also be fixed/planted, as is the "fiery streak of salvia" which runs around the Rainey home, a home of passionate people who choose to plant themselves in Morgana. Similarly, Cassie will plant her mother's name, Catherine (another artist and storyteller, another Katie), who resisted having her name diminished and ends up with it fully expressed as communal art.

The nicknames of the MacLain twins, Ran and Scooter, identify them as wanderers; while their given names, Lucius Randall and Eugene Hudson, send us to myth and history for sources. Lucius relates Ran to the twin of light, while the British Isles sings his story in the ballad of Lord Randal. In "The Whole World Knows," Ran, as does Lord Randal, complains to his mother of his pain, a lover's poison that kills him. Ran is not killed by the poison of his wife Jinny Love's betrayal, but Maideen Sumrall is (the maiden of summer/fall, the harvest virgin, is a common sacrificial figure in fertility myths).

Eugene Hudson MacLain has a decidedly unmythic name, the twin who proves his mortality by returning to Morgana in a coffin. Named after an explorer (as well as his maternal grandfather Hudson), Eugene wanders west, but his quest fails. Perhaps his first name relates to eugenics, a scientific approach to fertility; if so, science is not a successful alternative to myth in Welty's world, since his daughter Fancy dies. As in Hawthorne's tales, science and fancy fail to improve on nature. However, Eugene's romance, his Fancy, is lost to us, another silver apple that only the moonlight, obscured by the golden sun, could reveal.

King MacLain has been fragmented in his twins—historic and mythic, wanderer and king—each unable to understand the whole story, which results in the deaths of two sacrificial maidens—perhaps the female within each of them. The MacLain men, the "king's" men, represent the traditional male fertility of Morgana, but they will not be able to put the broken egg, from which myth tells us the two sets of twins are hatched, back together again. This begins the symbolism associated with the fragmentation of the generation of Morgana children born into the novel's time period. Denied their heritage, they struggle to shape their own lives as best they can. On the realistic level, Isaacs finds "the most important element of unity" in King's acknowledged and illegitimate children (37), but such a connection is ephemeral at best (as my mother told me, "A man thinks he's a father because some woman told him so").

While he may represent a mythic heritage of passion, which Virgie acknowledges in "The Wanderers" as the kinship she feels to him and Ran, King's social structure robs the illegitimate orphans of an inherited kinship to him or Morgana, while his wandering deprives his legitimate offspring of his parenting. King's responsibility for the "broken egg" is suggested in the word Morgana. *Webster's* defines morganatic as "relating to a marriage between a member of a royal or noble family and a person of inferior rank in which the rank of the inferior partner remains unchanged and the children of the marriage do not succeed to the titles, fiefs, or entailed property of the parent of the higher rank."

Perhaps this is why Ran and Eugene share the characteristics of the "strange children," the "rebel-victims" discussed by Ihab H. Hassan in "The Character of Post-War Fiction in America"; here, too, "dramatic emphasis is on the loss, the pain and bitterness of growth, the fall from uneasy grace" (31). Welty's language directs our attention to King's failure to be a father to his sons; when gods marry "among the daughters of men," need they be concerned with the fate of their offspring? Nor has he cared for the daughter adequately; her life is spent waiting for her Prince Charming. Meanwhile, it is the dwarfs who support her, the community of diminished gods and goddesses in Morgana. Isaacs argues that Morgana is "the protagonist of the novel, with its people as symbolic forces and resident deities" (39). Yet the king is seldom there until he is too old to resist its claim; the "peasants" keep the community intact and protect its sleeping beauties without his guidance.

So what happens after Snow White marries her prince? The patriarchal myth fails to continue the story, but Welty provides one version. Accepting King's wandering ways as validated by myth, Snowdie is a patient Penelope raising her sons. But she has weak eyes, offering them little re-visioning of that myth. King is willing for a conjugal visit but is driven back by the otherness of Halloween masks, another suggestion of the Celtic moonlight of Snowdie's untold story. If a father can't recognize his sons, how can they know their father, Eugene will ask in "Music from Spain." A biological definition of fatherhood is being challenged here as well as a general failure of parenting as a source of useful preparation for life's demands.

The Rainey family, as their name suggests, is more intact because they identify with the community of Nature. Fate, also a godlike wanderer in his youth as we learn in the last chapter, is a nurturing milkman whose wife Katie is storyteller and ice-cream lady. *Fata morgana*, a term that originally referred to King Arthur's sister Morgan le Fay in British myth, has come to mean mirage according to *Webster's*; yet within the myth that is Morgana, this Fate is one of the resident gods. The Rainey children, Victor and Virgie, have names that suggest the divine siblings Apollo and Artemis (called a virgin goddess because she is free of marital obligations). In our violent patriarchal world, however, Victor is ironically killed in the war. Yet Virgie survives death by button as a baby and her early wanderings, returning to Morgana to fulfill her obligations until her parents are both dead. When she is free to leave Morgana, it ceases to be the myth that encompasses her and becomes the *fata morgana* of its name.

Welty herself in *One Writer's Beginnings* identifies Virgie as the "subject" of the novel who "comes into her own in the last of the stories, 'The Wanderers.' Passionate, recalcitrant, stubbornly undefeated by failure or hurt or disgrace or bereavement, all the while heedlessly wasting of her gifts, she knows to the last that there is a world that remains out there, a world living and mysterious, and that she is of it" (111). Water and fire combine in the Rainey family, but planting both in the community lets the milk of human kindness flow—and even frozen it has the sweetness of ice cream. Virgie's heritage and parenting are intact, which assists her growth as fully human.

The Morgana Welty sees in her own Mississippi offers the possibility of a supportive community, providing parental love that nurtures and enables the next generation to grow and prosper. At the same time, such support could be a mirage. Does Morgana support its children or does it freeze their emotion and smother their passion? Has the Goddess been diminished to narrow-minded women who turn their backs on outsiders and demand that members of the community limit their vision to receive protection from the fearful otherness outside? Choosing to remain resident gods diminishes members regardless of gender: Ran is encouraged to ignore his wife's infidelity as "a thing of the flesh" and learns the lie well enough to let his own female insight die and to become—what else?—a politician. Welty places Morgana in her historical present and uses a female perspective to reveal its mythic marriages, but those marriages are inevitably patriarchal and morganatic. Her mythtelling, however, by making the myth new, reveals the pattern that shapes and controls Morgana. Welty's multimythic language is meant to uncover the face of the Goddess, "casting aside the gynophobic masks that have obscured her beauty, her power, and her beneficence" (Pratt 178); her realism, however, can only capture that face reflecting its years in a patriarchal marriage.

The MacLains and the Raineys are surrounded by other families who will fulfill their own communal and mythic roles, as their names suggest. Particularly important are the Starks and the Morrisons. The strength of Lizzie Stark, the goddess/queen of Morgana (her husband is Comus, the name of a minor satyr in classical myth), comforts the frightened children when they venture outside to "Moon Lake"; her virgin goddess/daughter Jinny Love reveals that in classical myth virginity did not preclude sexual activity. In "June Recital," Cassie Morrison is a Cassandra who has already learned to limit her intuitive vision by refusing to look out the window to validate it in the present moment, while her brother Loch (the Scottish name for lake suggests his later heroic role in "Moon Lake") fights even illness to see things meronymically—through direct observation and imaginative interpretation. The Morrisons' family role is to report the news for us, and the children have learned from both their newspaper editor father and their singer/storytelling mother to see historic and mythic Morgana.

Welty's Morgana must balance the story of our patriarchal reality—in 1949 when this novel was written of a war-torn world—with the story of community and love on the home front. She does this by ephemeralizing the historical moment and focusing on human relationships. The worlds interpenetrate, but at least in Morgana, Welty can focus on love rather than war. Joseph Campbell describes the use of a sanctuary and ceremonies to encompass levels of truth closed to

the advocates of Aristotelian logic, for whom A can never be B, . . . For the whole purpose of entering a sanctuary or participating in a festival is that one should be overtaken by the state known in India as "the other mind": (Sanskrit *anya-manas*: absent mindedness, possession by a spirit), where one is "beside one-self," spellbound: set apart from one's logic of self-possession and overpowered by the force of a logic of dissociation, wherein A is B, and C is also B. (40)

Welty makes her mythic Morgana such a sanctuary and schedules seven festivals that can be identified by rituals in her seven stories. At the same time, the titles of each chapter provide images that unite myths and capture Shakespeare's "seven ages."

Shakespeare's infant comes as a "Shower of Gold," suggesting both the gift of fertility that makes MacLain king and Welty's appreciation of the wealth of having children. King's twins are born on January 1, and their father visits at Halloween, linking the classical twin-faced Janus god of the new and old year with Samhain, which is the beginning of the Celtic year. The festival of birth, which claims the gifts of nature for the human family, is celebrated in the ritual of christening. Significantly, Snowdie "clapped the names on them of Lucius Randall and Eugene Hudson, after her own father and her mother's father. It was the only sign she ever gave Morgana that maybe she didn't think the name King MacLain had stayed beautiful." The ritual has been transformed, shifting the emphasis to their maternal heritage.

Shakespeare's "whining school-boy" must perform on Miss Eckhart's piano in "June Recital," having received his art education from this German refugee with her picture of Siegfried and the Dragon, while learning from direct observation with Loch Morrison the power of passion's fires. Frazer tells us that the fire festivals of Midsummer Eve were celebrated throughout Europe and probably reflected the anxiety caused by the summer solstice—the end of the sun's upward cycle and the beginning of its downward cycle (622). The Celts who inhabited the "Land's End of Europe" set their fires instead on May Day and Halloween, the festivals that divided the year for them (630). This might explain the paper maypole Miss Eckhart constructs to start her fire. Frazer further describes the associated ritual of young people leaping over the fires (625), providing a mythic image for the upstairs antics of Virgie and the sailor while the fire is burning. Also connected is the confirmation ceremony of the young girls in their music recital; each celebrates the awakening of passion, of the "fire . . . in my head" of Yeats' poetry.

"Sir Rabbit" humorously images King MacLain as "the lover," ironically celebrating the ceremony of physical awakening, appropriately set in the woods. Mattie Will provides us a fresh perspective on three versions: first with the relative innocence of the twins and later with the adulterous act of King MacLain, but throughout with the dialogic storytelling of Yeats' "Leda and the Swan" and her interpretations. This larger context helps Mattie to "will" her rape, to be a subject even when she is violated by patriarchal myth and nature's need to procreate. She controls the ritual by being the storyteller, transforming reality through shifting the perspective to her own, and she is rewarded with seeing through King MacLain, who is himself caught napping. Just as Virgie was freed of the "damnation" of the Perseus and Medusa myth by realizing the secret of the indifference of the gods, so too can Mattie will herself free of male dominance. Her story ends with the "mysterious" memory of the twins, not of the inherited worship of their driven father; she refuses to be destroyed by the realistic violence of life or wooed by the promises of patriarchal myth. As a Sojourner, standing outside Morgana, she embraces instead the unchanging, ever-regenerating natural world, taking on the God/*dess'* knowledge enough to see King in the past as his divided twin sons and in the future as a tired, very human old man—an old, diminished god in a new country, a new religion.

Shakespeare's soldier is but a boy scout in Welty's "Moon Lake." This chapter, included by David Young and Keith Hollaman in their collection *Magical Realist Fiction*, employs the powers of moonlight on the lake as it transforms Loch Morrison from a Morgana boy scout to a soldier of life itself. Again outside Morgana in nature's realm, the orphaned Easter is queen of life and death, Loch her hard-working hero facilitating the cycle of life. Such soldiering frees him to see freshly the world around him as Moon Lake mirrors Morgana's untold stories, reflected in the faces of unacknowledged orphans, of Easter and the apparently guilty black face of Exum McLane. "Moon Lake" captures the pain of rebirth, echoing the immersion of baptism as Easter/Esther plunges into the water but following this with the lifesaving parallel to the sex act, performed on her by Loch, which brings her back to life. Both rituals are needed here, because both death and rebirth must be encompassed in this harvest sacrifice if the victim is to be resurrected. The knowledge of otherness, of the dark, even of death itself, lies in the depths of Moon Lake, a sanctuary unplumbed by the sun. Loch goes East once he leaves Morgana, so Easter's name might have one more level of meaning, suggesting that facing death completes the quest for golden apples and begins the dark quest for silver apples that can return us to a new morning.

Without encompassing the whole story, Morgana is not likely to satisfy Shakespeare's justice in "The Whole World Knows." Morgana is imaged as a closed world; its justice is hierarchical and exclusive. Its ceremony of virgin sacrifice ironically defines patriarchal justice. Ran MacLain learns the pain of relationships when his community ignores his wife Jinny Love's betrayal because of her royal position as a love goddess and daughter of the town's matriarch. An outsider must pay the price to hold this goddess of love within the bonds of matrimony—to keep the community fertile and the heritage patrilinear. Maideen Sumrall's death comes alone and isolated; outsiders have neither communal protection nor male rescuers. Maideen is a suicide, passively accepting of her sacrificial role; that she won't live to tell her own story may be at least part of why Virgie hates her, as she admits in "The Wanderers."

Little is left for Shakespeare's last two ages but the falling action of Greek tragedy. If justice is lacking in the "Whole World," Ran's brother Eugene, who sought the Western garden in San Francisco, only finds himself mocked by the Golden Gate at Land's End. "Music From Spain," our first aural image, haunts Eugene with its otherness. This hero has raced westward, married and given birth to his Fancy, only to lose her to death and to turn his grief into violence toward her mother. Estranged from Morgana, from a mothering community, he pins his hopes on a "lean pantaloon" and follows an artist/father figure. Multimythic language has prepared us to see through the apparent otherness to recognize the mythic pattern of an Atlas ready to assist Eugene in his Herculean quest, but Eugene never understands, never gets beside himself. The otherness of the Spaniard bewilders him, an alienation symbolized as well by the otherness he sees everywhere on the journey. The Atlas who would help him remains foreign; they share only appetites, not languages. Achieving "mere oblivion," Eugene is returned to Morgana in a coffin.

Welty's finale, "The Wanderers," in its image of freedom to introduce the story of a funeral, rejects Shakespeare's promise of "mere oblivion" and interprets his "second childishness" as a cyclical new beginning. As Loch plunged into Moon Lake to seek Easter, Virgie dives into the river of life, willing even to learn music from Spain to enhance her own artistic talent, which found such little room for expression in Morgana. Her selling the cows is reminiscent both of her freedom from her personal and communal mothers and of the cows in Celtic myth who symbolize the wealth of communities; the rest of the story is now open to the free Virgin beyond the "Whole World" of Morgana. "The Wanderers" reminds us that even death can be a healing ceremony within the community. Virgie has learned to value communal and individual truths, mythic and historic truths, and her mother's funeral provides the ceremony that releases her mother's soul to wander and releases Virgie body and soul. If Virgie is Welty's "subject," as she says, then the subject of *The Golden Apples* is hope. Both mythic and historic limitations can possibly be overcome, and it is that hope which helps us survive. As Maideen's death suggests, we cannot live without love, without the support of the human family or the protection of a social structure; it is within these, within history and myth, that we must define ourselves and tell our story.

Throughout the generational cycle of Virgie and the twins, however, the stories of other characters begin and end. The funeral scene includes Nina Carmichael, Mrs. Junior Nesbitt, a younger storyteller who was convinced at the end of "Moon

Lake" that she and Jinny Love would "always be old maids" and is now "heavy with child." A pregnant storyteller promises us that the human story continues despite our individual despair.

"The events in our lives happen in a sequence in time, but in their significance to ourselves they find their own order, a timetable not necessarily—perhaps not possibly—chronological," Welty explains in *One Writer's Beginnings*. "The time as we know it subjectively is often the chronology that stories and novels follow: it is the continuous thread of revelation." That thread weaves together the mythic and historical stories of Morgana. Some characters in Welty's novel are peripheral to Morgana, however, and from the edges of the "Whole World" they challenge that communal exclusivity, as the name Sojourner (which connects Maideen and Mattie Will) suggests in its transience. "Colored" characters, as Welty calls them, are known for the most part only personally—by their first names; their familial and communal roles and myths are part of the otherness of the outside world. Exum McLane's last name reveals a patriarchal link that suggests yet a greater deprivation of heritage—not even a morganatic marriage is possible for offspring excluded both by illegitimacy and by cultural otherness. These characters provide correcting glimpses of the larger historic context in which Morgana exists, and which it ignores, imagining itself as "The Whole World."

Welty tells the sunlit story of America's quest for golden apples but only suggests obliquely the moonlight temptations of silver apples. Snowdie's silences, Loch's escape, Eugene's conception and loss of his Fancy, and Virgie's final moonlight swim chronicle Welty's indications of that quest, but its route lies beyond Morgana. We must turn to Naylor for that quest because her African American heritage well acquaints her with the American night. The magic of the full moon, of a Goddess cycle daring to reveal itself even within the patriarchal enclosure, lights her way through that darkness, as it will ours.

Shakespeare provides the language of dreams for Naylor's women, and Naylor dialogues with *A Midsummer Night's Dream* in "Cora Lee." On the other hand, Naylor's double marginality enables her to turn to Langston Hughes' poetry and other African American literary dialogues and to Kiswana Browne's African goddesses for mythic dimensions as invisible to most Americans as her own mother's ghost was to Welty's Virgie while it could be seen clearly by the black Juba.

Women's lives tell the communal story of Brewster Place. Basil and Lucielia, the infants in Mattie Michael's opening story, are not the focus of this cyclical novel. Rather, Mattie herself emerges still alive from the river of her life to smell sugar cane once again, a resurrection of the summer of her physical awakening "that lay under the grave of thirty-one years that could only be opened again in the mind." This time the fragrance marks her spiritual awakening, as this "ebony phoenix" rises out of the ashes of her life. Behind her is her patriarchal history of "[s]ugar cane and summer and Papa and Basil and Butch"; ahead is Brewster Place and her discovery of the female community and the goddess within her.

Awake enough to recognize that past as a nightmare, Mattie will still save from her memories the "other" stories that she failed to appreciate at the time. "Don't throw the baby out with the bathwater," my mother used to tell me, and Mattie lives to rescue one of those babies, Lucielia, and to dream a world of female (comm)unity.

While Naylor gives full attention to the historical realities, the *praxis* of Brewster Place, her focus on the women characters will slowly uncover the obscured Goddess story that comes consciously to motivate Mattie and is less consciously revealed in the others. If Welty told of Virgie earning her individual freedom from Morgana by paying her communal debts, Naylor will conversely show Mattie individually dreaming a potential community for Brewster Place. Naylor must move outside the cycle of individual lives to offer that promise of unity, which she does by framing the cycle. A historical introduction to Brewster Place in "Dawn" traces its creation by social politics and the "other" Americans who have shared its limitations before the "multi-colored 'Afric' children of its old age." A concluding section called "Dusk," while predicting the death of the geographical community, celebrates the ongoing dreams of its "colored daughters" and asserts that communal death will only happen "a second behind the expiration of its spirit in the minds of its children." Again we find ourselves, as with Mattie's memories, in the mind—in the possibilities of community rather than the limited realization of such dreams in contemporary life. To emphasize the realistic surface of this novel, therefore, is to betray Naylor's artistic accomplishment. Certainly Ann Petry's naturalistic classic *The Street* can be seen, as Gates and Appiah suggest in their preface, as the "silent second text" to *Women*; Awkward may be right that it "evokes and refigures" Jean Toomer's *Cane* in its fears "that the Afro-American folk spirit has met its demise in the urban desert of modernity" ("A Circle" 68). He argues as well that Naylor's novel "offers a bold criticism of the utopian resolution" of Ntozake Shange's choreopoem, *for colored girls . . .* , by presenting community as a dream unlikely to be realized in "an American society that is not radically transformed in terms of its debilitating racism and sexism" ("A Circle" 38). Each of these literary dialogues with Naylor's own tradition, however, helps to center her novel and strengthen the hope inherent in Mattie's dream and its attack on that "debilitating racism and sexism."

If Brewster Place is no improvement over Petry's Harlem street, Mattie's growing awareness of her female community does revise Lutie Johnson's rejection of community in her individual quest for survival for herself and her son. Mattie had similarly devalued the communal blessings she received from Lucielia's grandmother Eva Turner, who provides her a home and a heritage after her father has driven her North, but she comes to appreciate the Turners and the communal possibilities of Brewster Place. As Usha Bande observes, "Petry's Lutie is alone in her fight, but Naylor's women are bonded by their dreams" (5).

If the scent of sugar cane, which seems to introduce Mattie to Brewster Place, proves elusive, it triggers her memory like a Proustian madeleine and offers the folk wisdom Butch had shared with her that summer so long ago, that chewing cane too long leaves "nothin' but straw in that last round." Mattie will dream of Butch just before she learns of her son Basil's arrest; in the dream he "tried to pry open her mouth and scrape out the mashed wad of sugar cane." Folk wisdom—those old wives' tales—still haunts our dreams to offer us other ways to understand life.

Finally, if the dream of female (comm)unity is admittedly utopian, neither Shange nor Naylor offers more than the hope of achieving it. Naylor, however, must go beyond the individual insights of poetry and even the dramatic confrontations of a choreopoem if she is to offer us a "novel" pattern for society. Since the European myths blur together for her, taking shape primarily in the patriarchal hierarchy that excludes her twice over, she can see more clearly the hidden Goddess cycle and suggest its emergence when the socially empowered myths completely fail Mattie and nearly destroy her future hope as embodied in Lucielia. As Mattie's mothering skills grow, so too do the other women foster a sisterhood. "[O]ne character couldn't be *the* Black woman in America. So I had seven different women, all in different circumstances, encompassing the complexity of our lives, the richness of our diversity, from skin color on down to religious, political, and sexual preference," Naylor explains (*Ebony* 123).

While acknowledging the horrors of Brewster Place, Naylor herself turns the cycle of our seven ages into the resurrected hope of another Mattie. Like Mattie Will Sojourner, Mattie Michael is an outsider to America's empowered community; unlike Welty's character, however, Mattie's isolation closes her away from nature—except in a human sisterhood that can be a source of empowerment if its relation to nature is fully recognized. Naylor maps Mattie's growing awareness of this sisterhood through the short story cycle and Shakespeare's wheel of life, within which Mattie's new appreciation of Eva Turner will "turn her" perspective and her world around, reminding us too of the words of that ultimate outsider, Sojourner Truth, in "A'n't I a Woman?": "If de fust woman God ever made was strong enough to turn de world upside down all alone, dese women togedder ought to be able to turn it back, and get it right side up again!"

Naylor's double marginality is reflected in a double cycle pattern that reveals her double vision. While her circle of Goddess possibilities may be surrounded by the circle of patriarchal probabilities, it has not been subsumed by that larger cultural context any more than the African American has been subsumed into mainstream American culture. Rather, its resistance will reveal the other way of seeing life, a perspective from which shadows and dreams shift places with the nightmares of ghetto life. Naylor too chooses images to convey her story, not only the ambiguous but communal image of the novel's title but also the obscured images in each story of that unity in action. As she explains to Naomi Epel, "I will be struck by these images that haunt me and say, okay, that means

Figure 1
Gloria Naylor: Turning the Wheel of Life Around

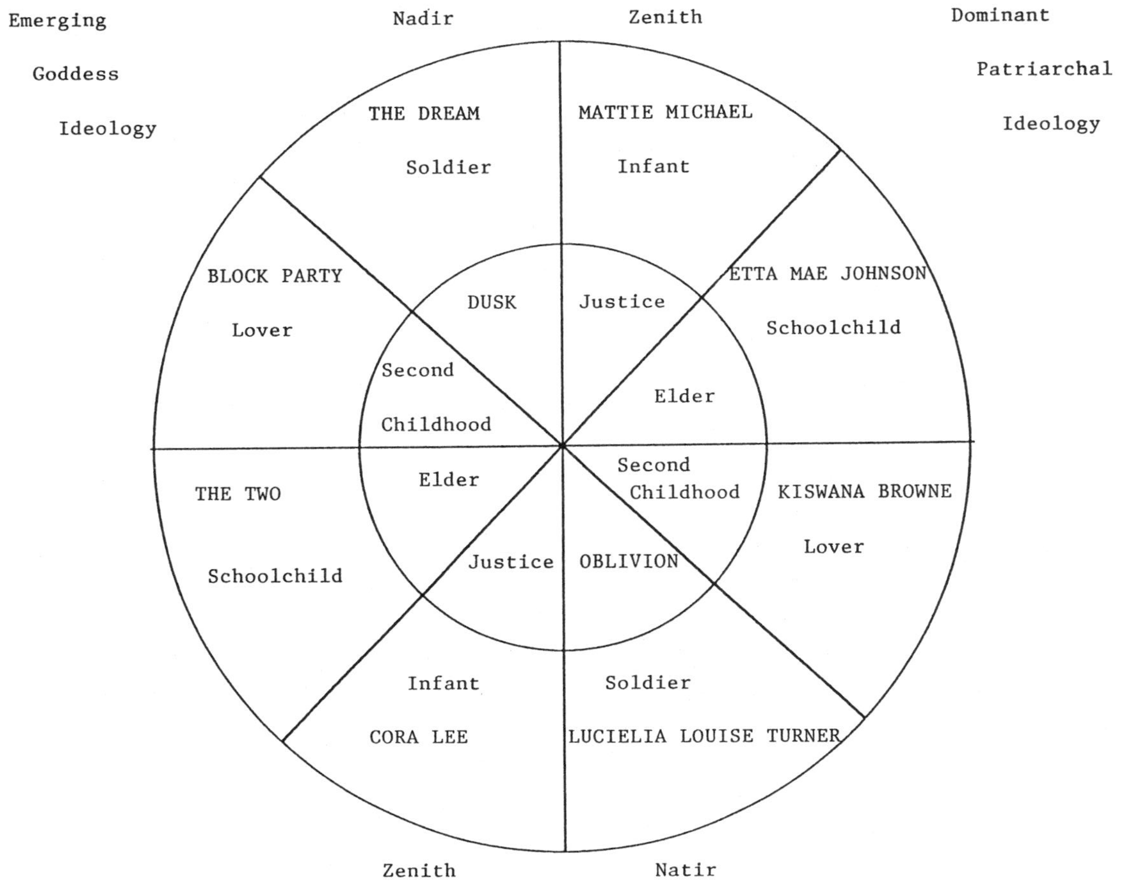

that's a story that's waiting to be told" (167). The image that triggered this first novel, she explains, "was the rocking of the women. Mattie rocking Ciel . . . the business of having an earth mother take this woman, who was in pain, in her arms and, through the rocking of her, bring her back to life" (167).

I have provided Figure 1 to help us visualize the cycle within a cycle that Naylor's wheel of life suggests, dividing it into eight rather than seven ages because her last quarter balances the seemingly inevitable fall of Brewster Place with the dream of hope and unity that embodies the emerging communal consciousness of its women. Naylor's "Goddess cycle" takes precedence after we pass the nadir, which is marked by the image of Mattie rocking Ciel, after which the persuasive power of patriarchal ideology steadily declines (I indicate this by labeling the larger circle by Goddess ages after Ciel's story). Minnie Ransom will allude to this last quarter in Bambara's *The Salt Eaters* (see chapter 4), asking, "Don't they know we is on the rise? That our time is now?"

Mattie Michael's chapter corresponds with Welty's "Shower of Gold" and Shakespeare's infant, and the olfactory image of sugar cane unifies her past and present possibilities. As Celeste Fraser points out, while Mattie is "an incarnation of the Mat(tie)riarch" in some ways, "Naylor widens the circle of permissible family in her representation" (98). Mattie's conception and raising of her son Basil shares the stage of her past with her acceptance into Eva Turner's home and the childhood of Eva's granddaughter Ciel; Brewster Place and Mattie alone is the present. As she is born again, she will encounter only Ciel in her new life, and she will mother Ciel in ways that redefine love, relationships, and motherhood itself. Her (s)mother love kept Basil a dependent and unruly child and kept her from having any adult love relationships, even from appreciating Eva's communal love, which she perceived as a financial debt.

The patriarchal story of this first chapter is one of violence, abandonment, and betrayal, and while she is part of that story Mattie has also betrayed both herself and her son by accepting the myth of the black matriarch. Matriarchy is just the reverse of patriarchy, a shifting rather than a balancing of responsibility and power; one cannot really be a matriarch in a patriarchal society. Driven away by her father's violence, Mattie simply isolates herself and her son, trying to shoulder her burdens alone even though she is socially powerless. Eva's goddess story provides her with a home and another model for mothering—unconditional love; yet she must lose both before she uncovers the beauty of this fairy godmother in her memories.

Mattie's "infant" communal self finds its first opportunity for growth in the story of Etta Mae Johnson, her own schoolgirl friend. This chapter corresponds to "June Recital," but Naylor's emphasis is on *unlearning* patriarchal ideology in order to see the other story of our lives. Etta has offered Mattie support in the past; now Mattie will return that support. Both women's lives reflect their patriarchal education; Etta is still living that story and believing she can only succeed attached to a "black star." Religion continues such education beyond her schooldays, while the blues music that haunts her carries the other story. Etta has learned to play the game too well; she is now recognized as accepting its rules by her current preacher lover: "These worldly women . . . understand the temporary weakness of the flesh and don't make it out to be something bigger than it is." But this time waiting for Etta is Mattie, with light and music and the love of a widened "circle of permissible family."

The community of Brewster Place women grows cumulatively; Mattie and Etta will reappear in later stories, expanding their definition of family until they can see their love reflected in the lesbian couple who so upset the other women still trapped in patriarchal ideology. Kiswana Browne, however, whose story corresponds to Shakespeare's lover and Welty's "Sir Rabbit," has come to Brewster Place precisely because of her communal love for this ghetto "family." Armed with her African goddesses and boyfriend and her imaginative appreciation of a shared culture, she has turned her back on mainstream education and values. Her mother, however, remains loyal to the system that has rewarded her with a home in the exclusive neighborhood of Linden Hills (the subject of Naylor's second novel). Kiswana too learns to balance her dream with the context in which it must be realized, as Naylor images in the pigeon that Kiswana imagines as carrying her dreams ever upward but that lands on a fire escape while she watches: "This brought her back to earth." Kiswana will not choose her mother's patriarchal path or even go by the name Melanie, which remembers her grandmother and her family's American heritage, but she will come to appreciate this woman who "swore before whatever gods would listen . . . that I would use everything I had and could ever get to see that my children were prepared to meet this world on its own terms." With her growing double vision Kiswana rejects those terms rather than her mother, whom she recognizes as "the woman she had been and was to become" while at the same time asserting, "But I'll never be a Republican"! Nor will she make Mattie's and her mother's error of perceiving love in terms of America's legal tender: the money her mother leaves behind buys only "a long sigh that caught in the upward draft of the autumn wind and disappeared."

Shakespeare's soldier and Welty's boy scout of "Moon Lake" take on a sex change in Naylor's story of Lucielia Louise Turner. Ciel has been a good soldier of her patriarchal society, taking back her wanderer whenever he returns to Brewster Place and caring for their daughter Serena or aborting a future child according to his wishes. Eugene, as that unmythic name again suggests, performs no heroic rescue; rather, turning her attention to him and away from her daughter results in Serena's death. But Ciel does have Mattie to turn to, and her communal promise has begun to shift Ciel's perspective even before the tragedy. When Eugene finds her love an insufficient reason for staying, she becomes conscious of "the poison of reality" that "drew his scent out of her nostrils and scraped the veil from her eyes." Yet when the ironic "serenity" of this union dies with Serena, Naylor does not blame Eugene.

"I wanted the reader to see that young man did care about the death of his child, but he had been so beaten down he couldn't come through for his family," she tells Toni Morrison in "A Conversation" (580). Eugene's name symbolizes society's culpability. Eugenics, *Webster's* tells us, is "the improvement . . . of hereditary qualities of a race or breed." American society had been "improving" on, or at least breeding, Eugene's race for generations; he is the product of ideological breeding as well.

At this moment of enlightenment, Mattie not only appears in Ciel's thoughts as a source of love but will physically act on that love to turn around the story empowered by Naylor. The rocking and bathing of Ciel provides an image of the mothering that enables us to survive tragedy, that releases us with a consciousness of unconditional love that enables us to wander. Morrison too explores the "thick love" of motherhood in *Beloved* in the story of a mother who kills her "best part" to protect it, to keep her daughter from being returned to slavery. At the end when Paul D. assures Sethe that she is her "own best part," however, the reader has come to know the importance of washing away the tragic past and acknowledging otherness, releasing what we love to life rather than to death. Each writer is echoing African cultural traditions, as Uchenda, a character in the Nigerian Chinua Achebe's novel *Things Fall Apart*, explains: "A man belongs to his fatherland when things are good and life is sweet. But when there is sorrow and bitterness he finds refuge in his motherland. Your mother is there to protect you" (124).

Naylor's imagistic language again links with Bambara's *The Salt Eaters* and the turning of the cycle when she describes the rocking of Ciel by Mattie: "And she rocked her back, back into the womb, to the nadir of her hurt, and they found it—a slight silver splinter." Turning the nadir into the zenith of a new cycle and rebirth, Mattie's love removes the splinter of white values, ripping a huge hole in Ciel's psyche but beginning her healing. So too will Bambara image splinters of white plaster imbedded in the clay of her people that prevent the potter's wheel, which is a loving community, from reshaping that clay when the tragic stress of living has turned it into a "crackpot."

The story of Cora Lee, then, begins the precedence of the Goddess cycle in Naylor's structural pattern. It also helps us read this circle as interactive; each story comments on and interpenetrates its opposing story. Cora Lee with her fixation on babies relates to Shakespeare's infant, but looking back across the circle, we realize that Cora Lee's and Mattie's stories are about both infants and justice. The young Basil must be tried and convicted by a society that has convicted him before he was born as illegitimate, a fate shared by Cora Lee's babies. Social justice is supposedly there to protect our children, but not in Naylor's ghetto or on Petry's *Street*.

Once we look back, we can trace the evolution of the Goddess cycle in each story. Mattie's story contains the justice of Eva Turner's intervention, rewarding Mattie's struggles in ways her society never will. Mattie herself is the wise elder fulfilling Eva's role in Etta Mae's story. "[S]econd childishness" can be seen in the relationship between Kiswana and her mother, for our children are the second chance that Nature gives us in this life. Finally, while patriarchy almost succeeded in achieving "mere oblivion" in Ciel's story, Mattie's loving care resurrects her, releasing her from that ideological slavery to begin her new cycle and ours with Cora Lee's story.

Cora Lee's education thus far has kept her an infant rather than taught her to be a goddess mother to her children. She has been wooed by the commercial America of baby dolls, and both men and children are playthings rather than relationships to her. In Naylor's growing community, however, Kiswana Browne intervenes to wake this dreamer to life, bringing "sisterly nurture to Cora Lee, another woman unbalanced in her mothering" (Andrews 289). Shakespeare provides the language of dream from three plays: *Romeo and Juliet*, *The Tempest*, and *A Midsummer Night's Dream*. Each raises the question of what in our lives is fantasy and what reality. Kiswana's African boyfriend creates a black production of the last of these plays, which testifies to art's ability to transcend social boundaries and provide its own "rare vision" of our world when another artist signifies its meaning. In *The Signifying Monkey*, Henry Louis Gates, Jr., argues that the tales of this African and African American trickster "can be thought of as versions of daydreams, the Daydream of the Black Other, chiastic fantasies of reversal of power relationships" (59). In her cyclical "reversal of power relationships," Naylor signifies on Shakespeare to unsettle our preconceptions about dreams and realities. Even Cora Lee's memory provides insight when she stares into her daughter's eyes and remembers her junior high Shakespeare with new understanding: "We are such stuff as dreams are made on, and our little life is rounded with a sleep."

Cora Lee emerges from this experience an infant goddess, still caught up with the "shadows" of patriarchy but nurturing new perspectives that offer the promise of change in her outward behavior toward her neglected children. As Jill Matus argues, "Even though her dreams show the absorption of cultural and gender stereotypes, the breakthrough, Naylor suggests, is that Cora is sparked to imagine and dream at all" (133). And while her unmarried motherhood provokes "friendly caution" in most of the women of Brewster Place, Cora knows she is accepted by Mattie—matured in her individual goddess cycle to justice—who "never found the time to do jury duty on other people's lives."

At least there is a friendly greeting possible for Cora Lee; greater communal rejection is experienced by "The Two" who provide the title for the next story. Just as Welty's "Music From Spain" revealed Eugene's inability to accept or understand the foreigner, the women of Brewster Place reject these lesbians: "They reached into their imaginations and, using an ancient pattern, . . . stitched all of their secret fears and lingering childhood nightmares into this existence, because . . . it was impossible for them both to be right." Naylor's own double vision underlines the irony of this judgment; as Ursula LeGuin points out in her androgynous science fiction classic, "Light is the left hand of darkness." Naylor shows the interpenetration of patriarchal and goddess *theoria* motivating her characters. Both, she suggests, could be wrong alone, but together they could find the right balance. Mother love must learn to release its children, and fathers need to return from wandering to accept communal responsibilities. We need to accept the coterminous realities of our linear and our cyclical stories, our history and our myth. Otherwise, we label one as dream, the other reality, or we reject one as alien or foreign and create a "woven barrier."

While Kiswana tries to involve the lesbian couple Lorraine and Theresa in her neighborhood meetings and Mattie and Etta Mae see through their supposed "difference" to appreciate sisterhood, it will be old Ben, failed father and drunken janitor, who offers mothering. Creating this relationship removes gender as the defining difference: "Naylor carefully separates the acts of individual black men from the patriarchal system in which these men might participate" (Fraser 98). Ben had good intentions when he allowed his own daughter to be raped repeatedly by her white employer, while his wife remained conveniently blind and accused the child of lying, but neither acted for her. He is there for Lorraine except when she most needs him, but if he cannot save either of them from tragic violence, he can protect the reader from identifying that violence as definitively male. If Ben himself is patriarchy's "lean pantaloon," he is also the goddess elder who has learned to love. Conversely, the pitiful gang of boys who must defend their six-foot grave-like turf reveal the "shrunk shank" of patriarchy. Headed for the "mere oblivion" that Gwendolyn Brooks predicts for Bronzeville youths who "Jazz June" and "Die soon," they "dramatize the closed economy of oppression within the wall around 'Black America'" (Fraser 101).

"What shall I give my children?" Brooks asks in "The Womanhood," which reminds us that the new Goddess cycle has reached Shakespeare's "whining school-boy," an apt description of these patriarchally educated gang members and a direct connection between Etta Mae's story and that of "The Two." Religion too is patriarchal in both stories, as we can see in the diminished "old wife's" tale with its lack of wisdom offered by the ironically named Sophie, spokeswoman for the condemning community. She confronts Etta Mae and then turns on Lorraine with Kiswana's goddess statue in her hands. Lorraine "stood like a fading spirit before the ebony statue that Sophie pointed at her like a crucifix," yet another sacrificial maiden, revealing the way both the Goddess and Christ's sacrifice have been perverted by hierarchical and dualistic ideology.

The rape of Lorraine and murder of Ben that conclude "The Two" make us eager to believe in the reality of the dream that constitutes most of the final chapter, "Block Party." The last quarter unites the lover and the soldier of the Goddess cycle, as Mattie's dream will reveal. The violent and concerted actions of the women to purge Brewster Place of Lorraine's blood and at the same time tear down the wall that isolates them from the rest of American society might remind us of "Onward Christian Soldiers" and identify the blood of Lorraine with Christ's gift of the mass to his apostles. Rape is love's opposite, but it has turned the women around in this dream so that they now love this outcast as themselves; they are willing to tell Lorraine's story now that she cannot. As Fraser argues, "Denied a voice to expel the pain, Lorraine retreats into a realm where she can no longer feel. The negation of voice effectively negates experience" (102). To create experience, therefore, Naylor gives voice to the dream that can offer these women an alternative. The untold story as we approach the patriarchal zenith, then, marshals the goddess soldiers to turn the patriarchal cycle around. This promise of rebirth rather than "mere oblivion" fulfills Sojourner Truth's prediction that "dese women togedder ought to be able to turn it back, and get it right side up again!"

The Goddess cycle reveals an approaching nadir, however much patriarchal propaganda about progress wants us to believe that the values of Western society have led us to our zenith. From the heavens, however, comes cleansing rain, and again the rituals of rebirth promise that the love of these survivors can bring us through the storm. The goddess soldiers balance the patriarchal decline into "second childishness"; as the men and children seek shelter from the storm, the women brave it to attack the wall. Instead of women attacking men, as Lorraine attacks her friend Ben, they direct their energies at the ideological wall that entraps them. Similarly, in Morrison's *Beloved*, when she is faced with what appears to be another threat to her children, Sethe turns on the white man who embodies that threat and returns to the support of her female community rather than murdering her own future by murdering her children.

When Ciel returns in Mattie's dream, we have one more link with the ever-renewing cyclical story of human promise. That Mattie's dream is communal rather than individual is indicated by Ciel's own dream of Brewster Place, which casts her in Lorraine's tragedy. Within the dream the women come to recognize Lorraine's pain as their own, and Cora Lee sees first the blood staining the wall that separates Brewster Place from the rest of society.

The women might appear childish as they ignore the rain and tear into the wall "with knives, plastic forks, spiked shoe heels, and even bare hands," but this affirmative communal act gives new meaning to Kiswana's banner for the block party: "Today Brewster—Tomorrow America." When Kiswana herself is handed a brick by Ciel, she "looked as if she had stepped into a nightmare." She tries to argue rationally that the bricks are wet only with rain, which should remind us that by the Goddess cycle "Block Party" dialogues with Kiswana's own story. The idealistic young woman who walked away from Linden Hills and a college education to embrace her people and her African cultural roots has indeed achieved the balance she needed to make informed choices. When Ciel answers her rational denial of the blood with "Does it really matter?" Kiswana sees through her own argument to recognize her own blood—her kinship with and her share in the communal suffering that motivates their actions. If that action is confined to Mattie's dream, the sun shining on Kiswana's gold earrings that greets Mattie when she awakes images its future fulfillment.

Nature's cyclical story only ends with the end of nature, and the human community is a part of that cycle. While we are alive, we are capable of change, of resurrections in this life. Mattie's earth mother rocking offered Ciel rebirth; Mattie's dream of the *rock*ing of a party removing blocks offers the community its chance to turn boundaries into thresholds as the women tear down the wall to purge its bloody memories. The blood is not in the bricks but in their minds; there, too, are the barriers to their rebirth.

2

The Word Made Man: Margaret Atwood

If female communities are not without their faults, they do offer some sanctuary: "for many of the women who have lived there, Brewster Place is an anchor as well as a confinement and a burden; it is the social network that, like a web, both sustains and entraps," acknowledges Barbara Christian (129). Still, the world beyond Morgana's boundaries invites exploration: "Father, Eugene! What you went and found, was it better than this?" asks Ran after he is "cheated" by Maideen's death into remaining in Welty's Morgana. Only Loch's and Virgie's departures seem to offer the promise of rebirth we see in Naylor's Ciel, perhaps because they too have been good soldiers who paid their communal debts. On the other hand, the wall between that world and Brewster Place discourages wandering, reminding us that communities can be closed from outside as well as from within.

The community of Gilead in Margaret Atwood's *The Handmaid's Tale* chooses with Morgana to empower its own culture, but as in Naylor's novel a wall must enforce that choice. This patriarchal community does offer the protection of Morgana, a freedom allowed only in the dreams of the Brewster Place women, but its sanctuary closes out the primary communal gift of love. Gilead does not release its children, which both Morgana and Brewster Place could do. Escape cannot be earned, only seized forcefully.

Although she discovers Gilead in the near future of twenty-first-century New England, Atwood departs less from the traditions of Realism than we might expect. The seeds from which Gilead grows are planted deeply in the *soil*ed world of New England, which already boasts similar Old Testament names in Goshen and Sharon.

Atwood goes East to find the veiled women who people Gilead and The Wall that encloses it, but each is as recognizable from contemporary reality as are the Japanese tourists with their cameras. Neither is beyond the walls of patriarchy: if the tourists merely observe, they participate in the preservation of that enclosure. As Addie observes in Lillian Hellman's *The Little Foxes*, "There are people who eat the earth and eat all the people on it like in the Bible with the locusts. Then there are people who stand around and watch them eat it. Sometimes I think it ain't right to stand and watch them do it" (79). Even though the Berlin Wall, which inspired Atwood to write this book, has since been torn down, its after-image should not be erased soon from our memories. Such images, verifiable by direct perception, and memories of an Old Testament past shape her pattern of our future, reminding us of St. Augustine's assertion that "the present of future things is expectation" (269).

Atwood's story of Gilead is told through the tapes of the handmaid Offred, a reluctant resident whose Gileadean name reveals her meronymic perspective. She may be "Of Fred," but she is also "Off Red," deviating from the role of the handmaid as symbolized by their red robes. She is also "Off[e]red" in more than one way—by Gilead as a procreative vessel and by Atwood as the "vessel of the holy spirit," the incarnation of the divine in the profane, which is the Christian definition of humanity. Off Red is eccentric, off-center, as can be seen at the Center in which she is held prisoner and trained as a handmaid, because her previous life offers her another perspective on Gilead's myth.

While Welty's female storytellers kept alive the story of Morgana, Naylor's mythtelling was needed to keep alive the dreams of the oppressed women of Brewster Place. The oppressed women of Gilead are denied the privileges of either oral or written preservation of their story, so the very survival of her tale attests to Offred's uniqueness. Preserved on already "obsolete" tape cassettes, her oral storytelling is retrospective in the past tense of the first chapter but switches quickly to the present tense as she recreates her life in Gilead. That the scholars had also found "The A. B. Memoirs" in Seattle and the "Diary of P." in Syracuse, New York, attests to the later spread of the Gileadean myth from east to west, but neither negates the importance of this "speaking voice," which "is a woman's." Atwood also appreciates the old wives' tales by which women have preserved their stories through centuries of patriarchy, an impossibility within The Wall of Gilead. She chooses this technically preserved oral discourse to give Gilead's silenced women a voice. A contemporary woman's voice is preserved in her short story, "Rape Fantasies," with which this novel dialogues. "Rape Fantasies" explores a female perspective on our society; its protagonist Estelle is nearly as estranged from the concept of community as is Offred. Trapped in a pink collar job in Toronto, Estelle is far from her mother's home in Leamington. She hasn't "been to church since they changed the service into English," suggesting that what is communicated there has lost its ritualistic significance for her.

Supposedly free to do what she wants, Estelle recognizes that the media shapes our attitudes, even toward rape: "The way they're going on about it in the magazines you'd think it was just invented, and not only that but it's something terrific, like a vaccine for cancer. They put it in capital letters on the front cover, and inside they have these questionnaires . . . RAPE, TEN THINGS TO DO ABOUT IT, like it was ten new hairdos or something. I mean, what's so new about it?" Her oppressed female community, centered in the segregated women's lunch room, romanticizes rape; she argues that "you aren't getting *raped*, it's just some guy you haven't met formally who happens to be more attractive than Derek Cummins."

Estelle recognizes that while society glorifies male-female relationships, convincing these women that only marriage promises them happiness, it simultaneously threatens them with the image of the male as rapist. Without a supportive community, they can resolve this contradiction only by romanticizing the rapist into an acceptable lover. Estelle, on the other hand, tries to establish a dialogue with the man she meets in a bar, asking "how could a fellow do that to a person he's just had a long conversation with, once you let them know you're human, you have a life too?" She believes that survival in a world in which men and women are free to threaten or love each other depends on establishing such a dialogue.

In the Gileadean world, rapists are defined as any man who has sex with a handmaid other than her assigned master and are ritualistically murdered, while all dialogue is forbidden to women. In such a context, the rapist may well be the only source of love possible for a handmaid; yet she is forced to be the agent of his death in the "particicution" (which is sometimes deceptively used to eliminate "spies"). In such a context, sex may be desired simply as a dialogue, a chance to challenge one's oppression. Compare, for instance, the explanation Harriet Jacobs offered in 1861 for accepting the advances of a white neighbor rather than her slavemaster:

I knew the impassable gulf between us; but to be an object of interest to a man who is not married, and who is not her master, is agreeable to the pride and feelings of a slave, if her miserable situation has left her any pride or sentiment. It seems less degrading to give one's self, than to submit to compulsion. There is something akin to freedom in having a lover who has no control over you, except that which he gains by kindness and attachment.

Offred will be repeatedly involved in illicit dialogues—with Moira, with Ofwarren, with Nick, with the Commander. The opening chapter, for instance, ends when the handmaids-in-training learned to lip-read and "exchanged names, from bed to bed. Alma. Janine. Dolores. Moira. June."

Naming has always been a human source of power, as is reflected in the tale "Rumplestiltskin." In that tale, remember, the ugly little man can claim the woman's child if she cannot come up with his name. When she is successful he is powerless—and angry. The ugly little men of Gilead claim the children of the handmaids *and* their names, keeping all power to themselves. The women's names provide their link to the Goddess (who was also denied Her names in our patriarchy until quite recently, as Patricia Monaghan points out) and tell their story in a single word. In this intensely patriarchal, dualistic, and exclusive future, that encoded myth must stand alone against the Judaic-Christian fundamentalism that undergirds the social structure.

The women of Gilead are robbed of their personal names when they earn their social definition of possession by the male, such as Ofwarren and Offred. Learning their previous names, we possess a key to each story. Alma means the soul, Janine the double-faced Janus/Sphinx, Dolores our Lady of Sorrows, and June or Juno the Roman Mother Goddess herself.

Offred's friend Moira connects with the three classical Moerae or Fates, the three Marys of the New Testament and Gnostic gospels, and the three (sometimes nine) Morgans of Celtic myth, uncovering the face of Robert Graves' nine-person White Goddess. The Moerae bestowed names in classical mythology and encompassed in its trinity the past, the present, and the future. Moira will also form a trinity "from the time before" with Offred and her memories of her mother, since they were all acquainted then. This maternal Goddess heritage provides essential support for Offred in Gilead, even though we learn eventually that all three are trapped in sacrificial roles within that society. With the silencing of Offred's mother, memory of the past is potentially lost; in Moira's degradation, future hopes are devalued and abused; even her own apprehension of the present moment is limited by Offred's confinement and programming.

Moira is cast by patriarchy as Mary Magdalene (literally named a Jezebel by the patriarchal Old Testament vocabulary of Gilead), while Mother Mary can be identified with Offred's silenced mother, who is both excluded from and controlled by Gileadean society. Offred, then, is cast as the Mary who listens to Christ (in the person of the Commander) while her sister Martha works. This interpretation is reinforced by the Gileadean identification of women household servants as the Marthas. Offred listens intently for the voice of Christian love throughout, answering the Commander's query about what the founders of Gilead might have omitted with the single word "love."

However, Offred is also a Mother Mary whose child has been sacrificed. Even when the memories of that child are resurrected as she learns of her physical survival, Offred must still mourn her female trinity of mother, sister, and daughter who are lost to each other. Her daughter's survival reveals the success of Gilead's Rumplestiltskins; the cost of this sanctuary is our children/our future. Gilead provides for the physical self only and for the benefit of the patriarchy: "This way they're protected, they can fulfill their biological destinies in peace. With full support and encouragement," the Commander explains.

Much is conveyed by Atwood's dialogue with the Bible, the only legitimized myth in Gilead. As Brian Stableford has observed, Atwood's novel borrows the style of a jeremiad from the same source as it borrows the name Gilead (97–98). Jeremiah 8:19 and 22 establish the complaint of this tale:

Behold the voice of the cry of the daughter of my people because of them that dwell in a far country: *Is* not the Lord in Zion? *Is* not her king in her? Why have they provoked me to anger with their graven images, and with strange vanities?

Is there no balm in Gilead: *is there* no physician there? Why then is not the health of the daughter of my people recovered?

Offred's tapes literally record "the cry of the daughter." The tale itself will provide a series of "graven images," from those contemporary images of oppression to the ubiquitous Eyes of Gileadean authority. The call for "balm in Gilead" provided by a physician reminds us that the New Testament Luke, identified with Offred's dead husband Luke, has been replaced in Gilead by doctors who offer the "balm" of their semen to impregnate the handmaids illicitly in case their designated owner is sterile. Such medicine emphasizes the irony of the passage's last question when applied to Atwood's Gilead.

Old Testament verses provide the text for Gileadean ceremonies, justifying the role of handmaid and defining the ritual to be performed to sanctify that role. Without the defined ritual, sex with a handmaid is damning; even with it, the proper attitude must be maintained.

From their Old Testament perspective, the mythmakers/media of Gilead rewrite the New Testament as well to justify their society. The Beatitudes become Orwellian Doublespeak as Gileadean words replace the music: "The voice was a man's. *Blessed be the poor in spirit, for theirs is the kingdom of heaven. Blessed are the merciful. Blessed be the meek. Blessed are the silent.* I knew they made that up, I knew it was wrong, and they left things out, too, but there was no way of checking. *Blessed be those that mourn, for they shall be comforted.*" Offred's words will later replace the music of the "Twisted Sister at Carnegie Hall" to preserve her story on tape, reminding us of Moira's lost voice and of the isolation of the "twisted" or "weird" sisters of their trinity.

Silences echo with past memories as Offred recalls the promise in 1 Corinthians 13:13 for the time of our lives: "And now abideth faith, hope, charity, these three; but the greatest of these is charity." When she discovers "the hard little cushion, FAITH," in her inherited room, she "wonder[s] what has become of the other two cushions." Near the end, when she despairs of escaping, she once more recalls the allusion and concludes that "[f]aith is only a word, embroidered."

As limited and manipulated as is the mythic dialogue in Atwood's tale, its power is maintained precisely because women have no recourse to language. "There was no way of checking," Offred had admitted, just as there was no way of passing on their own stories. Control of the media determines social values, and in this case women do not have the option of establishing a personal dialogue. Only from a larger context can their story be known, and that context will interpret as well as preserve their words. This becomes obvious in the satiric tone of the keynote speaker in "Historical Notes," where "[t]he voice was a man's" and the medium has altered the message. To challenge this, the small voice of Offred cries her jeremiad, prophesying our future fate.

Atwood dialogues as well with three other sources, two of which she establishes by prefacing her tale with quotations and one referred to implicitly by the title and explicitly in the "Historical Notes." This final dialogue, the keynote speaker tells us, originates as a male retrospective: "The superscription 'The Handmaid's Tale' was appended to it by Professor Wade, partly in homage to the great Geoffrey Chaucer; . . . I am sure all puns were intentional, particularly that having to do with the archaic vulgar signification of the word *tail*."

Atwood lets Professor Pieixoto condemn himself as a sexist with his own words, recording this far-future sexism while also paying homage to the literary past, to Chaucer's celebration of such socially powerless people as cooks and wives in his tales. He also lets them speak in their own voices, earning us our first vulgar English language. Linguistically, thematically, and formally then, he is a literary ancestor of this tale.

So too is Jonathan Swift, whose "Modest Proposal" ironically challenged the inequities of his society. Atwood's own modest proposal extrapolates from patriarchal myths, which still undergird our society, and sexual inequities, which still permeate our politics, economics, and social programs. As a daughter of an active feminist, Offred had never really appreciated the freedoms her mother had earned her, just as she had taken for granted the love of her family. When she loses both, "from the time before" becomes her haunting, mournful refrain.

The satirical extremes of her tale, however, are more closely paralleled in the realities of contemporary society than was the suggested cannibalism of Swift's savage satire. His invention concretized the hidden truth, while Atwood's invention merely had to reorganize blatant social truths by joining them in one place and time. Excepted from this realism is the particicution, although its roots do exist in our history, but it is the isolated exception that proves the rule.

The Sufi proverb, "In the desert there is no sign that says, Thou shalt not eat stones," reminds us that Middle Eastern and Eastern myths have long sustained oppressed and stratified populations, a connection reiterated in the "Historical Notes" announcement of "the well-known study 'Iran and Gilead: Two Late-Twentieth Century Monotheocracies as Seen Through Diaries.'" The proverb also indicates the obvious justification for this social transformation: the restrictions placed on scarce and desired objects. Fertile women had become both scarce and desired in pre-Gilead society. Atwood includes such current biological causes as nuclear radiation, pollution, and incurable viruses along with such social causes as the women's movement in general and pro-choice in particular to transform fear of the other into the demand for control of the other. When scarcity and desire demand, societies become restrictive and authoritarian.

To reflect the shape, the *mythos*, of that social pattern, Atwood's romantic neutral territory of Gilead draws selectively on the worlds of the imagination and the actual. Still, within that sanctuary Offred must face the same communal and individual needs of love and separateness; within herself she must face the same otherness; between herself and her context she must face the same demands of nature and society. Furthermore, she must face these human realities from the perspective of the handmaid role, of sacrificial victim, a role as confined within the given society as any woman has been in patriarchal history.

Just as Estelle and the other women trapped in Toronto's pink collar ghetto internalized their social values, even as they were devalued by them, and let the language of the media shape their fantasies, so too Offred and other handmaids will become programmed by Gilead. That women are the primary tools of their own programming, the Aunts of the Center in particular, reflects their common social powerlessness. Stableford notes that "we hardly see men behaving badly at all, and what we do see is counterbalanced by images of women behaving badly in all sorts of ways" (99), from which he concludes that "[t]he heroine, in seeking to live in this appalling world, is left without hope very largely because she cannot deny charity to her controllers" (100). While he has uncovered the ideology of this "appalling" social construct, he fails to note the connections between Gilead and contemporary society. He dismisses Atwood's feminist prophecy as a jeremiad against "the male of the species" despite his own evidence to the contrary. Gilead is oppressed by the ideology of the Old Testament, by a Christian fundamentalism that not only still exists in our society but is gaining power. Atwood extrapolates Judaic patriarchy from our multimythic story to examine the *idea* of patriarchy in its most dualistic and exclusive concretization. That the Gilead she describes could not exist in historic time and place is not suggested, however, as evidenced by her realistic images of gynophobic oppression and authoritarian confinement. The Actual and the Imaginary do meet in Gilead and suggest a future within our expectations.

This balancing of metonymic images and imaginative idea builds its own wall around Gilead, controlling the experiment. Gilead reflects in its extremes what is potentially possible in any patriarchal society. The images and actions are shaped by that idea; the social construct is expressed in clothing, rituals, language, and definitions of morality. An authoritarian order such as this superimposes itself, disregarding individual desires and needs. The Commander and the reports of continual warfare recalls our Army slogan: "There's the right way, the wrong way, and the Army way." There is no room for Love in Gilead.

Consequently, the remnants of goddess myths, New Testament myths of "faith, hope, and charity," and all but Old Testament myths appear in Gilead as "a heap of broken images," as T. S. Eliot has already observed of our contemporary "waste land." Not only have such images as "Hathor's Eye" been preempted by Gileadean authority, but also personal names have been stolen. Atwood has shuffled these images together with meaningless fragments; the language that could explain and connect them is denied Gileadeans, just as Offred must carry pictures of what she is to purchase from the grocery store. An illiterate society, which too we are threatening to become, is not an unthinking society. It is, rather, denied access to the shared language of literature, so that we cannot independently read and consider the ideas we are offered. "There was no way of checking," Offred complained, and even the surviving image of a word broken from its meaning and denied a context would not be sufficient to offer individual alternatives. Thus, although the handmaids share their names, each is fragmented—followed by a period; each must survive alone. Even "[f]aith is only a word, embroidered."

The above examples show how Atwood structures her prose to reflect the fragmentation of Offred's story. Often a sentence consists of a single word, paragraphs of one sentence. Recognizable images pile up indiscriminately to be ordered by the reader. The tale is divided into fifteen chapters, every other one of which is called "Night" (except for chapter V, which is "Nap"). The other chapters carry one or two words designating Gileadean places or rituals. Thus we shift alternately from public to private, social to personal, patriarchal day to the silent night, which allows Offred time to try to comprehend her own life. Even Gilead cannot control her night thoughts, which is probably why authoritarian societies reflect such a fear of the dark and patriarchal societies have always associated females and the dark. Even these seemingly orderly chapters, however, are fragmented again into forty-six sections.

Offred's prose is in marked contrast to the scholarly flow of Professor Pieixoto's remarks in the "Historical Notes." That difference reflects the larger patterns of the novel. While Offred's tale is complete without them, the "Historical Notes" are essential to Atwood's meronymic novel. Offred is trapped in her time and place, even after she supposedly escapes. Her vision cannot be comprehensive because of these limitations. The "Historical Notes," however, provide a probable future to Gilead. Readers who identify the broken images and historic parallels in Offred's tale and the revealing sexism and authoritarianism in the supposedly objective "Historical Notes" must finish her story, must recognize the *mythos* that shapes its past and present. As does Brecht's epic theater, this distancing from Offred as character to Offred as storyteller being critically evaluated by male scholars reveals revolution rather than resolution, a society in which the surface changes but its ideology simply finds new forms of expression. Brecht wanted his audience to see the patterns rather than the individual; so too does Atwood tell a handmaid's, not Offred's, tale.

Atwood runs a risk by trusting her audience to complete the reconstruction of the whole story. Such an open pattern assumes that readers of literature are looking for truth, are willing and able to enter into an otherness of perspective to expand their own. Women's literature has not often found such an audience; it is perhaps less likely to win over the male reader when it attacks patriarchy. Yet patriarchy is an idea, not a gender.

The female perspective in all of the novels we will be discussing does bring a different element into the literature that must be understood to appreciate the whole story. A recent example of critical failure of communication is evident in the movie based on this novel. Scripted by the British playwright Harold Pinter, the movie abandoned or transformed each of the linguistic and formal techniques we have discussed.

Admittedly, the translation of a novel into a movie demands artistic alterations. However, those alterations should be made in order to capture the novel's intent more effectively in the visual medium. Instead, the media manipulation of truth that Atwood's fiction has noted is evidenced in this movie. Atwood's structure is abandoned, and her images are reinterpreted to offer a decidedly male perspective on Gilead. The movie opens with the capture of Offred and the dissolution of her family, which exists in the novel only as a memory and assumes at least three different shapes as Offred tries to reconstruct it later. The effect of the movie structure, which then follows chronologically through her resettlement in Maine, is to offer a linear story of specific events, most of which chronicle her relationships to males. The "Historical Notes" are omitted, the goddess allusions lost, and we are trapped in Gilead's definition of reality.

Even that definition is altered as it is interpreted by Pinter's definition of Gilead. The casting and costuming of the women characters provide visual images of attractive, sexy bodies in bright red diaphanous robes for the hand-maids and short, sexy royal blue dresses accessorized with jewelry for the wives. The Aunts are shapely and made up, wearing tight brown suits, scarcely the image of the "childless," "infertile," "older" women described by Offred. Gone is the flat yoke over the breasts and the white winged hood with blinders that confined the handmaids; gone are the full-length sky-blue covers of the wives. Serena Joy, played by Faye Dunaway, is neither arthritic nor limping. Offred has a name, Kate (for Shakespeare's shrew?), and she visits the Jezebels in a sexy black gown rather than the tawdry leftovers and purple sequins of the novel. Imagine the transformative power of such images.

The novel's open structure and its admissions of unverifiable information and possible inaccuracies keep the possibilities open for Offred in a society anti-thetical to the order of the natural world. What appears at first glance as a tale with notes is really a novel retelling of the whole story that must be serially reconstructed. "I'm not sure how it happened; not exactly," Offred admits at one point. "All I can hope for is a reconstruction: the way love feels is always only approximate." While she seeks to tell the story of love, the scholars of the "Historical Notes" seek the validity of documented history: "We were assured by the experts who examined them that the physical objects themselves are genuine." But they too have to reconstruct a story fragmented into thirty tapes and taped over already recorded music that continues briefly.

Isaacs has compared Welty's novel with a musical suite, considering the seven stories as movements and noting varying tempos and a final coda (37). But Offred's music is atonal, broken, as the rhythms of her prose reflect the irreg-ularity of her existence in Gilead. How can one compose or be composed in such an environment? Professors Wade and Pieixoto even have to have a tape player "reconstructed" to access her story.

Broken patterns, reconstructed language, and programmed rituals describe the social realities of Gilead and are reflected in the way Atwood tells its story. The content may warn us more specifically about particular behavior encouraged in Gilead and other behavior forbidden, but we already know by the shape of the story that the artificiality of such a society isolates its population and smothers love. What product could be expected from such a society? It too is a "reconstructed . . . machine capable of playing such tapes" as those that carry invented and Old Testament guidelines for morality. In this fundamentalist tomorrow, we must recognize some fundamental problems of our own time and place—our emphasis on verifiable and physical reality, on the production rate of the human machine, on literal rendering and media rending of our myths. Otherness in Gilead is anything not defined by their monomythic structure; with only one story to tell they simply must repeat it indefinitely or cease to exist.

Gilead does cease to exist, but the myth that engendered it does not. It is waiting to be resurrected when scarcity and desire collide. It is still buried in our myths, carried in our language, and capable of being reconstructed to order the events of our lives until its story is our story. Atwood makes us aware of this very real possibility from the perspective of Gilead's most powerless—because most valued—member. This is the irony at the heart of Gilead, and the title of Aileen S. Kraditor's study of the nineteenth-century American women's movement, *Up From the Pedestal*, suggests that the female perspective on American history has pointed out before this patriarchal pattern.

Only the handmaid's perspective can really challenge and correct the dominant Gileadean patriarchal vision because it is justified by the fertility essential to human survival. Patriarchy requires confinement of the female by definition; only then can we control the future and accurately predict biological fatherhood by the appropriate male. However, even in the extreme confinement of Gilead, such a guarantee is impossible. This identifies the paradoxical premise of patrilinear culture. To be a member of the community in a matrilinear culture, one need only be born. The proof is in the directly observable act.

The idea of patriarchy determines the closed box shape it will take in the world of human events. Atwood captures that shape in Gilead, but in her own box of the novel she includes the context of American past and future as equally within that ideology; the form and language she chooses *are* the story. They concretize the idea just as it is concretized in history. She confines Offred's story to a retrospective, oral rendition with admitted inaccuracies. She then submits it to scholarly evaluation and further reconstruction by two male professors who are not objective. Finally, she provides us with all available written sources and expects us to let these sources dialogue with our prior knowledge. To initiate the dialogue, she provides three additional clues by the quotations that preface Offred's tale and the title of the novel. From such fragmented sources, each in itself only a part of the puzzle, can come the whole story that captured Atwood as she stood looking at the Berlin Wall. When the Word is made Man, when the female is denied the right to tell her own story and to have it read by someone with the ability to "enter into the nature of another being and judge his work by its own law," then we find ourselves in Gilead. Have we Americans ever lived elsewhere?

3

Mapping the Mind: Doris Lessing

"In the twentieth century SF [science fiction] has moved into the sphere of anthropological and cosmological thought, becoming a diagnosis, a warning, a call to understanding and action, and—most important—a mapping of possible alternatives," claims Darko Suvin in *Metamorphoses of Science Fiction* (18). Suvin's description of the jeremiad aspects of SF applies well to Atwood's novel. She maps such an alternative to warn us of the confining and fragmenting power of patriarchy, based on direct observation and memory. At first glance, Lessing offers an equally dark vision, but looks can be deceiving. "The artists have been so busy with the nightmare that they have had no time to rewrite the old utopias" (*A Small Personal Voice* 9), she complains. She has taken that time, publishing between 1979 and 1983 her *Canopus in Argos: Archives* serial utopia, revisioning myth and history. She turns to "space fiction" because her art needs a larger canvas.

The section of the universe over which Lessing stretches our story encompasses our galaxy, shifting perspective from Earth to other star systems, particularly those surrounding the two brightest stars in our skies, Canopus and Sirius. Sirius is apparently the brightest, owing to its white color and its relative nearness of 8.6 light years, although it is only about thirty times as luminous as our sun while Canopus, whitish-yellow in color and one hundred light years away, is actually 1,500 times as luminous as our sun. These images metaphorically communicate the limits of our myopic rather than mythic vision; we are taken in by appearances and misjudge based on inadequate knowledge. So too will the acquisitive Sirians seem superior in their material success until we become fully conscious of the ideological superiority of the Canopeans.

If physical descriptions provide one clue to the differences between Sirius and Canopus, quantum physics reveals Lessing's linguistic choices in naming her world. Light can be shown to be both a wave and a particle, depending upon the conditions of the experiment set up by the human observer, this physics teaches us. Sirius, also known as Canis Major, or the Dog Star, as part of the constellation of the Greater Dog, must be considered the particle in its materialism and imperialism, in its "dog eat dog" view of life. Symbolic of our own predictable future, it concretizes our particle/individual acquisitiveness as it experiments with "lesser" forms of life and conquers many particles of space.

Conversely, Canopus is identified with the Carina cluster, part of the more ancient Argo Navis constellation, mythically recalling the Greek Argonauts or, as *Webster's* offers, "an adventurer engaged in a quest." Symbolic of the quest(ions) we undertake to expand consciousness, it concretizes our wave/communal possibilities. Canopean adventurers ride the waves of space, adopting whatever particle form is necessary. The stories of *The Sirian Experiments* become historical predictions; the stories of Canopeans are mythic possibilities. Canopus further reminds us of the Egyptian canopic jars that held the internal organs of the mummified dead. It is the internal self that we share with the Canopeans; with them human consciousness is allowed to soar beyond physical boundaries. Love motivates these envoys to visit our planet, hoping to encourage our love.

That love is both the motive and the transformative power of Canopus becomes clear when we read the initial report from the envoy Johor concerning the continued interest Canopus shows in our planet: "I am a small number of the Workforce, and as such do as I must. That is not to say I do not have the right, as we all have, to say, Enough! Invisible, unwritten, uncoded rules forbid. What these rules amount to, I would say, is Love" (*Shikasta*). Through the pattern provided by the link with Canopus, we are enabled to share the SOWF (Substance of We Feeling) that energizes the Argive universal community. This greater whole to which Canopus belongs provides Lessing with the title of her series, which doesn't bother to mention Sirius.

It does, however, specify that the five novels we are reading are from the Archives. These, then, are the official documents of Canopean history, of which visits to our planet constitute a part. We are Planet 5, designated as Rohanda, or green, until negative influences block us from SOWF and transform us into Shikasta, or broken. We are part of the history of myth, which is itself part of the Argive universe.

Ironically, however, the reverse is just as true, since the written documents we have from Lessing, the novels, are a product of human consciousness, which is large enough to encompass even in its particle envoy (the author) that greater whole. The series, then, is a concretization of the human consciousness that explains what a human can know of universals. Lessing uses the physical universe as a canvas that maps and a language that expresses the story of that whole. Canopus and Sirius offer wave and particle manifestations of the light she can shed on human experience, while our small Planet 5 microcosmically expresses the macrocosmic universal community of Argos.

Lessing offers this literary cosmology to explore our interdependence within the indifference of the Necessity. Her physical approach discovers ready metaphors for invisible truths, and the actions predicated on those truths can be just as transformative to our lives as quantum mechanics has been. Heinz R. Pagels in *The Cosmic Code* explains that argosy:

Physicists have voyaged into the realm of quarks and other quantum particles from which everything in the universe can be made. Here, at the smallest distances ever reached by our instruments, they have discovered the basic laws that unify the forces of nature.

Understanding the world of these elementary particles requires combining the quantum theory and Einstein's special relativity theory of space and time. . . . [T]hrough the activity of science and technology the discovered order of the universe, what I call the cosmic code, becomes a program for historical change. The modern world is a response to the challenging discoveries of the quantum and the cosmos—discoveries which continue to shape our future and to transform our idea of reality. (14)

Lessing's first Argive novel traces the evolution of humanity from pre-history through World War III, told from myriad documents collected in the Canopean archives. *Re: Colonized Planet 5 Shikasta* interweaves myth and history in the past, present, and future of the story of our planet. The authority of the Canopean perspective is reinforced by the architectonic structure of the novel, which cites —as the subtitle informs us—"Personal, Psychological, Historical Documents Relating to Visit by JOHOR (George Sherban), EMISSARY (Grade 9), 87th of the Period of the Last Days." While Lessing relies heavily upon the patriarchal sacred narratives of Jewish and earlier Middle East traditions to create Shikasta, she also concretizes the more ancient patterns of a community extending to the stars—not just an Earth Mother myth but of a universal Goddess of Nature.

Linguistically, Lessing's series alludes to myth both by similar names and by revisioned but still recognizable stories; history is recorded in political and sociological jargon as well as in personal writings. Structurally, her euhemeristic reading, which marries myth and history, gains from the distancing of her perspective. The Sirians are not like our individualistic and material selves; they are an aspect of our story writ large. Our potential communal consciousness is manifested in the SOWF—Substance of We Feeling—which the Canopeans work to keep flowing and which motivates them to take on the burden of physical form.

That Canopean envoys are incarnations of Love is alluded to in the name of Johor, whose story also reminds us of Jehovah and Jesus. Although we would make gods of these leaders, their own humanity is revealed in the occasional failures who are just as likely to be seen as devils. However, the apparently superior Sirians seem godlike from certain ideological perspectives, as Lessing

ironically reveals. Canopeans discourage deification, echoing the biblical warn-
ings against idolatry and revealing their link with ancient myths of the deified
Universe:

When we turn to religions of immanence, whether we call them Witchcraft or Paganism
or polytheism or spirituality, whether we draw on sources from Celtic, Greek, Native
American, Eastern, or African mythology, we encounter the God/dess: the all, the interwoven fabric of being, the dancer, the weaver—we say—and the web of connection, the
pattern, the spiral. "She," we call her. But she is before sex; She whose name cannot be
spoken because she is the circle—before it is broken by a name that separates-out. (Starhawk 73)

Lessing describes the Lock with Canopus as connecting humanity with "their
Mother, their Maintainer, their Friend, and what they called God, the Divine"
(*Shikasta*). Canopeans see themselves as part of this greater pattern, a part indi-
vidualized in the Necessity of the physical universe to carry out by "voluntary
submission to the great Whole" the duties of love (*Shikasta*). Even Ambien in *The
Sirian Experiments* recognizes Johor in whatever manifestation—male or female,
human or other—might have been found necessary for the time and place. Thus
individual and communal goals from this perspective are no longer in conflict;
Johor's stress comes instead from the naturalistic demands of Necessity and the
emotional drain of despair.

   Lessing's tale of our present moment, which encompasses the entire series,
demands the historical reading of myth in *Shikasta* and the cultural concretization
of consciousness in *The Marriages Between Zones Three, Four, and Five*. The
larger context of the series maps our physical and psychic universe. Necessity
provides the only divine intervention, the unpredictability of nature: "When the
Gods explode, or err, or dissolve into flying clouds of gas, or shrink, or expand,
or whatever else their fates might demand, then the minuscule items of their substance may in their small ways express—not protest, which of course is inap-
propriate to their station in life—but an acknowledgement of the existence of
irony" (*Shikasta*).

   Lessing concretizes our potential for evil elsewhere—not as Melville's
"depravity according to nature," since nature is indifferent, but as our hunger for
discord, which the Judaic-Christian myths embody in the fallen source of light,
Lucifer. On her physical map Lessing identifies it with the planet Shammat, a
dreary rock in the minor star system of Puttiora. The physical and social insig-
nificance of Shammat obscures its psychic power—the "Degenerative Disease"
of individualism. Naming again images her message: the hypocrisy of "sham-
ming" and the rottenness of "putrefy." Shammat plays a major role in our degen-
eration from green Rohanda to broken Shikasta.

   Shammat also supplies the third heavenly perspective on our story, just as it
supplies the third intervening influence on our planet. It is the false light (Lucifer) that we may follow into a future of decay, which perverts the light of truth

and even clouds the light of day, the romantic and realistic truths of the Canopean and Sirian perspectives, respectively.

Viewing our planet through the Canopean Crystal reveals its psychic deterioration in the shadows of the surrounding zones that block its reception of SOWF. Ambien describes this aid to crystal-clear vision in *The Sirian Experiments*: "My guide was changing again, was showing how it had to change, and flow, and adapt itself, for all the movements or alterations of the atmosphere we were submerged in like liquid molded this Globe, or Rod, or Streak, or Fringe." So too our perspective must be dynamic, open to change, if we are to expand our consciousness.

Lessing also uses language to balance the realities she will be exploring. Estrangement and defamiliarization offer new perspectives; on the physical map of the universe, Earth is a minor entity. The Sirians and Canopeans refer distantly to our "Isolated Continent" and "Southern Continents I and II." The British Isles, Lessing's own home at the time, are merely the "Northwest Fringes" of a larger body of land. She estranges us from our attachment to appearances by ephemeralizing observable reality while concretizing levels of consciousness in *Marriages*. Equally invisible would be the Lock with Canopus through which we receive SOWF. Ideas become concretized in the Trial of the White Peoples of the World in *Shikasta*, challenging criticism of whites rather than ideology when recurrent oppression and slavery by all races becomes historically apparent. Conversely, the inhabitants of Planet 8 are literally ephemeralized, as Lessing makes us aware of the spaces in things. The physical universe that sustains us can retract that support, Johor explains:

All the old supports going, gone, this man reaches out a hand to steady himself on a ledge of rough brick that is warm in the sun: his hand feeds him messages of solidity, but his mind messages of destruction, for this breathing substance, made of earth, will be a dance of atoms, he knows it, his intelligence tells him so; there will soon be war, he is in the middle of war, where he stands will be a waste mound of rubble, and this solid earthy substance will be a film of dust on ruins. (*The Representative of Planet #8*)

Coterminous with the physical and social evolution of our species is the evolution of consciousness recorded in our myths, and it is important to picture the concretized maps Lessing offers us of both in her space fiction. Since the map of the particle/physical universe is already known, so that we can measure actual distances between us and each of her star systems, we must now map the coterminous light of Lessing's literary cosmology as a wave. Focusing exclusively on our broken planet in *Shikasta* and on levels of human consciousness in *Marriages*, Lessing encompasses physical and psychic Shikastan experience.

Critics who decried the complexity of *Shikasta* celebrate the mythic simplicity of *Marriages*, but few acknowledge the links between the two—beyond mentioning that Zone 6 did turn up in the former novel and thus suggests that the zones are located concentrically around our planet. What better language could convey basic patterns than mathematics? Such geometrical forms order our experience in Lessing's series. Let us turn, then, to the mathematical cities that appear at the end of *Shikasta* to link Necessity and Purpose. "I think that we are here for a purpose—to learn—and that there is a God: I don't think that we are purposeless," Lessing told a New York audience in 1984 (quoted in Tiger 223). Her series views a world that has lost sight of that purpose from a Canopean perspective that has not.

Lessing has expressed her admiration of the Victorian novel as "art which springs so vigorously and naturally from a strongly-held, though not necessarily intellectually-defined, view of life that it absorbs symbolism" (*A Small Personal Voice* 188). The symbolism "absorbed" in this series is most fully and clearly delineated for the reader in *Marriages*, as its mythic simplicity reveals the links between the sensual language of Nature and the sensible mathematical patterns by which she maps our consciousness. Sense, as does science, begins with our physical perceptions; myths also serve the scientific purpose of explaining our universe. The *mythos* preserves the recurring story, the pattern, while the myriad retellings and variations reveal contemporary recurrences.

The idyllic plans of shaped cities offered at the beginning and end of *Shikasta* are discussed by Claire Sprague in relation to Lessing's ongoing architectural symbolism: "The city is always the crucial center of human collective life. Historically described as female and entered by men, it is a construction normally out of bounds to the woman. Lessing has appropriated the fact and the dream of the city for women" (184). Sprague discusses particularly the initial Round City as "Lessing's most ecstatic example of devotional perfection" (172) then turns to, at the end of the Century of Destruction, Kassim's discovery of a city for which Lessing says, "There were no plans. No architect. Yet it grew up symmetrical and on the shape of a six-pointed star" (*Shikasta*). A third city materializes for his group when they spontaneously know "where the city should be. We knew it all at once. Then we found a spring, in the middle of the place. That was how this city was begun. It is going to be a star city, five-points" (*Shikasta* quoted in Sprague 174–75).

We will examine further the implications of these three figures—the circle and the five- and six-pointed stars—as they are absorbed into the mythic patterns of *Marriages*. Geometrical shapes, Sprague reminds us, will comfort Ambien II in *The Sirian Experiments* and heal Klorathy in *The Sentimental Agents*. In *Marriages*, they help us translate the symbolism of the zones that comprise Lessing's dynamic utopia. Ruby Rohrlich describes utopias created by women writers in her introduction to *Women in Search of Utopia*: "Unlike the planned, rigidly controlled, and static utopias, real and fictional, generally devised by men, these societies are subject to transformation as the world within and around them changes" (3). Order need not be static; even the universe depends upon a paradoxical order of chaos.

We can identify the Round City, the circle of perfection, with the marriage of Purpose and Necessity. Here, "because of this precise and expert exchange of

Figure 2
Doris Lessing's Zones as Celtic Zones and Judaic Rainbow of Systematic Ideologies

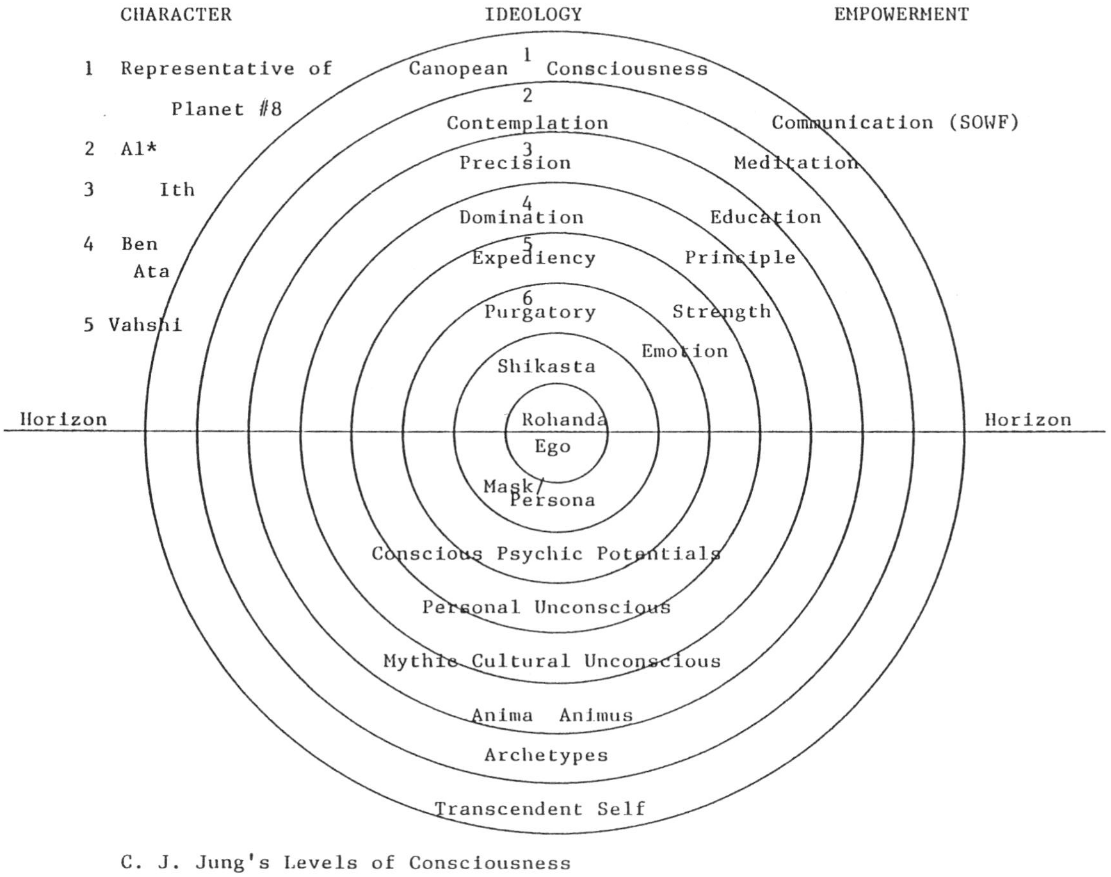

CHARACTER

1 Representative of
    Planet #8
2 Al*
3 Ith
4 Ben
    Ata
5 Vahshi

IDEOLOGY

EMPOWERMENT

1 Canopean Consciousness
2 Contemplation
3 Precision
4 Domination
5 Expediency
6 Purgatory

Communication (SOWF)
Meditation
Education
Principle
Strength
Emotion

Shikasta
Rohanda
Ego
Mask/Persona

Conscious Psychic Potentials
Personal Unconscious
Mythic Cultural Unconscious
Anima Animus
Archetypes
Transcendent Self

Horizon

C. J. Jung's Levels of Consciousness

emanations, the prime object and aim of the galaxy were furthered—the creation of ever-evolving Sons and Daughters of the Purpose" (*Shikasta*). Its pattern reminds us that civilization, or the "human city," is always within the circle of Nature and thus defined by that marriage of Purpose and Necessity. Many critics have read her submission to Necessity as pessimistic determinism, but Nature in Lessing's "strongly-held . . . view of life" is not without purpose and consciousness, however inscrutable Her ways may be to mere humans. Within that Wheel of Life can be found the concentric zones that surround Shikasta.

Phyllis Sternberg Perrakis discusses *Marriages* in relation to Lessing's interest in Sufism and to a revisionist version of the Myth of Kore, arguing that the fable "is not only an allegory of Jungian rebirth or mystical ascent; nor is it merely a sexual-political dialectic, as Katherine Fishburn reads it. Like a dream or visionary myth *Marriages* integrates all these levels of meaning and reference. . . " (100). The integration of these three levels can be mapped within those concentric circles when we balance a history of our social evolution from George Walford with psychology of levels of individual consciousness from Jung and Celtic myth of communal consciousness from R. J. Stewart.

References to Jung and Sufism fit comfortably into Lessing's formal choice of the fable, alerting us that the landscape need not be located in time and space. Unfortunately, the form also tempts us to forget that ideas do shape social and even physical landscapes inasmuch as those landscapes are altered by humanity. Our cultural ideologies, in fact, correspond to those ideas that shape Lessing's zones, when they are read as social critiques. Einstein's theory of relativity had already suggested that, given the right conditions, matter becomes energy becomes matter in a discernible pattern. Lessing transforms the psychic energy of our social and personal selves into matter in her mapping of Shikasta and the zones that surround it, geographically defining ideologies as human consciousness expands outward into the Canopean consciousness we call God and linking them spherically to Jung's levels of consciousness expanding into inner space and the Transcendent Self. Quantum physics reminds us that infinity lies in either direction. Figure 2 provides a map of these relationships within the coterminous image of Celtic Zones and the Judaic rainbow that established our covenant with God. As the rainbow rises from the horizon through the zones, its shadow image expands in the human psyche. Although our two-dimensional reproduction must depict concentric circles, our three-dimensional imagination should open these circles spherically—radiating outward from Shikastan probability or inward to rediscover Rohandan possibilities—to suggest the universal understanding each direction offers.

The ideologies associated with each zone come from Walford's study of systematic ideology, *Beyond Politics*, and his later comments as editor and publisher of the journal, *Ideological Commentary*. Walford images our social evolution as a layered pyramid, its base constituted of the three "eidostatic ideologies" and its apex shared by three "eidodynamic ideologies." The former include expediency, domination, and precision, which will correspond respectively with Lessing's

Zones 5, 4, and 3. The latter—revolution, repudiation, and reformation—correct imbalances in an individual society. Walford argues that precision is the most evolved ideology, dependent as it is on increasing knowledge of the world in which we live. Expediency depends on Nature and strength for survival, domination on the hierarchical empowerment of a controlling principle. The pyramid image, as are the gyres of W. B. Yeats, is in perpetual flux, turned by the corrective influence of the eidodynamic ideologies at its apex—in the head, one might say.

The dynamics of our social evolution are imaged in these ongoing attempts to maintain a balanced society. Walford's pyramid can be superimposed upon the Celtic pattern of the Triple Goddess given by Stewart, as we shall see in Figure 3, which attempts to translate Walford's systematic ideological evolution into geometrical mythic patterns by turning the circle three times. In the Round City of the Celtic Zone 5, imaged as a circle surrounding a square, divided itself into four triangles by a pair of bisecting lines, and dominated by an isosceles triangle sharing the base of the square, Stewart presents the Triple Goddess and the Fourfold Cycle: "The Triad or Triangle of the Goddess rotates around the Fourfold Cycle, through the Four Seasons and Elements" (60). This rotation echoes the flux of Walford's pyramid as consciousness adjusts to Nature's changing seasons and physical evolution. We will discuss Figure 3 later as mythic patterns in each circle.

First, however, let us map the zones on Figure 2. In Lessing's Canopean universe, release from our physical bodies initiates our journey through the concentric six zones that emanate in waves from our planet outward, each comprised of psychic barriers to achieving universal, or at least Canopean, consciousness. Jung's mythically informed psychology conversely draws us inward toward the Transcendent Self of full human consciousness. His argosy recalls the world of elementals about which Dr. Bramble speaks in Crowley's *Little, Big*: "The world inhabited by these beings is not the world we inhabit. It is another world entirely, and it is enclosed within this one; it is in a sense a universal retreating mirror image of this one. . . . The other world is composed of a series of concentric rings, which as one penetrates deeper into the other world, grow larger" (43). Six states of consciousness lie hidden beneath the persona, or mask, we offer the world. The ego must mask the god within, itself estranged from that light in our deepest unconscious.

Centering ourselves on the horizon, we move outward in Figure 2 from the ideal world that earth was meant to be, the Rohanda Lessing describes in *Shikasta* that receives SOWF freely and on which the self/ego would reach full consciousness. With the negative influence of Shammat, our vision of universals is obscured, as is our own consciousness. On Shikasta, we mask our inner self, presenting a persona that is determined by the ego's attempts to balance physical, emotional, and ideological demands. This persona must function for us in the world of *praxis*; the more demanding that world is the less likely we will find time to examine our own consciousness. When we do venture into the realm of mind, however, we meet with overwhelming despair in Zone 6.

Lessing's Zone 6 impedes the journey of our argonaut Johor in *Shikasta*; this manifestation of Limbo or Purgatory holds the consciousness awaiting return to earthly existence. To take on that physical existence, Johor must also make his way through this land of lamentations and blinding sands. Still attached to their time and place and personal relationships, these souls can draw only on Jung's Conscious Psychic Potentials, the ways they have been taught to perceive the world and themselves. However, inherited attitudes that help keep us intact in the face of historical probabilities hinder our ability to transform those probabilities by discerning alternatives from a communal, even a universal, perspective. Habit and training sustain, and stifle, us by narrowing our definitions of family and community.

Lessing combines her exploration of Zones 3, 4, and 5 in *Marriages*. Her title suggests strong connections among these zones, which can be related to Stewart's descriptions of the Fivefold Pattern or Wheel of Being of Celtic myth. Zone 5, assigned geographically to the Centre of Ancient Ireland located in the province of Meath, is imaged mythically as a unifying center circle superimposed upon the overlapping circles representing the four directions. The balancing circles inter-penetrate each other and unite in Zone 5. Stewart explains the intersecting circles as patterns of energy: "Celtic religion was primarily associated with the sanctity of the land, and the power of certain key location. . . . The land was primarily represented by a goddess. . . ; they had a whole vision of the sanctity of life and land, unified and harmonized together. . . . When the pattern was right, all went well; and when the pattern was disturbed, ills arose" (15–16).

Zone 5, then, contains all the potential of universal knowledge, but that potential is obscured by our lack of self-consciousness. Only her social ideology limits Vahshi, the Warrior Queen of Lessing's Zone 5, to her physical prowess; she is clearly capable of but not interested in thinking. When married to Ben Ata, king of Zone 4, she can "sit quietly and allow the beginnings of thought to live in her mind." She and Ben Ata balance each other, a balance that would produce a girl baby "because the strength of her wild femaleness could only give birth to itself." Socially, she manifests only the cunning and strength to live by expedi-ency that sustained nomadic tribes.

As Lorelei Cederstrom reminds us, "[Lessing] encourages the reader to look beyond the literal meaning of myth and religion and recognize those elements in them which are eternally recurrent because they represent basic configurations of the human psyche" (195). While the Wheel of Being is the macrocosmic sphere that embraces all of nature, Zone 5 is the microcosm, encompassing both center of kingship and triple goddess in the *hieros gamos*, or sacred marriage, of the king and the land in the Round City, which continuously rebalances as Nature r(evolves). In this world of expediency the other gender is simply the other self, a fellow warrior also fighting to survive in this expedient society;

Figure 3
Doris Lessing: Mythic Turnings of the Wheel of Life

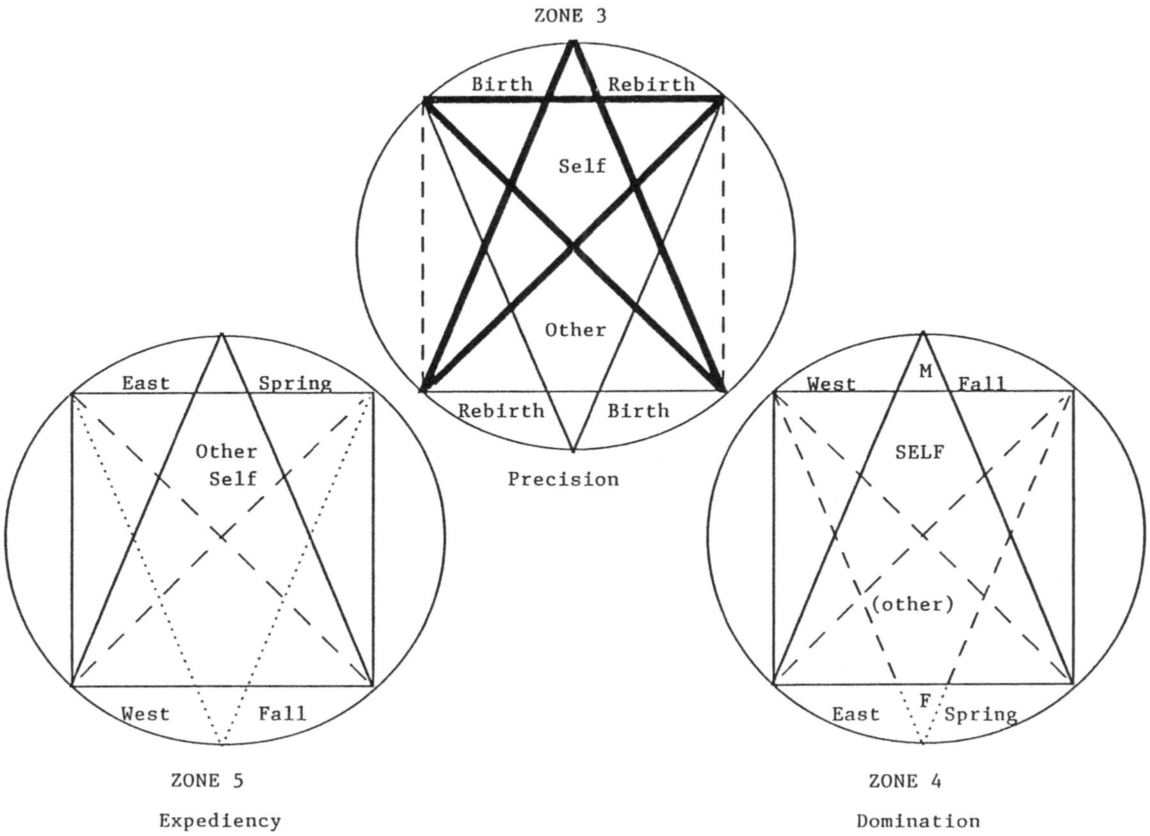

ZONE 3
Precision

ZONE 4
Domination

ZONE 5
Expediency

male and female, individual and communal, selves are superimposed and coterminous.

Jung's corresponding level of consciousness, the Personal Unconscious, examines the first level of our psyche that we are blocked from accessing,
revealing what keeps us, like Vahshi, from thinking or even wanting to think.
Jung identifies these blocks as the Shadow, repressed memories, and potentials disguised as complexes. Our fears, formative experiences, and hesitance
to explore otherness keep us from resolving inner oppositions and expanding
our consciousness.

Behind the Shadow lie the Mythic Cultural Unconscious and the Anima/Animus,
corresponding respectively with Zones 4 and 3. These zones re-create what Lessing previously imagined to be the "two ideal landscapes, male and female,
somewhat exemplary in both ways," which an earlier "very beneficial fantasy" had
revealed to her. She acknowledges this fantasy as the result of "a technique used
by certain schools of therapy" (quoted in Tiger 222). The Mythic Cultural Unconscious offers us the "absolute truth" of our cultural myths. Our finite humanity,
however, prevents us from knowing if such absolutes are indeed universal. A
monomythic perspective settles for the apparent and cultural level of truth, keeping
us from exploring deeper meanings by encouraging the assumption that our
perspective, our principle, alone defines truth. Lessing's Zone 4 embodies this by
empowering exclusive, patriarchal myth; its level landscape is marred by marching
soldiers and neglect of Nature's potential. The rolling land of Zone 3, imaging
Jung's Anima/Animus, allows differences to be expressed while achieving balance
in its communal consciousness—which includes shared consciousness with other
animals—but a comfortable apathy equally misleads its citizens into believing its
truths to be universal.

Zone 3 is west of the center in Ancient Ireland and is the seat of
"LEARNING, *Druids*, judgment, chronicles, story-telling" (14). Here Lessing
creates her ideal female landscape, and Lusik, its chronicler, narrates *Marriages*.
Its queen, Al*Ith, is first directed to marry Ben Ata. Perrakis and Cederstrom
both claim her to be the embodiment of the Triple Goddess, but a comparison
with myth and Walford's ideologies suggests otherwise. Vahshi is the Warrior
Queen who combines male and female in her fierce leadership and strength and
depends upon expediency to survive. So too was the goddess Inanna a warrior
queen, as well as many Celtic goddesses. As the sole pyramid acknowledged in
the Round City, she rules with no consort, denying otherness, as is represented
in the first circle of Figure 3.

Al*Ith, on the other hand, recalls Alice in Lewis Carroll's Wonderland, who
has penetrated to the other side of the mirror and would know best its opposing
landscape. The opposing, gender-defined landscapes of Zones 3 and 4 will both
be known well by Al*Ith because of her marriage, and she will find herself ready
to leave their imperfections behind for a solitary quest to the mountains of Zone
2. The story-telling of Lusik captures the story she has lived, just as the five-
pointed star represented in the second circle of Figure 3 images the knowledge

she has gained. Having learned to love the otherness of Ben Ata while she rejects the ideology of his zone, she realizes that the subsumed Other offers a supportive and balancing embrace when we must make decisions and another head to make the decisions obscured to us. Rebirth of the communal self sees this in the otherness of our children; marriage of the individual self sees it in our mutual quest for knowledge and survival, for Purpose and Necessity. Her society of precision has achieved an admirable balance, but Necessity is unpredictable and unceasing; only if we share our knowledge can civilization hope to survive.

Walford refers to expediency as the "only universal ideology" of the human family. Dominating authoritarian governments, such as Ben Ata represents, arise when social demands grow or where Nature is not as generous to her human children. While personal life is still primarily governed by expediency, the survival of the community demands limits be put on that life. "In order to function principle has to repress expediency," Walford explains as he traces the beginnings of dualism; "this pattern of two levels, one dominating the other, characterizes the many features which distinguish the new society from the old community" (*Beyond Politics* 83).

To correct the cyclical bias of expediency, authoritarian governments repress and repudiate the power of the physical world—and whoever is most closely associated with that world. Besides the effect on otherness of such oppression, the defensive stance toward nature imbalances these societies, as the history of Western patriarchy and Ben Ata's zone reflect. Lessing's patriarchal Zone 4 echoes the Celtic zone, located north of the center and the seat of "BATTLE, *Warriors*, conflict, struggle, pride" (Stewart 14). Ben Ata's exclusively male-dominated society is dualistic and hierarchical. Judaic patriarchy provides the six-pointed star that images this zone in the third circle of Figure 3. If the individual role of the warrior offers a key to Ben Ata's personal consciousness, the social ideology of patriarchy shapes his communal consciousness. The Jewish star, the first of the patterns Kassim discovers in the mathematical cities encountered after patriarchy's Century of Destruction in *Shikasta*, both absorbs and opposes the triangle of the Triple Goddess imaged in the first circle. This dualistic opposition symbolizes the lives of the women in Zone 4, as male is placed over and against female, and turns upside down the relationship of Man to Nature. Denying Nature as the concrete expression of the Purpose, of the divine ordering principle of the universe, patriarchy can thus be seen as enclosing its perception of Nature in the walled garden of the square, the box that falls within Zone 5. Nature so defined can be fully mapped by the human mind; its mysteries are only what we do not as yet understand. This square best images Pratt's "enclosure of the patriarchy" (39), for only that part of woman within the box, the body without the head, is acknowledged—although the potential negative magic of her otherness is suggested by the lower position of her head outside what is ideologically defined as reality. Man's head, residing also outside of but above this limited definition of nature, becomes patriarchy's divine image and only acknowledged authority.

R(evolving) the circle to place Man on top and the Goddess below suggests that our story begins with the Judaic Fall and nature's fall rather than the spring of the Goddess. Autumn and winter faces of Nature might well call forth the warrior king to ensure human survival, obscuring the cyclical recurrence that is our promise as creatures of nature. Fixed and two-dimensional, the symbolic circle of patriarchy suggests that rebirth only occurs after physical death. Thus our bodies become our enemies; the physical world, the Triple Goddess, the female within and made from us, threatens to trap us in a Pandora's box of the perishable gifts of Nature. We do not recognize that we have constructed that box, the walls of our garden of death. Only in a spiritual afterlife can patriarchy hope for the unity the Celtic *mythos* promises in the dynamic of self and Other. If self is separated from Other—if the triangle no longer represents the *hieros gamos* of king (consciousness) and land (body)—then the individual authority that denies otherness sees only a linear story leading to death. Humanity may be reborn cyclically, but only Christ is acknowledged as living after death, an individual reincarnation of human consciousness.

Cyclical and linear time, Michael Young asserts, "are best conceived as two often but not always complementary ways of looking at the same thing, two alternative conceptualizations of the same phenomenon which do not exclude each other" (14). Young has argued that Western ideology has shaped a "metronomic society," stubbornly linear and perceiving cyclical time as a threat that seems to rob us of our individuality (of what Lessing criticizes in *Shikasta* as our "Degenerative Disease"). Because of our metronomic fear, "the linear so much overshadows the cyclical, thereby hiding the vital, iterative past of its own constitution" (5), that we perceive only fragmentation and despair. Lessing's story of Shikasta, the "broken place" version of our planet, reveals that despair; Claire Sprague suggests the following line from Mircea Eliade's *Cosmos and History* as "an epigraph to *Shikasta*: 'History and progress are a fall, both implying the final abandonment of the paradise of archetypes and repetition' (162)" (169).

The patriarchal pattern that has dominated Shikastan society and that, we will learn in *The Sirian Experiments* (*SE*), has boxed Nature into the grid that the Sirian narrator Ambien II attributes to "the mind of the Northwest fringes, the mind of the white conquerors," has also trapped Shikastans within "a certain way of thinking" (277). The social and personal evolution of consciousness, of Purpose, no longer informs the physical evolution of Necessity because "between me and the language of growth and change was this imperious stamp. This pattern. This grid" (*SE, Worlds* 53). While the box would seem to protect us by locking out unpredictable Nature, it concurrently locks us in and away from the Canopean Lock that provides SOWF, the faith in Purpose validated by that very unpredictability, that promise of "growth and change."

Finally, the inflexibility of the patriarchal pattern, the need to remain at all times the acknowledged head and to confine Nature within its definitions, not only locks most of Nature out but also locks in the previously (r)evolving human consciousness. Thus the zones, when *Marriages* begins, have become territories of the Other, and the Providers must initiate union between them. Dualistic negation of otherness reduces us to the least of our own possibilities, a particle no longer riding the wave.

The fruitful union of Ben Ata and Al*Ith introduces the precision of a learning experience into Zone 4, exposing him to the female otherness, which he learns to love. The learning process stimulates personal and social r(evolution). When Ben Ata learns to love and respect the Other, he no longer denies expediency; he will marry Vahshi from Zone 5 and reunite with and accept the language of Nature as essential to making sense ecologically of the world in which we must live. "Well, Al*Ith," he admits, "I had to love her—after knowing you!" (*Marriages*). Vahshi's name suggests as well her Eastern origin, and this marriage of East and West, linear and cyclical perspectives, promises yet another rebalancing. Instead of our tradition of missionaries delivering the truth to heathens and pagans, we learn instead to encompass and embrace other ways.

Al*Ith's Zone 3 contributes most to this balancing, as imaged in its five-pointed star. Al*Ith herself is moving beyond social definitions toward the universal consciousness. As her mythic name (of Dame Alice as well as Alice in Wonderland) indicates, she is open to other ways. Her growing need for an active and individual pursuit of truth leads her to Zone 2, which corresponds with Jung's Archetypes as it begins her individual quest to discover the communal self in the human patterns that we acknowledge as true to each of us. Only an exploration of consciousness, a questioning of the self, still obscures her vision of the Transcendent Self and Canopean consciousness.

The social ideologies imaged in *Marriages* advocate neither a return to Celtic myth nor a rejection of Judaic traditions. Rather, they explore what each in the purity of its pattern has contributed to our understanding of ourselves and our universe. If Zone 4 provides the rage for order that drives our quest for knowledge and Zone 5 reconnects us to Nature, Zone 3 represents the balance that will overcome our fear of Nature's apparent ambivalence toward our survival, of Nature the Creator and Destroyer. Eventually, we may evolve with Al*Ith to a closer understanding of the Purpose, as is imaged in the mountains of Zone 2, the true landscape of divinity—high places worshipped as breasts of the goddess and as domiciles of the gods. Rising to the challenge of the climb, of the upward and outward quest of Lessing's space fiction, we acknowledge the imperfection of our finite understanding of Necessity and Purpose.

Beyond that physical expression our species can only imagine, as Lessing does for us when she braves the death of Planet 8 to explore possibilities. In that later novel, she will still insist that the archetypal pattern that survives as the representative of Planet 8 must remain flexible:

Nor were we something already fixed, with an entity that could not be changed, for we came upon a ghost or a feeling or a flavour that we named Nonni, a faintly glittering creature or shape or dance that had been, we knew, Nonni, the dead boy, Alsi's companion, and this entity or being came to us, and married with us, with our new substance, and we all went as one, but separate, in our journey toward the pole. (121)

Zone 1, of Canopean consciousness or Jung's Transcendent Self, is the seat of prosperity and hospitality in Ancient Ireland and is located in the East, in the position of new beginnings and the resurrections of Spring and Dawn. This can be read as the afterlife or as evolutionary, as the journey we can take from where we are—from Shikasta—to where we could be. A united consciousness recognizing the uniqueness of each part yet moving "as one, but separate" toward the dynamic ongoing transformations possible with a balanced society embraces both Nature and the individual quest for knowledge. Such shared authority has no room for a monomythic hierarchy, recognizing instead that "two heads are better than one." The Purpose is communicated and renewed continuously in the language of growth and change. Since no one of us can yet interpret that language fully, we must depend on each other if we are to survive until the universe has fully defined its purpose.

The geometric shifts within the Round City convey Lessing's evolution of consciousness. A flat representation of the Celtic Triple Goddess pyramid does appear to subsume individuality in its acceptance of the cycle of Nature as the expedient answer to all of life's mysteries. Challenging that answer from the north, where Nature is less inclined toward our survival, patriarchy asserts its opposition by tasting of the tree of knowledge. Fearful of the immensity and unpredictability of Nature's garden, it creates a walled garden to box in Vahshi's "wild femaleness" and to resist being subsumed—(s)mothered—by claiming control.

The new six-pointed pattern promises double the flexibility of the Triple Goddess triangle, and its mythic acknowledgment of the surrounding sphere is indicated by the Covenant and promise the Judaic God offers Noah after the Flood, a natural rainbow of concentric circles that are only half visible to the human eye. Denial of the other, however, erases the chthonic knowledge of the lower head, the other half of Nature's rainbow, which must remain buried in the unconscious. Without her head, woman is completely enclosed in the "box" of this limited perception of Nature. This static picture cannot afford to r(evolve); hence, the patterns that sustain us become fixed, as two-dimensional as medieval art revealed them to be, and dynamic growth becomes increasingly more difficult because of this lack of balance.

Fortunately, Lessing shows faith in evolution and in the emergence of individuals in the Coleridgean sense, simultaneously unique and collective, aware of integration into the whole. In *Marriages*, she images a social pattern that can possibly re-pair our broken planet. While the macrocosmic sphere of universal causation may well promise perfection, in our microcosmic sphere of human existence we can only strive for unity and balance, healing disturbances in the pattern and trusting each other to help keep that balance. Shikasta, Planet 5, houses the Round City as well as the five- and six-pointed star cities, because each when seen dynamically and in three dimensions can keep us in balance. However, it is the five-pointed star that unites our mythic traditions and reasserts the flexibility all such patterns must maintain to adapt to the "dis-asters" of Necessity.

In the Middle Ages, the five-pointed star already imaged our astral self, with its correspondences to the human and divine images (the points outline the head, arms, and legs of our physical pattern). Known as the love knot, since it could be drawn with no discernible beginning or end, it decorated the shield of the ideal knight Sir Gawaine to indicate his devotion to the perfect woman, the Virgin Mary. She was the Mediatrix, interceding for imperfect humanity, who would embrace her devotees with love and mercy while the dreaded Trinity demanded just punishment. Reading the image as our psychic Self, we can see that, while we may stand on our own two feet and make our own decisions, we often need the balance provided by the outstretched arms of the Other and Nature. That other head, whose feet are balanced in our hands, can also be called upon for decisions that may seem beyond our reach. This dynamic marriage of the completely integrated individual and Other and to the whole of which we both are parts promises diversity and unity, acknowledging and encompassing the other mythic patterns. Only if it continues to r(evolve) in the larger sphere of Necessity can it hope to survive and understand the Purpose of which we, as well as the physical stars, are Sons and Daughters.

In *Marriages*, Lessing offers an ideological pattern for contemporary society based on marriage to both the otherness of the physical universe of which we are a part and the other Self that is a part of us. Individuals who "sense" the limitations even of the best society are encouraged to journey outward, to learn from "the language of growth and change" and make sense of life. Utopia means no place; even the best society must be periodically re-vised and re-paired. Revolution can re-volve the circular bias, anarchy or repudiation can oppose the current hierarchy and reverse its linear bias (we reverse "pudentia," what we are "ashamed of"—which in our patriarchal language is female—"pudendum"), and reformation can reform the entire pattern. These eidodynamic ideologies can rebalance human society on its evolutionary quest to fulfill the Purpose.

Lessing goes neither forward in time nor outward in space in this series; rather, she uses a larger canvas to distance us and help us see better the present moment, its evolution from our human past, and its possibilities in the foreseeable future, depending upon which attitudes will shape that future. Canopeans are no saviors: they must work within the Necessity of a naturalistic universe and within the choices made by individuals and cultures. They embody full consciousness as preserved in song and story, parable and myth, in *Shikasta* and in *Marriages*. Art maps our quests, although we are still Canopean and Sirian—and Shammatan—because "it isn't or at all, it's and, and, and, and, and, and. . . " (Lessing quoted in Perrakis 100).

In Lessing's artistic transformations, the reality we intuit and the reality we experience are superimposed, and their interpenetration suggests that they are inseparable if not identical. Our world is both the potentially rich Rohanda and the predictably broken Shikasta, depending upon our perspective.

Each of these women writers expands Realism by reintroducing techniques from the Romance in order to explore the landscapes of the human mind. Focusing the lens of myth on our history, they capture the shadows of invisible realities that unite with, and are coterminous with, the observable realities. Symbol and myth, unifying shapes and structures, and allusive names and sub-headings dissolve the differences between what is and what can be. The language of legend removes distinctions between myth and history; mythic realism brings the world back into balance. Human consciousness can encompass both/all real-ities, as reason and imagination combine to expand our outlook beyond the limitations of either alone. The proof, the mythic realist might say, is in the pattern, the *mythos* that dynamically maps and shapes the argosy of our lives.

For Welty and Naylor, dialoguing with Shakespeare's seven ages provides insights into the cycle of life, the regenerative power of Nature, and the healing rituals of the community. The same cycle reveals, however, communal con-finement determined by patriarchy's ideological domination of American life. Those who cross the communal boundaries seldom return; even less seldom are we allowed to follow them. Only in our minds—in our art, our dreams, and the psychic circles of the individual and communal self in Lessing's *Marriages*—are the boundaries transformed into thresholds. Such possibilities, however, inspire us to move from *theoria* to *praxis*, with the loving support of the Other.

Refusing to be bound by the present moment, Atwood leaps into a dystopic future to diagnose our social illness, discovering again a community confined by patriarchal myths. Her fragmented, unverifiable narration forces the reader to reconstitute the story and uncover the same illness long after its symptoms have undergone treatment. Equally fragmented is the narration of Lessing's *Shikasta*, but the cumulative documents enlighten the reader patient enough to let them dialogue with each other to tell the whole story of our broken planet. Seeing every boundary as a threshold enables Lessing to span the universe, riding the wave of human consciousness through apparently solid walls that are revealed as but a dance of atoms. Dreams and shadows can solidify into future hopes, while contemporary nightmares pass with the silent night.

Part II

Realizing the Romance

The techniques of Romantic Individualism create a communal story in these contemporary novels, as they center us in our own traditions and offer through multimythic perspectives both the faces of the God/dess in our moment and novel patterns that promise cyclical regeneration. Mythic realists uncover the God/dess of Nature itself, a dynamic order implicit in the physical universe. By unifying gods and goddesses, the individual and society, and myth and history in the infinite variety of a universal community, the meronymic novel seeks to uncover the languages of that God/dess and the patterns of that order in its myriad particle forms. Expanding our perceptions beyond dualities, each novelist weds cultural perspectives, generating multimythic, multicultural possibilities.

The key to the language and structure of the meronymic novel is as simple and beautiful as Truth itself. Romantics might call it the language and links of love and marriage; realists might prefer the expression and pattern of type and community. If these patterns remain static and isolated, truths may remain hidden or be perverted and distorted into false myths. The meronymic visions of Welty, Naylor, and Atwood diagnose such a degenerative disease within our present society, the disease of patriarchy, which generates a duality and exclusivity that can only predict a future of destruction.

Lessing chooses to expand the canvas to help us see the larger picture, and her choice revives our hopes. Her naturalism blames the brevity of our moment for our despair, not the unpredictable Necessity that is indifferent to us and reminds us that we are free of time in our imaginations. Infinity lies in our microcosmic moment as well as in the vast universe. Not Nature but monologic, static ideology obscures our vision and shapes our social and personal worlds so disastrously.

We are not gods, Lessing reminds us. We cannot afford to be indifferent to our membership in the universal community or the human family. If we are to survive, we must learn to live within Necessity while we appreciate and are regenerated by its hidden order and visible beauty; we must learn to love the human family to realize the full promise of its past in the experience of the present moment in hopes of shaping a better future. She challenges Western social values with a compendium of formal documents filled with fragmented particles of truth. With the assistance of archival and Canopean explanations and notes—the closest she can offer to an omniscient narrator—we can order the information and recognize the pattern and can discover the language of Nature and read the cosmic code.

In the remaining chapters, we will follow Lessing's lead and listen to the multicultural and multiethnic voices who trace the human spirit, the love that could unite us, through communal, historical, and personal versions of our story. Part 3 will explore a microcosm of the world community in the cultural diversity of ethnic America. Before we turn inward to discover that enriching otherness, however, Part 2 moves us outward to our multicultural heritage and relationships. Beginning in Joseph Conrad's "Heart of Darkness," Butler's African American perspective will shine light on our past marriages and future possibilities for survival and community. Latin American magic realism provides Isabel Allende with a balancing perspective in which to realize the romance of history in Chile and to find room for the whole family in an expanding house of the spirits. Finally, we return to our Anglo-Saxon roots in the British Isles to research past and present, prose and poetry, and love and marriage in an effort to reclaim the language of trees and flowers, of growth and change, in A. S. Byatt's *Possession: A Romance.* These writers enable their characters to realize the romance anew in our moment, as reality transforms expectations and uncovers new American dreams.

4

Signifyin(g) Science Fiction:
Octavia E. Butler

Butler must turn to the romantic form of science fiction to find traces of that uniting communal love. "Cautionary tales," says Butler: "That is what I hope I am writing" (Louis 66), placing herself in the best African tradition. Her novels explore otherness, reflecting her own double marginality and revealing that "the thing most needed to make homo sapiens viable and whole is 'alien' to the species: compassionate and rational thought" (Louis 66). Being raised by women ("her grandmother, her mother, who still works as a maid, and an aunt were the most influential people in Octavia's life"—Mixon 13) has taught Butler much about kindred, compassion, and survival. But as with Naylor's women, she has learned her lessons on the dark side. "My mother and grandmother were survivors" whose "lives seemed so terrible to me at times—so devoid of joy or reward. I needed my fantasies to shield me from their world" (quoted by Mixon 13).

Yet women survivors fill Butler's fantasies. Alanna in *Survivor* epitomizes this when only she survives capture by the enemy Tehkohn. Such fantasies help center Butler in her traditions, help her understand the world of her female kindred rather than escape it. "Mothers are likely to teach their daughters about survival as they have been taught, and daughters are likely to learn, even subconsciously," she adds (quoted by Mixon 13). Shielded within the Romantic tradition of science fiction, she could look back from a fresh perspective and explain how her female kindred found the hope necessary to bear racial and gender oppression.

Butler's Patternist series goes beyond fantasy, however; it stretches three hundred years back into historical Africa in *Wild Seed* through a scarcely recognizable present in California in *Mind of My Mind* before it leaps into a possible future. In that future is realized an extended community that overcomes racial and gender prejudices, an achievement that depends upon as radical a change in our thinking as would Lessing's shape cities.

Unlike Atwood's dystopia, Lessing's and Butler's futures are not extrapolated from our history; rather, they result from transformations of that history that create new possibilities. Within our moment, however, can be explored the attitudes and ideas that could initiate such a transformation of history. Butler chooses to revive the Goddess cycle that already sustains our dreams, offering the promise of balance and marriages as she mythically re-visions African American history. While Welty's diminished goddesses, as members of the dominant culture, can be discovered in her Mississippi back yard, Butler must reconstruct her story because, like the handmaids of Gilead, oppression has fragmented the members and myths of her kindred. Speculative fiction allows her time and space to arrange those fragments and trace that community to its spiritual survival in today's African Americans despite historical efforts to disperse and destroy it.

Both Lessing and Butler expand their revisioning of our story beyond one novel, making us conscious that even a meronymic novel is part of a larger story. Lessing echoes her commitment to the Celtic Zone 5 of human endeavor by writing five novels to complete her map of our universal truths. Butler's series is even more open-ended, as it ventures further into our future in *Patternmaster* and *Clay's Ark* but heads for another planet into a Patternist universe in *Survivor*. *Marriages* and *Wild Seed* both stay home, however, revealing in their language and structures patterns that unite the communal and individual self and balance our dualistic ideologies. While *Wild Seed*'s locales can be more easily found on our maps, it too takes place in the human mind. We can only know the past there; even Butler must imaginatively recreate her heritages of Africa and of slavery. They come, as James has said of Romance, "only through the beautiful circuit and subterfuge of our thought and our desire" (32).

As Sandra Y. Govan argues, *Wild Seed* draws on more than one literary tradition, "neatly defin[ing] the junction where the historical novel, the slave nar-rative, and science fiction meet"; the novel "stands on the foundation of tradi-tional form and proceeds to renovate that form" (82). Butler herself has ack-nowledged her use of such romantic patterns as "the chase, the game, the quest, the test" here and elsewhere to explore "the struggle to grow up or deal with some change" (Jackson 5).

Butler marries her Judaic-Christian cultural heritage to African myth, particularly of the Ibo and Yoruba tribes to which most African Americans could trace their beginnings, to identify the God/dess and learn again the language of Nature. But her history demands another language for her fragmented culture as they learn to survive within the lesser necessity of an oppressive society. Signifyin(g), as Gates explains in *The Signifying Monkey*, is a deliberate distor-tion of the language that depends on the shared understanding of a third perspective from which the social and physical information can be judged: "Signifyin(g) turns on the play and chain of signifiers, and not on some supposedly transcendent signified. As anthropologists demonstrate, the Signifying Monkey is often called the Signifier, he who wreaks havoc upon the Signified. One is signified upon by the signifier" (52–53). As a rhetorical strategy, it does not claim omniscience; the monologic voice is avoided when the novelist is seen as the Signifying Monkey "who dwells at the margins of discourse, ever punning, ever troping, ever embodying the ambiguities of language" as "our trope for repetition and revision, indeed our trope of chiasmus, repeating and reversing simultaneously as he does in one deft discursive act" (52).

The double marginality of race and gender locates Butler "at the margins of discourse": the very existence of her voice initiates a dialogue with the accepted expressions of a white male society. However, the rhetorical freedom of her position is discovered in recognizing her as the Signifier. We gain most if we are willing to accept our role as the signified, to receive her message as a fresh perspective on our shared human story as told in her family, her community, her myths.

The Signifying Monkey tale comes from African myths of the trickster, that mediary who claims direct communication from the gods but often tricks us with his stories. A common figure in world mythologies, the trickster is defined by Paul Radin as

at one and the same time creator and destroyer, giver and negator, he who dupes others and who is always duped himself. He wills nothing consciously. At all times he is constrained to behave as he does from impulses over which he has no control. He knows neither good nor evil yet he is responsible for both. He possesses no values, moral or social, is at the mercy of his passions and appetites, yet through his actions all values come into being. (xxiii)

Although she first creates Doro in "an adolescent fantasy of mine to live forever and breed people" (Kenan 499), Butler brings the trickster to life in this Nubian who has survived centuries. In her signifyin(g) within the novel, she dialogues with this patriarchal figure—born human but now using his trickster powers to control select humans as their god—by creating an equally exceptional woman, Anyanwu, who is not taken in by his stories although she is subject to his controlling power. By combining mythic allusions with signifyin(g), Butler can be both Signifier and Signified within the novel to uncover hidden meanings.

Furthermore, her own mediary position as doubly marginalized lets Butler record the lost otherness of her cultural traditions while challenging the gender dualism within those traditions. The meronymic marriage of Doro and Anyanwu can balance this dualism to some extent, but their descendant Mary must destroy Doro in *Mind of My Mind* if the infant community she unites is to escape patriarchal domination.

Jung defines the trickster as "a collective shadow figure, an epitome of all the inferior traits of character in individuals" (in Radin 209), revealing our monologic fear of that shadow; but he qualifies himself by adding that "the shadow, although by definition a negative figure, sometimes has certain clearly discernible traits and associations which point to a quite different background. It is as though he were hiding meaningful contents under an unprepossessing exterior" (in Radin 210). This remark is particularly useful in understanding the speculative signifyin(g) of Butler's fiction. The enslaved African is the shadow of our American communal consciousness.

The first "numinous figure" Jung posits behind the shadow is the anima: "in proportion as the shadow is recognized and integrated, the problem of the anima, i.e. of relationship, is constellated. . . . [T]he integration of the shadow brings about an alteration of personality" (in Radin 210n). The emergence of the anima that makes relationships possible could be read as the contemporary emergence of African American women writers, who offer to lead us back to the goddess within each of us. She in turn promises an integration of the shadow, of the other, which can transform personality and society. Yet, Jung specifically observes, "even the most rudimentary insight into the shadow sometimes causes the greatest difficulties for the modern European" (in Radin 211). Our otherness, which we hide behind the shadow of fear, echoes the otherness we envision behind the shadow of difference in the world outside. Until we integrate both shadows we cannot transform ourselves or our society. Is the "modern European" or the Euro American ready for that?

Doro has found the secret of regeneration in the theft of other bodies, beginning unconsciously with those of his parents when his own was weakened by sickness. He becomes his own god; his survival is the purpose, from his perspective, of the existence of any other life. He supports a community of followers, selected by him and valued at first simply by how well they promised to satisfy his hunger. His instincts identify "good seed" with which he begins the selective breeding project designed to feed him well for the eternity he hopes to survive. As such, Doro embodies patriarchy and individualism; it becomes increasingly difficult to discover any love in him.

The special abilities Doro discovers and nurtures in his eugenics project are only a by-product to him, but they reveal the human potential that our society neglects, enamored as we are with external sources of power. Note how many ways he reflects the values of the very society that will exploit his kindred. He does not interfere with that society's history; he too spreads his business concerns from Africa to America. Subsumed cultures often survive within a dominant culture by ignoring it as much as possible and pursuing their own concerns. Yet they are inevitably changed by immersion in that culture; Doro becomes increasingly isolated from community as he becomes more American, although his patriarchy has African roots as well.

A father gives life, but he must use the bodies of others—as vessels in which life is created or from which it is stolen—to do so. Doro is thus both adored and feared, an unpredictable patriarch who uses and rewards others whimsically, demands strict obedience, and eventually takes their very lives. Even more frightening to Anyanwu is his power to claim the lives of her children, her future. An-yanwu's mythic connection to Doro is revealed in their names, both of which re-late to the Sun, and Doro will call her Sun Woman although in *Mind of My Mind* her descendants will call her Emma, which means grandmother. She may be as glorious in her uniqueness as is Doro, but she is more concerned with her communal self, with her relationships to others. While Doro orders his people to increase and multiply only to supply his own appetites and demands periodic human sacrifices, Anyanwu gives life directly to countless children. Loving and accepting even the pain of having to watch those she loves die, she reshapes her body to hide her age and marries repeatedly. Indirectly, she draws upon her power within and her knowledge of nature for her own survival and that of her kindred.

Anyanwu too improves the human species—not by selective breeding but by genetic inheritance. She improves those not biologically descended from her as well, as Butler like Naylor expands our definitions of family. In this, Anyanwu is similar to the many strong women in Butler's fiction "who see and act upon possibilities beyond the human experiences they know to affirm consciously chosen community" (Williams 72). When Doro finds her in Africa, she is the medicine woman of a small tribe. Her gifts of love are offered freely. As such, she is a face of the Goddess. "I used in particular the myth of Atagbusi, who was an Onitsha Ibo woman," Butler explained in an interview. "She was a shape-shifter who benefitted her people while she was alive and when she died a market-gate was named after her" (Kenan 499). This shapeshifting is an immanent power from within, while Frazer's recounting of the Ibo myth gives the externalized version: "They think that man's spirit can quit his body for a time during life and take up its abode in an animal. This is called *ishi anu*, to turn animal" (Frazer 601). She, on the other hand, marries herself to the animal empathically and physically, seeing things from the perspective of the other, as Margaret Fuller asks of apprehensive critics who "can go out of themselves and enter fully into a foreign existence" (1587).

Although gifted with natural abilities, Anyanwu bestows her gifts lovingly and develops them humanly, through the use of reason and hard work. She has learned to repair physical damage by focusing inward and "seeing" the injury until it rights itself; she ingests poisons to learn their antidotes; she tests nature in various ways to learn what it has to offer humanity. Only by tasting the flesh of the dolphin and the leopard has she learned to shapeshift. While these are gifts celebrated in African myth and techniques reflected in rituals, the rational description of their processes given by Butler links them as well to scientific possibilities. Anyanwu uses her own body as her laboratory; her experiments are often painful and her knowledge inductively arrived at during her long life.

Furthermore, she has spent those hundreds of years sharing her gifts with others by marrying and having children and by serving her people as healer and wise woman. Her power from within genetically enriches her children, and she draws on it personally to support her community physically and psychically so that they can develop and share their own gifts. Integrating the shadow of Doro's otherness into their own communal strength will also prepare them to take on the work of love, which Anyanwu had borne alone for centuries. Anyanwu offers the anima key to relationships, even choosing not to live without Doro.

Anyanwu's legacy enables Butler to signify the Pattern in *Mind of My Mind*, a symbiotic support system that costs the Patternmaster any independent life, a willing sacrifice to communal needs. In his analysis of the trickster within, Jung had posited just such a conclusion for our society because of our fear of otherness: "the recognition and unavoidable integration of the shadow create such a harrowing situation that nobody but a saviour can undo the tangled web of fate" (in Radin 211). Yet the few gifted individuals who sacrifice themselves for the greater community do not offer us a possible social pattern; even their gifts depend on unpredictable Nature. This ironic Pattern, given birth by a contemporary Mary who is neither virginal nor successful in love or marriage, signifies on the options offered the African American within our society. Butler can imagine a nurturing past rich in the traditions of her people, but her expectations of the future are limited by an oppressive present.

Butler's rhetorical and mythic "punning" and tropes disguise her story as the Shadow, the otherness of science fiction. As a black woman writer, she is perceived herself as a shadow in white male society. Read as signifyin(g), however, these first two novels in the chronological order of the Patternist series reveal a fresh perspective on African American slavery and its aftermath as well as a new perspective on myth through the interwoven traditions of the African American. Within the time and place of slavery, we find Butler's female kindred offering the support of communal love, shapeshifting when necessary for survival or to understand the other, and committing themselves to the cycle of life. They keep love alive, even in their patriarchal masters. The same will be true in her more straightforward depiction of slavery in *Kindred*, a novel set alternately in California today and in Maryland before the Civil War, which immerses its romantic element of time travel completely into the historical connection of a woman's first-hand experience with the slavery of her kindred. In each case, female kindred survive oppression and exploitation to keep hope, and the race, alive.

In *Wild Seed*, Doro too is a slavemaster, but he is also kin to those he oppresses, a father who has absorbed the patriarchal selectivity and dualism of the larger society. Like that society, he has become self-centered, acquisitive, abusive, uncaring of any but a select few. Even they are subject to the unpredictability of his necessity, his godlike demands. The intracultural truth of his trickster role is his link with the power of the dominant society—what in Lessing's terms would be his alliance with Shammat. Recognizing the "part of myself from which [Doro] was created," Butler finds his destructive violence not so much between himself and Anyanwu as directed at "the people around them who are not nearly so powerful" (quoted by Hine 209). Inasmuch as Doro can be brought back to his "inner otherness"—his anima of relationships—he is still capable of love. If not, his existence is a threat to the community unless he is absorbed by the Goddess and reborn.

While African myth identifies Doro and Anyanwu for us, they are equally linked with the Old Testament Abraham and the New Testament Virgin Mary by Butler's signifyin(g). Anyanwu's role will indeed pass to a Mary, who then gives birth to the Pattern that saves and nurtures her community at the cost of personal sacrifice. An earlier type is equally present, as Sandra U. Govan has noticed: "They are a black Adam and Eve, and those whom they beget will themselves beget a new race" ("Connections" 83). Anyanwu marries both Father and sacrificial Son, both Doro and Isaac (whose name identifies Doro as Abraham as well). She is the Holy Spirit of this Trinity, linking the two by her love.

The Bible provides both structure and images for *Wild Seed*, as its three books marry myth to history to yield that love. "Covenant 1690" signifies Abraham's covenant with God by associating it with Doro's breeding project as well as the thriving slave trade that links Africa and America. Anyanwu finally submits to Doro's control by marrying Isaac, which provides the ironic close of this section as she begins "to make the children who would prolong her slavery."

In "Lot's Children 1741" Butler's irony becomes increasingly bitter. Genesis 19:36 reminds us that "both the daughters of Lot were with child by their father. The first-born bore a son, and called his name Moab; he is the father of the Moabites to this day. The younger also bore a son, and called his name Ben Ammi; he is the father of the Ammonites to this day." The Moabites are described as idolaters but also as a strong, progressive people who for a short time subjugate the Israelites themselves (Judges 3:12–14). The Ammonites, equally idolatrous, are nomadic and cruel and become enslaved by David as well as denounced by the prophets Jeremiah and Ezekiel. So too will Doro have children indiscriminately by his daughters, breeding an increasingly gifted people when he is lucky and creating monsters at other times. This book is set in his New England village ironically named Wheatley, but Anyanwu's presence there has gentled the irony by offering Doro's slaves the succor of her female arts.

The first line will reverse that: "Doro had come to Wheatley to see to the welfare of one of his daughters." Nweke, Anyanwu's daughter as well, is beginning the Transition, a wrenching maturing of her gifts that she is not destined to survive; Doro's contributes to that outcome by relieving her of her virginity. In doing so, he breaks an unspoken covenant he has honored with Anyanwu, as Butler continues to signify on her biblical parallels. Both Nweke and Isaac die as a result of the Transition and Doro's intervention; with all covenants broken, Anyanwu chooses to give up her burdensome humanity and escape Doro's slavery by becoming a dolphin. Butler's mythic dialogue divorces the goddess from a patriarchy that would betray and diminish her. "If Doro had not found her an adequate mate, he would find her an adequate adversary. He would not enslave her again. And she would never be his prey."

Anyanwu's slave narrative has passed through its first section of depicting life in slavery and reached its leap to freedom, nor does she need to tell that story of nearly a century of freedom. Butler's account will resume when Doro rediscovers her scent once she has resumed human form and tracks her down. "Canaan 1840" is set on Anyanwu's Louisiana plantation. As God offered the land of Canaan to his chosen people, so too did Doro offer America to his, but there the allusion becomes ironic. "For they are my servants, whom I brought forth out of the land of Egypt," we are told in Leviticus 25:42; "they shall not be sold as slaves." Only with Anyanwu do these chosen people find their Canaan; in the heart of the slave society of the South, she has gathered around herself a multicultural family and protected their freedom even from Doro by her shapeshifting. When he finally penetrates her disguises and invades their sanctuary, she must find a way to save them. But she can only escape alone, and she will not desert her family for only personal freedom. Nor can she live without freedom, so she chooses as did Demeter to express her grief by withdrawing. Her willingness to sacrifice herself teaches Doro "to recognize love, to reveal love; through love, she forces him to change" (Govan, "Connections" 83). He realizes that he does not want her to die, and that truth keeps him human by revealing the context in which love must exist.

Change is not a one-way affair, however. Anyanwu has been changed continuously by her association with Doro. "I don't believe in pure good or pure evil characters," Butler has said; nor does she believe in pure societies: "So what I see is a system that takes in the best aspects of any system out there" (Jackson 6). Doro reminds us that all life lives by devouring other life, while Anyanwu teaches us that we must give back when we take, we must sacrifice for others. Few of us enjoy receiving our mother's demanding training when we are young, but all of us recognize the message. It is perhaps even more difficult the more gifted we are, the more our "difference" promises us power.

While Anyanwu teaches Doro to discover his capacity for love, he teaches her to expand her definition of kindred and to accept cultural differences. The complexity of this issue of kindred is matched by the complexity of the concept of survival in Butler's novels. Neither the obvious restrictions of a slave society nor the apparent freedoms of today's society encourages communal love. The marriage of Doro and Anyanwu offers the greatest hope Butler can give us; their children may find a unifying Pattern within which we can communicate honestly and help each other develop our individual gifts. Such a community depends, however, on both our mothers' and our fathers' truths.

"I usually put my characters into positions that show us how well they've learned" the lessons of their mothers, Butler has said (Mixon 12). Social survival is not synonymous with social power. Survivors often perpetuate the very society that denies them power. Their children enrich the slavemaster, increasing his property. Yet their children's children may transform that society; they have already been transforming it invisibly as the shadow within. Children of slavery must within themselves resolve the apparent duality of black and white; the real Necessity has created in them a biological answer, and their combined mythic heritages offer psychological and social answers.

As Morrison reminds us in *Beloved*, slavery became so oppressive that mothers chose to murder their own children to defeat the perpetuation of that system. While the death of a slave may lessen the slave society by one, however, it also eliminates the potential personal power of that slave's descendants. Every life is of inestimable value; every particle holds part of our future potential. As Morrison's Sethe learns to let go of the past, her daughter Denver learns to live in the present and thus give us hope for the future. Society does not decide which particle will be blessed with the gift that we need to survive. This complex examination of the interrelationships of kindred and survival is typical of Butler's fiction as well. She began writing science fiction partly because "I was free to imagine new ways of thinking about people and power, free to maneuver my characters into situations that don't exist. For example, where is there a society in which men and women are honestly considered equal? Where do people not despise each other because of race or religion, class or ethnic origin?" (quoted in Mixon 12). Not in our society, in which mothers are again choosing to murder their children. Nor in our earlier history: Hawthorne had attributed such thoughts to Hester Prynne in *The Scarlet Letter* for gender-related reasons of oppression, and Mary E. Wilkins Freeman offered in "Old Widow Magoun" the wisdom of a grandmother who allows her granddaughter to eat poisoned fruit rather than delivering her to the whims of a patriarchal father. Doro may be the only African American slavemaster we have encountered, but his white counterparts have not disappeared from our social realities.

Despite the patriarchal lineage reflected in American names, American slaves were denied marriage and could be sure only of their maternal heritage. "Because of the system of slavery in which the Negro male was systematically used as a stud and the Negro female used primarily for purposes of breeding or for the gratification of the white male," Kenneth B. Clark argues, "the only source of family continuity was through the female, the dependence of the child on his mother" (70). Doro, like King MacLain, is a wandering father; it is Anyanwu who supports her kindred, offering the Christian covenant explained in Hebrews 8: "I will put my laws into their minds, and write them on their hearts, and I will be their God and they shall be my people. And they shall not teach everyone his fellow or everyone his brother, saying 'Know the Lord,' for all shall know me from the least of them to the greatest. For I will be merciful toward their inequities, and I will remember their sins no more." The unconditional love of Christ, of goddess mothering, of Anyanwu's personal sacrifices, promises a loving, nurturing community.

Butler's women recognize that their acts affect not only their own survival but also that of others in this pattern of kindred. All actions must be undertaken with the consciousness both of self and other and of the kinship between the two. Kinship includes male and female, black and white, oppressor and oppressed. It argues that no denial of social power can rob the individual of personal power, and that personal power can be used to effect social change. Butler reminds us that the past is constantly influencing the present, that social change is slow and depends upon personal action for its impetus. Speaking from behind the shadows of racism and sexism, she can testify that influence works in both directions within time and space. White America has been just as transformed by its social choices as have been the black slaves involved against their wills.

Despite her "escape" into the Romance, Butler cannot offer happy endings. Her historic connection is too strong to give her such freedom. We are permanently married to each other in this life, she reminds us, whether or not we acknowledge that relationship. Like Welty she recognizes a morganatic marriage when she sees one. As a doubly disinherited member of the human family, her meronymic shade of gray is much closer to black than to white. Responsible personal action, Butler contends, depends upon awareness of all our kindred—our membership in the human family—which must be balanced against any consideration of individual rights. As long as we must survive in a society that is out of balance, controlled by a static ideology that excludes its own otherness, and unable to adapt to the chance and change of life, the individual will be confronted with insoluble paradox. Since each person has the power to act and thus to affect everything, the lack of social support places the weight of the world on each of us. We are neither Atlas nor Hercules, neither Anyanwu nor Doro; we need each other to bear that weight.

Even looking through the lens of love, which celebrates our kinship with other members of the human family, Butler's women barely survive to keep hope alive with their children. The necessity imposed upon them by their social oppression is not balanced by any sacrificial love they offer their kindred; they can never give enough. Her women still choose to serve as healers and teachers, helping others through their compassion. Her contemporary woman is the culmination of a female heritage at least as old as Demeter, affirming rather than denigrating the value of the other, defining the community as a composite of kindred individuals each with personal power independent of social power, each needing to accept limits on power voluntarily if we are to survive together. But her goddesses are only human; they cannot survive forever in such a world.

As we read her meronymically, we begin to appreciate the stylistic complexity of Butler's fiction. At the same time, however, we begin to understand the darkness of her vision. Even science fiction fails to provide her any escape; rather, it reveals the ideology that has shaped her oppression. "We can only imagine what we truly know," Marge Piercy explains in her often dismal meronymic novel, *Woman on the Edge of Time* (1976). Who "truly knows" the abuses of people and power better than the doubly marginalized black woman writer?

Signifyin(g), which is without a "transcendent signified," combines with her SF techniques and mythic allusions to trap Butler's gods within the human story. This ironic language offers no cosmic code, only the chatter of the jungle. It is a chatter that we have heard without comprehending, and Butler records it so accurately that we must listen, must return to the heart of darkness to recognize our own darkness—the shadow of fear that obscures love. The folk tale of the

Signifying Monkey offers the rhetorical pattern that helps us understand these novels. The monkey is oppressed by the lion, self-appointed king of the jungle. Knowing that the elephant would be the natural choice for such a position, the monkey signifies with his trickster stories to persuade the lion to take on the elephant instead. In this way he survives by rhetoric when he could not have survived a confrontation. He wins by proxy, as the lion will lose to his second, the elephant. Yet all three remain animals in the jungle; all three will continue to confront each other as long as they live. He buys us only time and space.

So, too, does Butler operate only in our time and space despite her mythic allusions and speculative form. Imagining what she knows, she creates a community of Patternists tied to earth by their Pattern, by the very kinship that supports and makes their growth and change possible. The Pattern is described as a "little sun," reminding us that it is the product of a dual heritage from Doro the Sun Man and Anyanwu the Sun Woman. Our kindred make escape less attractive than the struggle, however; beyond suicide lies rebirth through our children. Anyanwu's slave narrative, like that of Harriet Jacobs, includes hiding for years in order to ensure the survival of her children. Goddesses both, they exemplify the power of love to transform reality.

Butler's signifyin(g) becomes more ironic, however, when we shift from idea to act, from romance to realism, and look more closely at the effect of time and space on mythic possibilities. Not hidden behind the shadow of blackness, other patriarchal masters carry on Doro's tradition of selectivity and violent oppression. The children of Anyanwu, taken from the lush jungles of Mother Africa to the social jungles of America, lose her protection and balance. To choose love is to choose social suicide; as Naylor suggests, rape seems to have taken its place in the walled ghettoes of today. Butler will assail those walls in a later novel, *The Parable of the Sower*, showing that "if you live behind a wall, you will die against it" (Louis 65). That novel again offers a cautionary tale, expressed alternately in the prose of its main character Lauren's life and the poetry of her self-composed religion. "If we do not heed 'The Book of the Living' we may end up in the book of the dead," Frances D. Louis concludes in her comments on the novel (65); indeed, Leslie Marmon Silko, sees a similar fate in *Almanac of the Dead*.

Butler's Patternist series offers little to change this bleak picture of human possibility. When the Patternists are forced to return to their confining homes, their venture into the heavens has added an additional burden—a degenerative Clay's Ark disease that diminishes their ability to communicate until their descendants end up living like animals. Those who leave earth, like Alanna in *Survivor*, find the same oppression among humans wherever they go. Alanna's companions are religious zealots who seek gods with their own faces and decide all life forms they meet, therefore, must be animals. When Alanna marries a blue Tekhohn on the new planet, she is an "abomination," as Old Testament patriarchs had taught them. Even that planet is racist, for blue Tekhohns claim superiority over green Garkohns.

Butler only "really know[s]" oppression and dualism. Boundaries seem impenetrable if you are one of the monkeys. Your only hope lies in finding elephants strong enough to shoulder the burdens of the world—or the burden of the worlds—and being clever enough to talk them into helping you. Taken from the home they knew, slaves found themselves very short on elephants. Alanna must go elsewhere to find one in the blue Tekhohn Diut. In *Wild Seed*, however, Butler finds one in Africa, signifyin(g) that the goddess, as quietly powerful as the elephant, is greater than patriarchy. But even Anyanwu is human; she succumbs when left alone and homeless in the contemporary California ghetto in *Mind of My Mind*. Nor is she mourned by her daughter: Mary's response and her description of the violence of her madonna role suggests the beast Yeats saw "slouching toward Bethlehem":

By the time Doro was dead and I began to try to give back the strength I had taken from my people, the 154 were already dead. I had never tried to give back strength before, but I had never taken so much before, either. I managed it, and probably saved the lives of others who would have died. So that I only had to get used to the idea that I had killed the 154. . . . Emma died. The day Rachel told her about Doro, she decided to die. It was just as well.

Butler's signifyin(g) dissipates the shadow of fear to reveal the truth of the anima, the supportive pattern of female kindred, but that pattern remains confined in the human consciousness. Still shaping the social realities is the ideology of oppression, of the exclusive individual or group that like Doro tries to guarantee its own survival by defining the rest of the human family as not-human and claiming sole ownership of them and what they may produce. Rejecting kinship with the Other, this group depends on force and confinement. Nature is diminished, her language obscured. How can we read a cosmic code in a ghetto?

Butler's women are survivors, but she offers little hope that our survival can be accomplished through love in such a violent jungle. Like Welty, she reveals the diminished role of the goddess in our lives. Yet even Welty's Morgana acknowledged possible rebirth through immersion in Moon Lake on the margins of Morgana, which would free both Loch and Easter, both hero and victim, both God and Goddess, to enter a wider world. That world may have been feared, foreign and obscured by shadows, but it did provide a larger alternative and could be reached through Nature. Butler too argues that we must coexist, marry the anima to the animus, one the shadow of the other. As Jung concludes in his discussion of the trickster as the shadow within, "the problem constellated by the shadow is answered on the plane of the anima, that is through relatedness. In the history of the collective as in the history of the individual, everything depends on the development of consciousness. This gradually brings liberation from imprisonment in . . . unconsciousness, and is therefore a bringer of light as well as of healing" (in Radin 211).

Can we penetrate to the divinity within? Only, Butler suggests, if we can dissipate the shadow of the trickster, recognizing the "numinous figures" behind the rhetorical signifyin(g) instead of fearing the shadow or ignoring the message. In the marriage of anima and animus, in "a system that takes in the best aspects of any system out there," we may yet realize the Romance in our time and place.

5

Magic Realism:
Isabel Allende

In 1988, my mother died. One sister had survived her, and when I arrived for the funeral she met me with an apology. After the death, she had gone through my mother's diaries and ripped out two pages. We both knew what was on those pages—the story of an illegitimate child. When the pages were gone, reality was transformed: neither history nor he will ever know that he is not the son of his legal father. The potential power of the written word, of my mother's diaries, awed me then as it awes me when I read Isabel Allende's *The House of the Spirits*. In this translation of a work written in another language in a part of America I had never visited, the refrain immediately made me feel at home: "in her notebooks that bore witness to life."

Some feminist critics might be disturbed by Allende's women characters, who seem to accept passively their social inequities and hence allow these to continue even as they continue to love the men holding power. So too were my students disturbed that Anyanwu could love Doro. While Allende and Butler offer graphic examples of gender inequities, our common story cannot ignore any of its parts to please an ideology; it must come from a realistic "witness to life." The way her primary narrator Alba constructs the story of our century and her family as much as the romantic or spiritual realities she draws to our attention explains the real magic of Allende's realism.

Language itself is a social construct, reflecting the values of the dominant ideology (Cf. Jameson, Lakoff, & Wittig). All language is metaphorical, not a transparent, neutral system that expresses "the thing in and of itself." While control of the media can be used to program people, control of the language is earlier and even more pervasive in its influence. The imperative of the dominant social ideology not only creates the metaphors that shape our expectations but also presents them as objective absolute truth, while all such "truths" are already value laden.

English and Spanish share European origins, but their cultural homes also create linguistic differences. Allende uses language to represent ideological differences between Clara and her husband Esteban. He prefers English and considers Spanish "a second-rate language, appropriate for domestic matters and magic, for unbridled passions and useless undertakings, but thoroughly inadequate for the world of science and technology." This helps us identify those functions assigned by the patriarch Esteban to women as well as to the language of his own country. Clara, on the other hand, receives psychic messages that a pendulum spells out "in Spanish and Esperanto, which proved that these, and not English, were the only languages of interest to beings from other dimensions." Clara would share these insights with the world, not wanting others to be limited to "English and French, which were languages for sailors, peddlers, and money lenders"; but her letters are never answered, just as her values are never shared even in her own home by her own husband. For this reason, their granddaughter Alba must balance her family history based primarily on Clara's notebooks and other family documents with her grandfather's oral reminiscences.

Just as Lessing compiles the documents of human history in the Canopean archives, Allende compiles the documents of this representative human family on her grandmother Clara's table so that Alba too can see with clarity—can see more than that clairvoyant grandmother who regularly entertained spirits and was now in spirit entertaining us. The story had to wait for Alba, the third generation, to complete it: "That's why my Grandmother Clara wrote in her notebooks, in order to see things in their true dimension and to defy her own poor memory."

Young and Hollaman discuss "magical realism" as "a hybrid that somehow manages to combine the 'truthful' and 'verifiable' aspects of realism with the 'magical' effects we associate with myth, folktale, tall story. . . . What matters is that the domination of any one way of looking at things is, at least temporarily, put in jeopardy" (2). Allende has created such a hybrid, with which she penetrates while simultaneously sharing and celebrating the cultural and linguistic differences that would seem to separate us. Although as an English-speaking North American unable to read her work in the original Spanish I can never fully appreciate Allende's cultural subtleties and linguistic accomplishments, with the help of Magda Bogin's fine translation and attention to linguistic patterns, images, and mythic allusion we can discover her many similarities to our other writers in her unique version of the meronymic novel.

Allende's fiction is also bound to European traditions and transformed by America. Boundaries drawn on a map are part of the patriarchal construct that separates and opposes people who share the same geography, whose connections are visible while the social realities of nationalistic borders must reshape nature. Challenging those boundaries helps reveal our interdependence. Borders make the starvation of an entire people outside of them possible. Care, respect, and responsibility can treat these borders as thresholds again, as we learn to live in tune with a planet that finds room for all in more than the two dimensions of a map. We need not wait to be carried across such thresholds by marrying men, either. Therefore, when we discuss Atwood's Canadian fiction or Allende's Latin Amer-ican fiction, we are still home, turning other borders into thresholds to share more of the multiplicity and diversity that is America.

From both its Incan and Spanish traditions, Chile has been redefined through patriarchal, dualistic ideologies. The power of naming given in Genesis to Adam in Incan myth is assigned to the Creator's two sons, Imaymana and Tocapo Viracocha. The myth specifies that "neither the Creator nor his sons were born of woman and that they were unchanging and eternal" (de Molina in Osborne 56–57). Although Allende must work within these already existing metaphors, her naming reveals connections among and roles of her characters.

Alba, her mother Blanca, and her grandmother Clara have names that play on the color white, while Clara's adds the dimensions of clarity and clairvoyance. Clara's mother Nivea might be linked as well, since snowy is *níveo*. Clara's sister Rosa's name suggests their linking as Snow White and Rose Red, and this fairy-tale dialogue further clarifies their sisterly relation to the "bear" in both their lives, Esteban Trueba.

The mythic dialogue begins with this naming, then, and the women of the family will both embody and transform the myths as they repeat them in their lives and their storytelling. Rosa, "the most beautiful creature to be born on earth since the days of original sin," is compared to a merwoman and an angel, to European and Indian myths. Looking like Aphrodite rising from the sea with her seaweed green hair and fair skin, she also embodies the Araucanian Serena, a mythical merwoman who sometimes has a fish tail and is reminiscent of the sirens as she is seen "holding up a mirror and combing her hair. Some say that whoever sees the Serena lives but a short life" (Osborne 116). In one of the many ironic reversals of the novel, Rosa's life instead is shortened, by poison meant for her politician father.

Imaginary animals are common to Latin American mythology, although Jorge Luis Borges doesn't mention the Serena in his discussion of sirens and mermaids in *The Book of Imaginary Beings*. He does, however, tell of the Chonchón, which is shaped like a human head with ears large enough to be its wings and which is "supposed to be endowed with all the powers of wizards" (99). Native to Chile, the Chonchón offers an absurd image by which we can interpret one of the events in Allende's novel. Clara's parents are killed in a car accident when she is pregnant with her twin boys Jaime and Nicolás, and her vision leads her to find the head, which then supervises their birth. Extolled by women as "the first feminist in the country" while others said "if she lost her head during her lifetime there was no reason why she should find it in death," Nivea's power is returned to her daughter's home and preserved in the basement for many years with the other magical items collected there.

Among those items are the books left by Nivea's brother Marcos, who himself is resurrected when he returns to visit after being proclaimed dead. The books will later provide Blanca with tales to be transformed as she passes them on orally to Alba: "This was how Alba learned about a prince who slept a hundred years, damsels who fought dragons single-handed, and a wolf lost in a forest who was disemboweled by a little girl for no reason whatever." These feminist transformations of European folklore reflect not only how women might revise events but also how Chile adapts and adopts what it receives from other cultures. If Serena sounds like Siren and her images echo European mermaid folklore, we must remember that Araucanians are also an oral culture; by the time their folklore is recorded "it is virtually impossible to determine what part of the reported mythology belongs to the original strata of belief" (Osborne 116).

Imported myth opens and closes this cyclic story: "Barrabás came to us by sea." While Barrabás is simply the caged and severely neglected dog shipped to Chile by Uncle Marcos, he is also the resident mythical beast of the novel, haunting the house in body until he is murdered on Clara's wedding day and in spirit from then on, after his hide is made into a rug. His name, too, deserves examination. In Spanish, *barrabasada* means mischief or a rash act, while in myth Barabbas is associated with Christ's crucifixion. In both references are clues to the ongoing mythic and realistic animal images interwoven with the spiritual images from Catholicism and spiritualism throughout the novel. Humans, Allende seems to suggest, are "imaginary animals"; we are animals with imaginations, with the ability to transform our reality by seeing it freshly and preserving that vision in our arts. Our animal nature might commit mischief and break laws, but the love that is God made human in Christ would never let that prohibit our sharing any heaven that love might provide.

Our animal nature is what betrays us, while our reason alone—not its imaginative powers that come with the balancing perspective of romance—is admired by realism. This patriarchal denial of the body and worship of a transcendent Father removed from nature reinforces our estrangement from the universe in which we must live. Naturalism further emphasizes the irrational animal within us who is driven by nature and environment, a reductionist view that robbed us of the divinity of that animal's larger role as an essential part of the greater whole. By extension, this has devalued all human gifts, while it has made Nature the other Shadow that we fear.

Animals with imaginations create art; our claim to divinity is that creativity is married to the language skill that enables us not only to see the world freshly but also to name it and tell its story anew, transforming the story, if not reality as well. Thus it is not in the Church that we locate the divine element in Allende's novel, but in the loving spirit and the imaginative powers of her characters. Nor is our animal part belittled; rather, ideology again divides and threatens to conquer us. While the novel begins with Clara's journal entry on her family's participation in a noon mass at the Catholic church, we are given only an imagistic description of the rituals and the objects involved and clear indications that religion is a social affair for this family, with a father who is an atheist and a mother who "preferred to deal with God without benefit of intermediaries."

Animal imagery links an appreciation of nature to women's imaginative art. Each generation produces its artist, beginning with Rosa, who embroiders fantastic animals on tablecloths, to remind us perhaps of the Chilean popular art form, the *arpilleras*, which would become an important export during the 1960s when the Christian Democrats then in power set up women's centers in which middle- and working-class women worked together in "a sort of country-wide communal cottage industry" (Agosín 139). The popularity of these embroidery-paintings led to even more women's centers when Allende's uncle, President Salvador Allende, came into power: "For the first time, women were in the midst of history, until then forbidden territory. So in spite of the various economic and political problems that developed during the government of Allende, it was a period of renaissance for women and for popular culture. We were reborn out of an iron silence" (Agosín 139).

Rosa is dead long before Allende comes into power, which takes place during the early adulthood of her grandniece Alba; this does not negate the connection, however, because Alba's meronymic perspective purposely condenses the events of her family from the beginning of the twentieth century into the time and place of her storytelling: "memory is fragile and the space of a single life is brief, passing so quickly that we never get a chance to see the relationship between events; we cannot gauge the consequences of our acts, and we believe in the fiction of past, present, and future, but it may also be true that everything happens simultaneously." That simultaneity is picked up in Blanca's artistic parallels to Rosa. She chooses to sculpt the animals: originally as a distraction from her migraine headache, she forms working people and household animals from the clay, but eventually she specializes in "incredible crèches full of monsters which, against all logic, sold like hotcakes." Finally, Alba carries on what Clara has finally decided must be an inherited trait of "craziness" by connecting the art to the "house of the spirits" itself. She begins a mural on her bedroom walls with paints that her grandmother gave her. It eventually embraces the entire room, filled with the flora and fauna that echoed the embroidery and statues of her maternal ancestors.

The imaginary animals, the order achieved even in fantastic art, balance the many times within the novel when the people act like animals. Nor is that a simple condemnation of their behavior, because the physical acts of love are celebrated quite as much as the imaginative expressions. Only when the spirit is perverted—by rage, revenge, or whatever—or when ideology substitutes for humanity will even the "house of the body" be difficult to love. Barrabás is never described in flattering terms; yet it is clear that Clara loves him deeply.

In this microcosm of one family, therefore, Allende is able to describe the human family. No need to spread that family across the universe and to extend our lives indefinitely, since our lives are already extended by the lives of our ancestors and our descendants; Allende eschews even the appearance of universal truths by confining her story and her narrator to her precisely defined earthly home, so that we can see that our truths are microcosmic and must be understood within the context of the universe that kindly houses us. This shift of perspective helps us locate that home, to find in its architecture and its people—in its body and spirit—the images of our ideologies. It prevents us from assuming any such ideology to be the universal truth; rather, we must examine our interdependency within the physical and spiritual worlds that surround us.

Such exploration of the microcosm must not be confused with the fragmentation of reductionism that Henry Lewis Gates discusses in *"Race," Writing and Difference*. As Gates points out, when we look at a forest only in terms of the lumber it will produce, we are applying economic reductionism and ignoring the whole of which that lumber is a potential part; so too, when naturalism reduces humans to reactionary bodies, it ignores the whole of nature in which both body and spirit live coterminously. When we look at a microcosm, on the other hand, we are limiting the expanse of time and place precisely so that we can examine the whole story within those parameters. Beyond that, with Nivea we must "deal with God without benefit of intermediaries." That there is such a beyond is not rejected; from whom or where did the last of the Mora sisters learn of Alba's impending fate?

Allende's magic realism is as rooted in the time and place of central Chile as is its recorded history, stretching back from Alba and her contemporaries through the European immigrations (primarily Spanish) and the earlier invasions of the northern Incans from Peru to the southern Araucanian Indian stock whose descendants farm Tres Marías. Alba is the only member of the family left in the house (although she is pregnant with its future generation), and it is therefore in her that the whole story of the past must be reconstructed to define expectation.

Boundaries become thresholds stylistically as a story of mothers and daughters opens doors where others see only walls. Doors, walls, and homes are appropriate metaphors for entering Allende's novel *House*. Butler's women have been so uprooted and dispersed that they must create a pattern of consciousness within which to feel at home; Allende's women are that pattern. As she traces generations of women in the same place, chronological time fades in importance and St. Augustine's present of consciousness fills the rooms of the house with ghosts and evolving images, with myth and history from the lives and writings of the women who "bore witness to life" within—and outside of—its walls.

House is more easily translatable than many novels precisely because it is permeated with the images of women's art as well as the documents they leave in the house. The primary dialogue is metaphorical. Houses provide the unifying images, beginning with the urban home Esteban Trueba gives his wife Clara when they marry. Periodically, however, the family relocates to Esteban's rural farmhouse in the South, Tres Marías, which in its way equally houses spirits, although those still residing in human bodies are neither acknowledged as relations nor treated as fully human by the dominant society.

Members of the family lead us to other houses as well. Most significant are two houses of the body—the Christopher Columbus Hotel kept by Esteban's prostitute friend Tránsito Soto and the decadent *fin de siècle* house to which his daughter Blanca is taken by her husband, the French Count Jean de Satigny, in the far North. Thus each house has its own *doppelganger*. Finally, Alba is housed briefly but tortuously by the oppressive military government under Colonel Esteban Garcia, her grandfather's illegitimate grandson. The prison is ironically divided as well: Alba experiences tomblike isolation in the "doghouse" and a compassionate community in the women's concentration camp.

Each of these houses is detailed imagistically to represent concrete as well as ideological possibilities in which humans live. Each contrasts with its double and contains contrasting rooms that help us understand the ways in which we learn to adapt. The home Clara receives as a wedding present from Esteban is ideal as the center home of the spirits precisely because it will grow and change with three generations of women and yet will always remain the home of Esteban as well.

Allende suggests earlier patterns, but it is with Clara that this story begins. Clara and Rosa ironically parallel Snow White and Rose Red: the romantic view of love as an unattainable goddess not meant for this world is expressed in Rosa's death from her father's poison. When we kill off Rose Red, the healthy body of women, by denying an animal nature to the spirit, the spirit usually dies too. In this case, the spirit lives on in Clara. Clara learns from her mother Nivea, another Snow White, to reveal only her spiritual beauty. Rosa's death silences her for nine years until a vision shows her the way to resurrect Rosa in her own and Esteban's lives by marrying him. While Esteban worships the dead Rosa—even exhuming the dead but miraculously preserved body that he really loved and that ironically crumbles to dust as he kisses it—it is Clara he loves for both body and spirit, however little he understands her. It is Clara's love and contemporary realities that transform his houses and clarify his vision, at least momentarily, before he too dies.

Esteban's three houses image his patriarchal fragmentation. Just as patriarchy denies the apparent matrilinear heritage of Nature, so too does the social pattern superimpose its truths on the body of Nature herself. His houses represent both our individual and ideological needs. In his marital home with Clara, Esteban houses his love, his spirit, and he has every intention of leaving such an impractical reality there at all times. His body is served by the prostitute Tránsito Soto, but her Christopher Columbus Hotel explores such patriarchal passion with mental constructs; she need only feed the fantasies and illusions of her clients and they provide bodies themselves from the many women subservient to that ideology. Esteban's body actually finds its home in Tres Marías, the southern farm of which he is the patrón. There he claims Nature for his own and rapes at will. Not even a morganatic marriage is provided here, reminding us of Butler's Doro, who simply harvests or destroys what Nature helps him create, although the stubborn native stock of Esteban's farm often ironically claim their heritage themselves by providing their children with his personal if not his patronymic name. Nature herself will reassert her sovereignty over Tres Marías twice in opposition to Esteban's claims, first with a plague of insects, which is averted by the native knowledge of Pedro García, and then with an earthquake.

The natives also return, whenever the patrón is absent, to their ideologic expediency of living with what the Goddess provides. They remind us of their Araucanian ancestors, whose ability to adapt (as we have seen in the Serena myth) and yet to survive intact led mythographers to describe them as "having put up the most obstinate resistance first to Incas and later to Spanish domination" (Osborne 114). Yet, as we have learned from Welty's novel, even the Goddess community is transformed and diminished within a patriarchy. While the women seem to expect and accept being used and abused, the men are denied patriarchal empowerment, reserved exclusively for the Spanish descendants.

Each generation of overseers at Tres Marías is progressively more distorted by this denial. Old Pedro García still retains the magic of his original heritage, which enables him to talk to the insects that are destroying the crops and get them to leave when the new science has failed and to heal Esteban's broken body after the Goddess has challenged his claim to Tres Marías with an earthquake. His son, Pedro Segundo, given little power and expected to tolerate Esteban's rape of his sister Pancha, saves his love for only Clara. Next, Esteban's unacknowledged son Pedro Tercero loves Blanca and fathers her child while also becoming a political revolutionary. Tercero is not simply taking on the patriarchal right to rape, however; his other heritage is clearly seen in the mutual love the half-siblings share, which does not need to, and in its incestuous nature could not, receive the social stamp of marriage to validate it. He remains true to Blanca, as she does to him, despite later relationships. When they are finally united, that marriage must be consummated outside Chile—in their new American home in Canada.

Finally, Esteban's unacknowledged grandson Esteban García will challenge the very survival of this Trueba microcosm by his need for revenge on the father who has denied him his social heritage. His rage will lead to Alba's imprisonment, depriving her of her spirit's physical and familial homes. In the distorted face of this revolutionary we see the ultimate perversion of the human animal by patriarchy, as he tortures the bodies in his attempt to destroy the spirits of other members of the human family. Alba traces his violence to its undeniable roots in her own family's complex heritage, which helps her let go of her own hate and recognize that "my revenge would be just another part of the same inexorable rite." Refusing to perpetuate that patriarchal heritage, she uses her storytelling art instead to reconstruct the familial house of the spirit.

Once Esteban is married he seeks out prostitutes, a patriarchally legitimatized form of rape that keeps it in its proper location. Not natural sex but the perversion of that sex to suit the progressively distorted tastes of the patriarch fills these houses, and Allende's novel will trace that perversion by following the woman who realizes its business potential, Tránsito Soto. Again, her name is a clue to her role: Tránsito's meaning of transit or traffic captures the transitory nature of such love, while Soto means a grove or thicket, which is a common patriarchal reduction of women to their genital geography. However, Soto might also make us consider the meaning of *sota*, which is foreman or overseer, because Tránsito, with the help of a small financial investment by Esteban Trueba, grows to be the ultimate Madam. Her house, the explorative Christopher Columbus Hotel, uncovers the real nature of her business. No longer does she provide women for her customers; she realizes that patriarchy has so devalued women that they are willing to give their bodies for free. Her hotel, therefore, houses these transitory romps in rooms decorated with appropriately perverted art and myth, revealing the uses and abuses of the spirit that are also the product of patriarchy but kept in its hidden houses.

As such, this transitory overseer demonstrates once again that the devalued humans who serve the dominant society are most in danger of becoming vehicles of that society. Her final service of engineering Alba's freedom, however, shows that the people caught in the middle can turn both ways. Similarly, Pedro Tercero rejects serving his patrón to become a revolutionary whose song inspires the people, while the more damaged Esteban Garcia, denied love as well as social recognition, tries to take both by force. Pedro is uncomfortable and stressed when he is put in a position of social power in the new but doomed Marxist government, while Esteban Garcia thrives within the restored patriarchy. Meanwhile, Tránsito Soto survives by recognizing a practical social truth; as did James Baldwin's Ida, another exploited woman in another exploited part of America, she too has "decided that the whole world was just one big whorehouse and so the only way for you to make it was to decide to be the biggest, coolest, hardest whore around" (*Another Country*).

An even more hidden and perverted mental construct which uses and abuses the body and spirit, so ephemeral that Alba has trouble believing that it really existed, is that in which Blanca is forced to live temporarily when her father marries her off to the French count Satigny after he discovers her pregnancy. As his name's inclusive suggestions of both Satan and satin suggest, Satigny's northern house unites the worst of European and Incan patriarchal myths, excluding the Goddess altogether in its perversions and homoeroticism. That the Incan ideology is patriarchal becomes clear in the myth of "The Children of the Sun," in which the Sun father sends his two children to found his sacred city and provided the following instructions: "When you have reduced these peoples to our service, you shall maintain them in reason and justice with devotion, clemency and tenderness, playing in all things the part of a loving father to his beloved children, modelling yourselves on me" (de la Vega in Osborne 38). That even this manipulated Indian population, if left alone, is capable of returning to an expedient Goddess culture is made clear by their native art forms that Blanca appreciates, but Satigny's offer of the temptations of his house transformed by decadent art seduced them away from such a course. Blanca, alone and pregnant, finds the strength to leave and to return to the house of the spirits to give birth to Alba.

Still, Blanca does not let Alba know that Pedro García, rather than Satigny, is her father until much later, and then only in a passing remark while seeking Pedro's assistance. She taciturnly responds to her daughter's request for an explanation, "Better a dead father than an absent one." The complexities of that simple statement might well sum up the complexities of the family's survival in a patriarchal society.

Meanwhile, Clara's transformations of Esteban's wedding gift helps their family home retain its links to the spirit without being redefined by his attraction to European ideologies. With only the Incan image of idealized Indian warriors to represent his Chilean heritage, he envisions classical structure, statues of Olympic gods, and a French garden. The house, then, is his artistic attempt to superimpose European values on his married life. The pervasive influence of the deeply rooted Clara transforms it, however. She houses the spiritual activities of such members of the larger human family as the Mora sisters (whose name reminds us of the three fates we discovered even in the memory of Atwood's handmaid) and The Poet (who would later be awarded the Nobel Prize by the artistic world while he is assassinated by the leaders of his own society). The house itself images in its rambling, hacienda structure Clara's inclusive art of making room(s) for everyone.

The novel refuses to be ordered either by patriarchy or by chronology, the linear stories chosen to structure the movie version of Allende's story. Sentences expand to encompass past and future; when we learn of Esteban's architectural intentions we are told simultaneously of the changes Clara will make in the future to transform the house. Reunited with the physical as she marries Rosa's fiance, Clara can now find her voice and her art in her notebooks and her house of the spirits. Alba, too, will root her art in that very house and her story in those very notebooks. As she tells her grandfather when he suggests that she escape from the horrors that he finally realizes are in the social ideologies dominating Chile, she has no intentions of leaving the geographical and human truths that are best housed for her in her country, in her ancestral home, in her traditions.

Within this complex yet inextricably interwoven pattern of symbols, Alba relates the history of her family. Coterminous with these truths ordered by art and organized (as is Clara's journal) by events rather than chronology, we can detect the chronological history of Chile and of our own twentieth century. Although atrocities of our century are ephemerally mentioned in passing, usually by the outward-looking Esteban, the atrocities within Chile are described in graphic detail. Mentioned also are the foreign arts and sciences, business and industry, and foreign exportation of Chilean arts and humanity. Blanca's brother Nicolás (Saint Nicholas or Old Nick himself?) represents the spiritual heritage that Esteban cannot control and that he therefore pays to have sent elsewhere. (Ironically, the business sense Nicolás inherits from his father will make him a successful guru in that elsewhere.) Women's art is disseminated as well, but by popular demand rather than money.

This historic and chronological framework is realistic and pervasive, but it is also minimized so that we can focus on the microcosm instead of its context. A more immediate context is the physical reality of Nature, which is well represented through mythic allusions to the stories of its human creatures, both Araucanian and Incan, and to the Europeans only as they have adapted to and adopted these geographical boundaries. We can follow Alba's familial story because time has been opened to the eternal moment, as Alma's memory is extended realistically through the family documents, predominantly maternal but also—by her request—supplemented with Esteban's near century of eye witness accounts from his patriarchal perspective. This is supplemented by her own direct observations, both of the storytellers who provide the documents (so that we can understand better the ideological elements that affect their perspectives) and of the present moment as the current realization and transformation of that past. Alba's continuing residence in her grandparents' house of the spirits offers the healing love within which future possibilities can be encompassed and endured.

However, the violent death of her loving uncle Jaime, self-appointed sacrificial healer of his community, reminds us that some social ills promise nothing but destruction and that one individual cannot solve all the problems of the human family. Jaime's name might mean to remind us that *jamás* is Spanish for never. Nor is his the only failure of love in the novel. Esteban's sister Férula repeatedly fails to save those she loves or herself from isolation and even death, dying herself in isolation. Despite—or more likely because of—her strict adherence to prescriptions for Catholic sainthood, which is revealed imagistically, she must watch her mother's body rot away infested with gangrene and reclaimed by the natural lifecycle of insects. She drives away her only brother not once but twice, first when he turns to Tres Marías for escape and again when he sees her love for Clara as competition and exiles her.

In a society that denies both women and the body, the lesbianism he suspects her of is to Esteban a final perversion of all values; in this familial rejection of the female self can be seen the patriarchal exclusivity within which he would control the spirit as well as the body. Clara's tribute to Férula as she performs the healing ritual of laying out the body after death equally represents the response of the spirit freed from such ideological blinders: she remembers only the unconditional love given her by this sister-in-law. Thus even Férula, named for the ferule with which the children were disciplined in the British school to which their father sent them to learn European values, is finally recognized for the face of love distorted by patriarchal expressions and perceptions. Still blind to what he has done, Esteban cannot understand why his sister would die in squalor when he had sent her money to guarantee her survival elsewhere, although Clara tries to explain: "Because she didn't have anything else."

Clara's house of the spirit could offer what else Férula needed rather than sending her where else she would be hidden from sight. There is no elsewhere in Allende's novel; there is only blind rejection of the whole determined by the patriarchal exclusivity of the society that shaped Esteban. As life and love work together to show the real and predictable distortions and perversions produced by that destructive ideology, Alba's story reminds us as well of love and alternate possibilities. To survive her present moment and help shape the future, Alba must reconstruct through her art the whole story of the preserved history and mythic images and tales she has received.

Alba shows how these seemingly conflicting perspectives have shaped her moment of time but offers neither the passive, accepting love of an expedient societyn or the revolutionary efforts of the Marxist challenge to the long-established government as an answer. That seemingly dynamic challenge is itself polarized by class, as she realizes when she is first rejected by the revolutionary sister Ana Díaz because of her aristocratic family. Her love for Miguel draws Alba into the group of young revolutionaries to which he belongs; her refusal to betray him wins Ana's later friendship when they are both incarcerated in Colonel Garcia's prison. Love, not ideology, sustains each of them in this period of torture.

More than those individual animal loves, however, the unity of the women and their mutual protection of the children produce the art of their songs and rituals, while the compassion of their jailers heals Alba's body and encourages her to write. Master or slave, jailer or prisoner, the human story must include both; the human imagination must use its reason to examine the moment and its gift to express that moment fully so that we can survive and understand what threatens to distort and pervert our message. As the images of society express our ideologies, the images of myth express our imaginative spirit. We must read both to reconstruct human history accurately and picture our possible futures. Only then can we make truly informed choices, knowing that they must be as dynamic as the world in which we live, responding to the changes of that world with the love and compassion possible in a diverse but united family.

To conclude that Allende's novel, or any of these novels, is apolitical is to deny that the personal is political. Literature must reflect the world as perceived by the author, not as the author might wish it to be. Clearly the novelists do show, from that perspective, the effects on the human family and its world of the current dominant ideology, and they draw our attention to alternative ideologies in the process of storytelling. Allende's women extrapolate from the human story of growth and change within their own Chilean home what must be true of the rest of the human family. They do not presume to interfere with personal perceptions of God; they are content with accurately recognizing the microcosm rather than mapping the macrocosm.

At the same time, an understanding and appreciation of our place in nature and our ordering gift of art to contribute to whatever universal order there might be can provide much comfort while we live. Each woman tells a version of our story, which cyclically balances and regenerates itself even as the linearity of our chronological history inexorably records the apparent changes. The infinite variety of human faces and expressions of each moment becomes the ever-increasing pageant of imaginary animals encircling the holy family in Blanca's crèches or filling the walls of Alba's bedroom; we admire the creativity of the artist who selects and orders the pageant and appreciate the particularity of each animal and rich diversity of the scene just as we appreciate Nature's own diversity. Even the most distorted face is recognized by borrowed parts from more familiar beasts. If the cyclical repetitions of the past in Allende's story of the human family threaten to make us merely the latest version of another time and place, art shows us that each moment is novel; each makes new combinations that continue to transform the universe itself. Each allows us to celebrate life as we live it.

The Americas comprise what we still call the New World because here the European ideologies find themselves away from home and must contend with the native ideologies on their own turf. To reflect this social development, the developing genre of the novel must be dialogic imagistically as well as linguistically. This is the elsewhere to which Europeans travel, have traveled, and will travel; yet when the globe adds the third dimension, any map reveals that we are still here on the same planet, in the same global village all the time.

Here also is the elsewhere for Europeans, a fresh beginning that offered a new Promised Land and a possible Eldorado of gold(en/and) apples. In America Butler's homeless Pattern can discover a past of which the dominant society has remained ignorant and which can inform our present and possibly transform our future. Alba's story, constructed in the present moment from the documents of her familial past, reveals that moment, as Michael Young would say, as "more a dash than a dot, and the stretched simultaneity of the present is what makes possible the sense of movement" (10). Human consciousness can understand that present because it can stretch with memory and expectation to the before and beyond that promise change.

Thus, a further dialogic must be established temporally, as Allende does by ordering her chapters by a pattern of events repeated with variations in each generation, while recording those events in chronological order disrupted repeatedly by Alba's observations on what is to come. Cyclical and linear time, Young asserts, "are best conceived as two often but not always complementary ways of looking at the same thing, two alternative conceptualizations of the same phenomenon which do not exclude each other" (14). Allende's history of Chile is recognizable, while her focus on events balances our social commitment to history with a more noticeable pattern of cyclical time within the family history. Concentrically, that history can be seen within the history of the prior Incan invasion, and that within the earlier presence of the Araucanian natives, while all are embraced by Nature, who speaks most clearly from the open fields of Tres Marías.

6

Repossessing the Romance: Antonia Susan Byatt

The social structure of the Americas cannot be comprehended within the linear ideology of Europe; yet its history must be recognized as simultaneous with the history of Europe. While Europe was evolving its patriarchal societies, the inhabitants of what would look to Europeans centuries later like a new world were also evolving. To understand America, we have had to expand our perspective to appreciate its own history, reminding us that European history is simply one story among many. If this is true of place, we must then consider its truth in terms of ideology and time. Already Frazer's *The Golden Bough* has collated myths and suggested a repetitive pattern that would place the Judaic-Christian cyclical story of death and resurrection among similar stories in other cultures. We seem much less willing to consider recorded history as also one among many, similar to some and sharply differing from other patterns; yet such an insight is needed to encompass difference and expand future possibilities.

As American readers, we are already hybrids of European ideology and our experiences in this New World. To understand how European explorers could claim America and "begin" its history, we must examine the time and place from which we received the label of the Other, that Elsewhere that asserted exclusive possession of America. Only then might we see through that otherness to recognize our links, even our identity, with each other and, ultimately, with other forms of life.

A meronymic perspective turned back on the European home of our language detects the reverse image, the negative, of the picture it would project on us. When we accept that America is the New World, then Europe becomes the Old

World. In temporal terms, then, Europe by its own definition is trapped in the past.

The British writer A. S. Byatt explores these links to the past in *Possession: A Romance*, which is primarily concerned with what is open to the quest for knowledge. Since quest literature is one version of the Romance, and the mystery novel is another, Byatt turns to the past century for the form of her novel. She must balance poetry and prose, past and present, and numerous shades and meanings of the word "possession" to complete her quest. As Jay Parini asserts in his review, "*Possession* is a tour de force that opens every narrative device of English fiction to inspection without, for a moment, ceasing to delight" (11). This is not simply "literary game-playing," as Donna Rifkind calls it (77), but an attempt to reunite the fragmented traditions of narrative style as she reunites past and present.

In 1990, the same year *Possession* appeared, Byatt coedited and introduced *George Eliot: Selected Essays, Poems and Other Writings*, and that introduction reflects her stylistic and ideological similarities to Eliot. Included is an Eliot essay that views civilization and religion as "an anonymous blending of lifeless barbarisms, which have descended to us like so many petrifications from distant ages, with living ideas, the offspring of a true process of development" (xxi). Without sacrificing the precision of language and direct observation of the social moment that mark her realistic style, Eliot borrows from the Romance to accentuate the differences between "lifeless barbarisms" and "living ideas." Similarly, Byatt as the intrusive Romancer repeatedly shifts our perspective in *Possession*. Like Hawthorne, whom she quotes in her prefatory material, she finds historical distance an aid in clarity precisely because the appearances of the past social milieu are more easily identified and penetrated.

Byatt argues that Eliot's interest in poetry alters her style as "her interest shifted from the exactness and definiteness of her earlier realism to the system of correspondences, and general truths, and similarities and connections that make up the general reality" (*Eliot* xxxi) and notes "the recurring web of metaphors in *Middlemarch* that links and combines the diverse parts of the social organism in the novel. And that self-conscious web of metaphor itself is a conscious poetic strategy of universalization" (xxxii). This "recurring web of metaphors" describes Byatt's *Possession* as accurately as it describes *Middlemarch*.

In *Possession*, the Victorian poet Randolph Henry Ash writes, "we live in an old world—a tired world." This linear exhaustion that her character perceives reveals Byatt's conscious introduction of growing metronomic despair into the earlier time period of her novel, a despair that nearly paralyzes her contemporary characters and sends them into the past in their quest for knowledge. To counteract this despair for her contemporary characters, Byatt creates a Romantic quest to resurrect the living past rather than the moldering remains of yesterday's story. This heritage lives on in life and art rather than in objects and historical records.

To lead us on this quest for knowledge, she fills her novel with contemporary characters possessed by the past. These researchers, collectors, even spiritualists, try to document, to prove, and to find material evidence of a hidden relationship between Ash and another Victorian poet, Christabel LaMotte, a love that had created new life both literally and figuratively in their futures. This, then, is a search for love; yet, the linear bias of the researchers threatens to validate only evidence concretized and particularized, offering such fragmented results that we as readers and Byatt as the intrusive Romancer have to revise their accounts, to see again for revision that evidence and bring the whole story to "closure, if not finality," a phrase that Roland Mitchell uses to describe the appearance of Ash's death mask. The novel will end with the final page, just as life apparently ends behind the mask of death, but such endings are seen as the stuff of comedy rather than tragedy.

It has been said that tragedies end in death and comedies in marriages. To understand the tragicomic view of life Byatt offers in her novel, we must venture beyond the lives and deaths of the two Victorian lovers as recorded by linear history to discover with the wisdom of retrospect the "marriage of true minds" and the union of love they shared. Because of the real limits of such reconstruction, which is inevitably affected by the observer and by the lack of concrete, objective evidence, Byatt eschews the artistic withdrawal of the Realistic novelist from the text and returns to the Romantic option of authorial intrusion. She thus achieves satisfying closure by offering hidden information available only to the artistic insight that can imagine the Other, creating "imagined lives" for historically defined characters based on the realities of what we know of their history and of our present moment.

In her article "Imagined Life," Maxine Hong Kingston discusses this artistic process, which fuses imagination and history to reveal the story of our shared humanity in the characters we construct, as a necessity in our dehumanized time: "Now, I don't want to leave you with the impression that to imagine life means that you only invent ways to befuddle and blur and to find what is not there," she assures her reader. "To live a true human life today, we have to imagine what really goes on when we turn on the machines. . . . We deliberately weaken and divert our imaginations to be able to bear a world with bombs" (140). Kingston also explains why she attributes, when she attempts to fill in the silences left by history and even her mother's stories, only specific experiences and motivations to the "real life" of her paternal aunt in the "No-Name Woman" section of her book, *The Woman Warrior*: "Unless I see her life branching into mine, she gives me no ancestral help."

In hopes that her Victorian poets can offer their spiritual and/or biological descendants, Roland Mitchell and Maud Bailey, the "ancestral help" that reveals the cyclical recurrence of their attraction to and for each other and the real heritage such love can leave though art and life, Byatt's meronymic Romance must balance the validated realistic evidence with the other evidence of the Romantic imagination. Seemingly by magic, however, she will be assisted in that ordering process by life itself, as the mutual interests of Byatt's researchers unite them in their quest. As in the storm that temporarily unites the researchers, Nature, stubbornly surviving even in the streets of civilized London but freer to express Herself in the wild North and in Brittany, reintroduces the cyclical story of life.

Unrecorded human actions often hold the key to understanding the relevance of the past to our lives; the literary artist alone can penetrate the silences and provide the words that describe and therefore concretize those actions and make them available as our other history. Thus, Byatt's Romance takes us into Nature, human and otherwise, and eavesdrops on such secret moments, venturing with imagination into the time and place where both Realists and angels fear to tread. Yet Byatt never escapes into fantasy; rather, her romantic fantasizing reveals hidden historical truths, claiming a more complete revisioning of reality. At the same time, it shifts our focus to what is often dismissed by Realists as the emotional but that may well be the moral context of the recorded moment, the invisible element of consciousness that motivates human actions.

Possession and love have had an ambiguous linguistic relationship over the years; yet the title of a text, as Barthes says, is "the prince of signifiers," and Byatt's title is no exception. Thematically and stylistically, this one word captures the perspective of the novel and orders its "recurring web of metaphors." That we will be at least as much in the linear past as in the present, that we will attempt to "thoroughly possess" both times, and that we will express them both in the complementary languages of Romance and Realism, poetry and prose, is established by the epigraphs Byatt begins with from Hawthorne and Browning. Hawthorne identifies "the attempt to connect a bygone time with the very present that is flitting away from us," while the Browning poem explains her use of poetry in the novel. Prose, he argues, is for "Dealers in common sense" who depend upon their "helpful lies" to validate their own interpretations of reality. Such self-justifying language is apparent as each researcher offers a different interpretation of the shared past. Prose that purports to describe reality objectively is therefore shown to be as much if not more of an artifice, a construct, than the most romantic narrative of the artist. Furthermore, each observer defines even that limited reality differently; their shattered fragments of ideology reflect different faces of the artifact each examines as proof of his or her own position.

Ash himself suggests another advantage of including poetry, or what he calls "singing of the Language itself." Poets love language, he argues, while novelists must concern themselves with "the betterment of the world." Byatt as the meronymic novelist will do both. She must consider her readers more than does Ash, who admits that he writes for himself only. For those readers fascinated by the realistic elements of her Victorian setting, Byatt recreates the styles of Victorian literature in her collection of poetry and tales and even plants suggestive allusions to actual poets of the period, a simple feat for this accomplished Victorian scholar/writer. Christabel's name and story comes from an unfinished poem by Samuel Taylor Coleridge; but Byatt's Christabel, who has been compared to Emily Dickinson in the reviews, also bears a strong resemblance to Christina Rossetti, not only in her sisterly attachment to Blanche Glover, which recalls Rossetti's "Goblin Market" in its gothic intensity, but also in the suggestive love poems of this spinster poet who turned down more than one marriage proposal. Maia, the name she gives to her daughter by Ash, recalls the final stanza of Rossetti's poem, also named "May":

> I cannot tell you what it was;
> But this I know; it did but pass.
> It passed away with sunny May,
> with all sweet things it passed away,
> And left me old, and cold, and gray.

Rossetti was known to admire Algernon Swinburne greatly, and though the character Randolph Ash has been most often identified by reviewers with Browning, he and Swinburne share poems entitled "The Garden of Proserpina." One stanza of Swinburne's poem seems particularly apt for the "tired world" that Ash perceives and its demands on lovers and artists:

> From too much love of living,
> From hope and fear set free,
> We thank with brief thanksgiving
> Whatever gods may be
> That no life lives forever;
> That dead men rise up never;
> That even the weariest river
> Winds somewhere safe to sea.

That both Swinburne and Ash appeal mythically to the Garden and to Proserpina, the daughter who must live with death, may further link them and offer clues to this tragicomic history.

Poetry emphasizes the imagistic language that Byatt will employ throughout the novel as well as in the poems themselves, drawing not only from Nature and images preserved in myth and symbol but also on the creative richness of that Christ-like Romantic imagination, which offers "[w]ord[s] made [hu]man" through their continual recreation and expansion of meaning in a living language "left to grow in precision, completeness, and unity, as minds grow in clearness, comprehensiveness, and sympathy" (Eliot xxii). This increases what Richard Jenkyns has called "the solidity" of the novel, however; "she suggests that those who genuinely love literature may apprehend the real world more keenly" (214).

The meanings of possession developed throughout the novel will serve to demonstrate that meronymic language, since they speak to the materialism and exclusivity of our society's "lifeless barbarisms" and of the obsessive power of our "living ideas." Byatt's characters find themselves wanting to possess the relics of the past, often irrationally opposing social laws to do so. The novel is filled with purloined letters, from Roland's first irresistible impulse to take Ash's drafts of a first letter to Christabel to Mortimer Cropper's scheme to rob the grave of Ash's wife Ellen of Christabel's final letter.

Each thief is motivated by other desires for possession. Roland wants to "possess the knowledge" promised by the letters, not only the information reported but more importantly the living emotion captured even more in the scratched-out changes of the earlier versions than in the final draft, which he will read much later. The ever-changing expression of the living love of a dead man is captured in the process rather than in a final product that provides only the information that history can record. On the other hand, Cropper wants only the physical evidence, the relic that once was possessed by the great man and would now belong to him. That relic will be sealed in his collection, while xerography and other reproductions can let others possess it.

Through the legalities of inheritance, meanwhile, the letters are in the de facto possession of Sir George and Lady Joan Bailey, although we will later learn that their relative and Roland's co-researcher Maud Bailey has through Christabel's will a legal claim of possession. Another case might be made for Lord Hildebrand Ash, who is enlisted by Cropper to claim and sell him the letters. Cultural claims are made by James Blackadder, who feels that English documents should remain in England, preferably in his Ash Factory in the basement of the British Museum.

The material possession of the letters allows the plot variations of the Quest, the Race, the Chase, and the Mystery to be developed, while gothic variations of the Romance explore the concepts of demonic possession when characters find themselves tempted to betray social definitions or rational desires. That such possession is associated with women is reflected in Ash's poem "Mummy Possest" and may remind American readers of the immensely popular novel by James Gould Cozzens, *By Love Possessed* (1957), in which the female characters are subject to similarly irrational possession (Cf. Shinn, *Radiant* 15–18). Christabel offers an image of such possession as well when she describes a worm kept in a jar to be studied as "Possessed of a Restless Demon—or hatred of Jarpanopticons," much as she herself will find the safety of a small house and the social roles of women confining and will also be "possest" by passion.

Ash, conversely, "always looked so self-possessed," as Roland observes, and Maud will seek that attitude as well when she fears the loss of autonomy that falling in love seems to promise. Looking at the future in the light of knowledge, Roland finds himself able to anticipate Ash's style because after years of study he "was possessed of his characteristic habits of syntax and stress." Then, conceptually, one can possess a knowledge of patterns that recur cyclically, but one is possessed by the unique occurrence of strong emotions. Love cannot treat the beloved as a possession, as Maud warns Roland, but lovers can let down the barriers, cross the thresholds when invited to do so, and take possession of each other.

Only things can be owned, however, and even of those we can be dispossessed, as the dragon is dispossessed of the golden apples in the Garden of Proserpina poem that opens the novel. Nor can the whole truth be possessed, except possibly in a Romance, because some information will always be lost and some feelings will never be expressed. Repeatedly, Byatt's Romance reveals that our society is obsessed with the idea of possession.

Perhaps most important in our metronomic society is the desire to possess the past, while the contemporary level of Byatt's novel reveals that instead we are possessed by that past—by the belief that our world is the decaying remains of that world, that our talents could not match the Great Men of that time, and that our little story can only weakly repeat the stories already told. The contemporary central character, Roland Mitchell, is a good example of this: "He thought of himself as a latecomer"; in his quest for knowledge "he had done what was hoped of him" but "saw himself as a failure and felt vaguely responsible for this." He lives with Val, but is not sorry when she leaves him. When she comes back, however, he denies such feelings. His life has not led him to hope for love; he would be quite happy with "solitary activity and free watchfulness." Such a confined, little life can make even the grave attractive, as is suggested when we read the imagistic future implications of the "solitary bed" both he and Maud will fight for as each seeks to preserve autonomy. Love can survive even that little death in the cyclical story of their shared bed; it promises the rebirth to each other that such withdrawal aids by protecting and regenerating the self.

Ash is the central character in the past the researchers study, and his own fascination with an even more distant past in turn shapes his writings. He sees such research as "the business of every thinking man and woman," even while admitting its limitations in his letter to Priscilla Penn Cropper, an American spiritualist and great-grandmother of his later biographer, Mortimer Cropper: "A lifetime's study will not make accessible to us more than a fragment of our own ancestral past. . . . But that fragment we must thoroughly possess and hand on." Possessing and passing on our past thus becomes our work as human beings; yet life is what happens while we work, the actions that will in turn define who we were to those future generations who seek to inherit our knowledge. In contemporary England, Byatt creates a cast of characters who consider their lives empty, passing on only the tales and poems, the written story, of yesterday; life itself finds little or no consciousness of its immediate value when its human members accept that for longer than they have been alive the world has been deteriorating and was already in the lives of their Victorian subjects "an old world—a tired world."

The novel's alternating temporal structure reveals the continual domination of the past, while the architectonic structure suggests that the importance of the written word has come to outweigh that of personal action. Characters representing varying perspectives live only to research these documents preserved in archives and libraries, museums, and private collections. However, to "thoroughly possess" this fragment, Byatt counters the ideological hierarchy with yet another meronymic balancing act. She ephemeralizes the science and history that dominate European linear records of the nineteenth and twentieth centuries, assuming prior audience awareness of such materials. She visits archives and museums, ferrets out personal records and physical evidence. The stimulus of the living past encourages her contemporary characters to act, and their actions resurrect that Romantic imagination as they retrace the patterns of the past. She allows her own living language the flexibility of Romance, of poetic narrative, so that she can reimagine as well as recreate the past in the present.

Her empathy for the hidden, cryptic, and silenced stories of women and her appreciation for the truths inherent in our language and our literature enable Byatt to make room for the whole story. The Victorian Ash is not a major poet; rather, he is a man who "tried to write justly, to see what I could from where I was." Where, however, were Victorian women likely to find justice? Christabel receives little attention, except from Byatt's contemporary feminist critics. Thus, the balance that Ash could achieve by trying "to write justly" could not come easily to Christabel, as he himself implicitly admits when he writes that her later rejection of him might well come from "the injustice of the different fates of men and women." Other women of Christabel's time, without her strength and talent, would remain trapped by those very emotions within the safe houses they found for themselves in a patriarchal world. Love and necessity offer her a moment of eternity, but the social realities will punish her theft of that moment by her later isolation.

Nor is Roland typical of his power structure: he is an unemployed postgraduate with a romantic perspective on life. It is he who adds the claims of love to each debate, arguing for instance that the Baileys should have possession of the letters, which they would sell to buy Lady Joan a new wheelchair. Perhaps the novel's most romantic element is that Roland achieves a happy ending —discovering the poet in himself through his understanding of Ash, discovering love with his fellow researcher Maud Bailey, and even being offered three substantial positions in Hong Kong, Barcelona and Amsterdam, suggesting that available elsewheres may appreciate him more than does his native England.

If her meronymic blend of Realism and Romance provides Byatt room to house her story of love, however, neither that content nor the typical plots are as important to her novel as the language. Providing in this expanded home of language room for dialogue and confrontations is only her first step to "thoroughly possess[ing]" the fragment of the past. Dialogues do not promise comprehension; confrontations do not result in marriages. Byatt will transform such dialogic confrontations into *conversations* that expand the understanding of each participant by exposure to the other perspective; Maud and Roland recognize the mutuality of the letters of Ash and LaMotte, which reveal their whole story only when read together as an open-ended *correspondence*. For Ash and LaMotte themselves, she will create poetry and tales that evolve because of their relationship, although only Ash, less encumbered and imprisoned by social mores, can benefit fully from the growth such love should offer. Cropper acknowledges that transformation when he comments on Ash's "mid-life crisis" as a turning toward "Life, Nature, and the Universe. It was a kind of Romanticism reborn." Ash equally acknowledges the limits on LaMotte when he takes on a female persona in his poem "Mummy Possest" to explain that "Women have no Power / in the cold world of objects Reason rules" and presents spiritualism as the way women can gain knowledge, a threshold to "*our* negative world, where the Unseen / Unheard, Impalpable, and Unconfined / Speak to and through *us*." Only in a reversed world do women find power to possess, briefly, the things they love.

The ability to balance love and fear determines whether or not people can come together—whether or not, in fact, the divided self can achieve harmony. The Romance dares to tread on these territories of emotion, as marginal as they are to the dominant society, in which can be found coterminous boundaries and thresholds by which to enter or leave such enclosures. In their fear of being completely excluded, most women in this novel accept the available comfort of small houses or the protective silences within a patriarchal marriage to avoid exposure. Not even Christabel LaMotte initiates such exposure, and after love draws her out into the open, the dependent Blanche Glover considers herself "superfluous" and commits suicide. Christabel will become a "witch in a turret," her daughter knowing her only as an aunt that she sees as "a spinster in a fairy tale."

Only Byatt, the intruding Romantic author, can offer us the whole story, but her linguistic marriages of concept and phenomenon, of emotion and action, and of process and product prepare us to accept such information as reality. These inclusive techniques help her craft more than the imagined lives of two Victorian poets, more than a critique on the dominant ideology, more than a tour-de-force Romance, and more than a clever exposition of contemporary literary criticism. Achieving "closure, if not finality," for Christabel's story, as Coleridge never did, she reminds us that in literature the concept captured within the Word lives on cyclically, however dead the phenomenal expression sharing the space of that word may be, so that new phenomena can be easily imagined as contemporary expressions of ongoing human truths. Encouraging us to let go of things, she resurrects the hope that can help balance our fear, the Romance that can be *real*ized once again in our time and place and can enable us to enjoy Proserpina's Garden of Life married to Death. From the past Byatt recalls for us the passion of life, which creates both art and life itself and allows us to possess it at least for the duration of her novel. If *Possession* is Byatt's "thoroughly incarnate" idea, perhaps "la mot" that Christabel would offer as the object of our Quest into the Past might be the title of Christina Rossetti's poem "Echo":

> Come to me in the silence of the night;
> Come in the speaking silence of a dream;
> Come with soft rounded cheeks and eyes as bright
> As sunlight in a stream;
> Come back in tears,
> O memory, hope, love of finished years.

The meronymic perspective Ash gained on life through his love for Christabel led to his *Ask and Embla* poems, the title of which easily translates to refer to the "ash" and "ember" of their passion. However, it also suggests that we should "ask" the "emblems" of the text for clues as well as the content. Pictorial emblems explained in the language are common in English poetry, and other contemporary writers like John Crowley have also treated the novel as a visual artifact. Byatt's twenty-eight chapters and the final postscript each begin with an emblem of two woodcut flowers, with a single smaller woodcut flower indicating breaks within chapters. Marching in twos above the chapter headings, however fragmented the lone flowers may reveal the chapters to be within themselves, the emblems promise a series of pairings, if not of sharings. Even oxymorons may be resolved naturally from a wider perspective. To all appearances, however, each of the paired flowers is a double of the other, while the single flowers within the chapter are diminished copies with one rather than three blossoms and robbed of their supporting stem, emblems of the diminished and isolated God/dess, now fragmented as well.

The language of flowers is mentioned more than once in the text, particularly in the "wild North" where the poets consummate their love. Retracing the steps of the lovers, Maud and Roland visit a jewelry store run by an old woman, who shows them brooches carved in this language and identifies the flowers that mean "Mental Beauty and Enduring Affection" as a gift "Better than old hair." While they visit the location of the past lovers' tryst, the potential lovers of now are reminded that the most enduring aspect of love is in our memories, the love of the spirit. Furthermore, the natural image of flowers, a metaphor for that love, is to be preferred over the metonymic relic of the loved one's hair; the recurrent memory can be preserved, while the dying body is beyond our reach, a relic only. Living objects deteriorate and decay; only the dead can be locked unnaturally into a moment of perfection and idealized.

The language of flowers has explained that physical love, however much a necessity, remains in the linear moment, as does the idealized beloved. Enduring beyond that moment, however, is its power in our memory to transform reality. When she ages, Christabel will miss not the passion but the "trusting *minds* which recognized each other." Passion is the recurring pattern of history, of the body; the spirit expresses itself in words, and it is through our words we "recognized each other." The ideological critique hidden here, however, is that kindred spirits housed in the body of the Other may never meet in a society that silences what is not apparently like itself.

The flowering of nature is always new, and always recurring, unique to each flower yet common to the whole world of nature, a promise that such is true of human nature as well. So when Ash realizes his love for Christabel, he finds words for everyone, and his talk of nature to a countryman makes Christabel remark that he is "in love with all the human race." In their love the universal love of Nature is discovered; in the joining of two spirits the Spirit of Love itself might be discerned.

Form is as important as content, even in emblems. That the emblem is a woodcut might lead us to the language of trees that permeates the novel and establishes a silent dialogue with Robert Graves. A more obvious mythic dialogue with his *The White Goddess* will be seen in the "whiteladies" and "chilly mortals" who embody Arianrhod, the Snow Queen; similarly, Byatt will trace the abstraction, idealization, and division of women into partial selves preserved, as in Christabel LaMotte's tale, in *The Glass Coffin*. In the same book, however, Graves posits a Druidic alphabet based on the first letters of the naming of trees and on their mythic associations, which in turn relate to their physical properties. Ash is the Norse tree of life, with roots in the underground and branches in heaven. Christabel is the alder, which Graves explains was associated with fire, and hers is the fire of passion, which Ash does not have with his wife Ellen, the love that unites body and soul and creates new life. Together they will create their daughter Maia; apart, the memory of that passion will endure in their poetic creations. In the Rowan Tree Inn, also known as the mountain ash, the contemporary researchers will find their moment of community, after escaping from the cemetery where the yew, tree of death sacred to Hecate, trapped Mortimer Cropper, the collector of dead things. Sabine de Kercoz, Cristabel's Breton cousin, also mentions in her diary the Druidic tales collected by Christabel's father, which may be themselves "the vestigial memory of an other world where women were powerful, before the coming of warriors and priests." This Druidic language of trees may help to balance the contemporary patriarchal language of the novel.

The text visually displays the varying forms of its compiled documents. Most chapters begin with a poem, from either Ash or Christabel, whose content gives clues to its matter. As for the titled chapters, 9 announces Christabel's tale of The Threshold, which must be crossed to enter 10, The Correspondence; 11, 16, and 21 each consist entirely of a single poem; Ellen Ash's Journal is in 25; and the final title announces a POSTSCRIPT 1868. Chapters 17, 22, 23, 24, and 28 lack epigraphs or titles; each is confined to the contemporary scene and apparently without romance as well, unless we as readers can learn to see it.

The appearance of the text establishes the dialogue between and within poetry and prose. Within the prose, correspondence is italicized, while journals and diaries are ordered by dates. Those dates become meaningful when in the text we learn the significance of *November Tales*, which Christabel uses with her *Tales for Innocents* to separate the gothic despair of our fears from the saving grace of our love. In the journals, November is a month for recording such fears, while Christmas entries offer rebirth and regeneration. May provides a name for Maia as well.

In both the poetry and the prose, textual differences reflect patriarchal empowerment. Mortimer Cropper, the collector of relics, footnotes heavily, cross-referencing to past and present, previous source and later personal observations. Ash's two loves, Christabel and Ellen, write indirectly, Christabel preferring "riddles" while Ellen's journal "baffles" the reader. The riddles may be worked out, while the hidden or disguised report of the journals may be as lost as the letters Ellen burned or need as much digging as the letter which was buried with her. The gender messages reveal that women are not allowed to speak their thoughts plainly. Men, on the other hand, own the language: "The first men named this place and named the world," Ash writes in "The Garden of Proserpina."

The Romance creates its own order; yet individuals within that form may never achieve even a temporary respite from the ideology that has shaped their time and place. Fergus Wolff continues to devour whatever he can; Mortimer Cropper remains the grim reaper of relics from the past. Ironically, words will often speak much louder than actions. Safe within the construct of language, even the most marginalized member of society can express herself, if only in a hidden journal or in letters burnt or buried by others. Byatt will chose the omniscience of an author of Romance to resurrect those words. However, in the world of *praxis*, no third alternative can long withstand the censure of the ideology within which she must order her story.

LaMotte's *Tales for Innocents*, her contemporary double and critic Maud Bailey felt, were derived from the more frightening elements of European folklore. She writes parodies of both the content and conventions of folklore in her tales. For instance, when a hybrid boy is transformed by the traditional princess into a prince, she writes that "we must go no further, having reached the happy end." Such an ironic tone is common to both poets in their prose writings, whether in the open-ended letters or in the abruptly closed tales that choose to realize the romance while admitting a happy ending to be a contrivance. Parody sets the tone for the poets' contemporary doubles, Roland and Maud, who also embody as do the other researchers conflicting critical approaches to literature. Mortimer Cropper's ideological bias is evident in the title of his biography of Ash, *The Great Ventriloquist*, a title that defines him as well as his subject, as Maud notices. He is isolated by his materialistic greed even to the end of time (as defined by the novel's end, of course), while other characters, whose differences appeared to be equally unresolvable, have successfully paired and re-paired.

Byatt does not validate by her inclusivity any character's individual interpretations. As the author of a Romance, she determines the ordering pattern within which their documentation is placed, and the connections established by that pattern—the correspondences that grow from juxtapositions, oppositions, and similarities—will constitute the whole story she offers for our social "betterment." Pairings may have to substitute for marriages, but the *fin de siécle* patriarchal marriage has taught us to be cautious of institutions.

To tell the Victorian love story, therefore, Byatt must venture beyond recorded history and realistic source materials; the other Victorians who betrayed social conventions knew enough to hide their tracks well, and within that enclosure the women write baffling accounts designed never to betray the silences of their marriages while still perhaps reaching a kindred spirit who will understand. Ellen Ash's journal will find that spirit in Beatrice Nest, for instance, but even Beatrice decides the time may have come for such secrets to be told. Byatt's whole story, unavailable to any single re-searcher, emerges cumulatively to order the chaos almost magically. Multi-mythic references abound, naming provides effective clues, and literary dia-logues involve a remarkable number of American and English Victorian and Romantic writers, as well as the more modern Graves and the more distant Renaissance and Metaphysical poets. Fairy tales are regenerated, not simply retold, and the language itself is explored as poetry, one word at a time.

In this love story with a happy ending, in the poetry and passion of the past that results in a living child with descendants in the present, and continuously—in the cyclical stories of myth and literature, the flexible language of poetry and storytelling, the haunting images of art—dualities are paired and blended, brought together and allowed to drift apart to achieve what balance they can in a world out of balance, while the memory of love endures and enriches them. Biological and spiritual heritages of our linear construct of time blend with cyclical recur-rences preserved in the language of myth, the art of literature, and the original language of growth and change, finding a rich diversity of expressions in the present moment and promising more of the same tomorrow. When a poet dies, even Nature fears death, the epitaph on Ash's grave suggests; conversely, when Nature resurrects the flowers, even poets believe in tomorrow.

The dominant ideology of today's society does not make us feel at home in the world. If our quest for knowledge is met with love, however, we will realize the Romance in our lives and see it in the lives around us, as does Roland. We will steal from life the things that we love, but we must be willing to give back the object and keep instead the enduring memory. Maud claims the letters for her Women's Centre in Lincoln; Blackadder would bury them in the British Muse-um, where the workers in his Ash Factory, also jokingly called the Crematorium, can sift through the remnants rather than the romance of the passions of the Past. Beatrice Nest hopes only to keep her fragment of that story, Ellen Ash's Journal, tucked away in her nest, a sisterly gesture of protection to keep Ellen from being exposed. Only when they let go, deny this need to possess the apparent reality, can they join forces to succeed with the quest.

As the Romance tells us, the hero must be the pure knight who acts from love, and Childe Roland offers that perspective of innocence. Roland sees romance everywhere—in the love between Sir George and Lady Joan Bailey, for instance—and finally sees that all of us live our particular romance. Never, however, does he lose track of that self, the simultaneous necessity of a solitary bed that a linear consciousness of death promises but that the romantic per-spective of the lover finds almost as attractive, as full of potential, as the moment of love that messes up the bed and our carefully ordered lives. In the "fragment of the past" that is Byatt's story, then, form is content and the past is the present; when the Romance is realized in our lives, we realize that reality is in itself a Romance and that life is a construct that needs to be retold in the present mo-ment and can be transformed with each retelling.

This discovery, made by expanding their perspective to give equal weight to Realism and Romance, leads these novelists to search for the language and form in which the story of the physical universe and the imaginative animals called human beings who are a part of that universe can be told. To the logic by which our society defines the rational mind, they add the logic of metaphor that governs romance and imagination to discover the patterns by which balance is achieved and our interdependency acknowledged. Realizing the romance in this world and marrying the members of our surviving family to each other promises the comforts of home without confinement. Such a home could help us survive long enough to discover the healing rituals we need.

"To oppose something is to maintain it," Estravan reminds us in LeGuin's *The Left Hand of Darkness*. "You must go somewhere else; you must have another goal; then you walk a different road." LeGuin follows her own advice in that novel to create the world of Gethen in which the human family has become androgynous. These writers decide instead to walk the same road, recognizing the opposing Other as our opposite in another sense—as our mirror image. Shifting perspectives instead of planets, they examine what we have done and are doing to shape this life we share in the belief that elsewhere is nowhere; we must share our other goals here and together to shape a different tomorrow.

Butler, centered in her traditions and looking for a communal home, shows a culture already robbed of its time and place, uprooted from the natural African home of its myths and subsumed within a foreign and dominating society that has forgotten its myths. The mythic memory of an expedient society, a society that lived within and learned from the natural world, determines Butler's "new way of thinking about people and power" in her fiction. Our inner gifts could empower us and help us empower each other in a symbiotic society that draws its life from the center, from the current Patternmaster who, like a spider spinning a web, shoots out connecting threads of power. This community of consciousness may not have a social expression yet, but telling the story introduces its possibility.

Love is preserved and transmitted through the images transformed and ordered in art, and over time love may work its magic even on the most perverted distortions of our family, as evidenced by Esteban Trueba's overwhelming love for and from his granddaughter Alba, which finally wrests him from the ideological lie that has shaped his life. Communication of this truth can help us transform as well our social patterns—dynamically, as needed—to assist our survival by sharing the whole story with all members of the family. If we cannot communicate, if the Pattern is too diminished or too unimaginable to sustain us, then we will remain isolated and silenced.

Our future depends upon how well we communicate the past, since both are constructs of the human consciousness. Allende's women have stayed at home in their world and sought to understand it within their time and place, expressing that understanding in their art and writing. As each generation passes on the stories of the spirit to the next, that generation learns to adapt to and adopt what they must from history and nature, from the stories of the body that houses that spirit. With this awareness, Alba can capture the linear and mythic truths in her moment. Both the animals that unite through marrying (spiritually if not legally) and the imagination that inspires oral and written stories and various art forms find rooms in which to survive in Allende's house of the spirit, because her women accept the interdependency of body and spirit, despite the terrifying face the animal might be wearing at the time and the absurd ritual that must be performed to offer a healing pattern.

Can even love see beyond its metronomic moment? Byatt seeks such knowledge in her Romance, but our brief moment threatens to be lost if we cannot distinguish the lifeless from the living, the relic from the memory. Still, the balancing act of nature itself assists her, couching her story in the larger language of trees and flowers. Acknowledging the value of the past in fulfilling our quest for knowledge, she offers the living words of poetry, of correspondence, and of tales, and helps open doors to the closed patriarchal homes of the women who baffle us, hiding within their moments and carrying their secrets to the grave. From her meronymic perspective, even the devalued members of our society may gain the courage to come out of the enclosure of the patriarchy and find their own work, our shared work, of keeping this world going and telling the human story.

Each of these novelists celebrates the imaginative art by which human creatures preserve life's story of growth and change. If balance eludes the inner self, it can be achieved linearly by marrying oppositions and recognizing ourselves in our shadows and doubles. If poetic truth eludes the prosaic lie, then poetry and prose can alternately offer their stories, enlarging and explaining each other and expanding the story cumulatively, even if authorial intrusion is needed to tell the whole story.

Is it best to accept the diminished Goddess—the small freedoms within prescribed boundaries, the possibilities of the stolen moment, the resurrected savior whose promise of a better elsewhere after death makes even being buried alive before death acceptable—than to live without love? Who will then understand us, what we meant and who we were among the particles of our time and place? And what do we leave our children but the linear promise of decay and a confining protectivity? Byatt reveals a deceptively attractive patriarchy, retaining the facade of past glory to hide the futility of its diminished present, filled with seemingly superfluous people living vicarious lives. Butler pictures an isolated Pattern of sacrifice in an otherwise mute world, while Allende offers unconditional love in isolated houses surrounded by crumbling societies and haunted by their own ideologically perverted doubles.

The meronymic romance cannot escape the realistic nightmare; it can only comfort us and provide at least a temporary home for our body and spirit until Necessity forces us into the dangerous streets of a fragmented world. It can, however, remind us of our dreams. Such dreams, when communicated, are the stuff that life and the future may be made of—if we don't forget them.

Part III

Reinventing the World

From within our ideology, we see ourselves as the avatars of progress. From without—meaning either outside or devalued and disempowered inside—our ideological grid, the picture changes drastically. Progress seen only linearly leads to entropy, boxing life in by denying its living romance. Our wonderful gift of human consciousness is directed at making each of us happy in our living graves, in smaller and smaller boxes. Boundaries that keep us from loving each other proliferate over the face of the Goddess, of Nature, isolating us and obscuring her beauty. The spiral of social evolution threatens to become the closed circle of a shrinking world as we retreat from the shadow of our fears behind walls that deny even the goddess within.

As living bodies, most of us feel very uncomfortable boxed within that shrinking circle in safe houses. Yet the meronymic novel must tell that social truth as well—the truth of fearing the quest for knowledge lest it yield only an infinitely shrinking series of Chinese boxes or release us into infinitely empty spaces. Instead, we bank the fires of our passion in the brick fireplaces of silent patriarchal homes, dismiss our dreams as fantasy and explore our nightmares as symbolic reflections of daily life. Nature frightens us; we try to control rather than commune with her. Things proliferate to fill our empty spaces; music blasts to hide our silences. The novelists in the last chapter only uncovered the love housed within our limited communal patterns, our divided family estates, and our alternately shared and solitary beds—love still attached to Shikastan acceptance of limitations, enclosed within ghetto and patriarchal walls, diminished and narrowed until it appears to be a debt that must be paid if we are to continue our lonely quest.

For those people closed out of the patriarchal home, the ideology surrounds and shapes their lives at the same time it devalues and excludes them, leading them, like Mortimer Cropper, to depend upon reproductions to disseminate their story. They, however, produce subjects rather than objects, who like Mary and Alba and Maia may survive and transform that world. For people inside the houses, life has become so frightening and the goddess so diminished that women dread the messy violence of conception and childbirth, feel inadequate to the anticipated demands of parenthood, and depend upon silence to protect their dreams.

As Atwood reminds us, fewer and fewer children are being born in those houses. Simply in order to survive and perpetuate itself, patriarchy may yet again force itself upon Nature, box its women in even more severely if it feels threatened. When children become one more of the products that need to be reproduced by a materialistic society, what will nurture the human spirits trapped within the houses of those bodies? What about the children already starving outside the patriarchal home? Until we can make every child feel at home in our world and offer that child future hopes and dreams—or at least a happy ending—are we not perpetuating instead the material proliferation of an ideology out to own the world, to fill up all our empty spaces with its things while objectifying even its own children?

How do we turn our boundaries into thresholds? Feminist critics Monique Wittig and Teresa de Lauretis urge us to find the in-between spaces in the hegemonic discourse of our society's gender construct in order to negotiate new spaces for ourselves. The magic of romance haunts such in-between spaces. Our society laughs at, and fears, such magic; yet our popular art forms reveal that the boxed-in, buried alive members of our society are hungry for magical escapes, obsessed with graphic nightmares. In-between spaces may house more than just women.

Yet how can gender be only a social construct, Diana Fuss asks, when there really is biology? We must theorize about how society acts upon the body, she reminds us. Ideologies may provide the hidden agendas of society, but they are not abstract once they control society and shape the world in which we live. While patriarchy may idealize women on pedestals and elevate the spirit by placing its god in heaven, the body becomes its real obsession because the spirit is now out of reach. Possession of our own body/family/community and perception of the rest of the world as objects and otherness—the not-human—legitimizes our claim to own the world and our justice in using it as we see fit.

Bound by the pattern of patriarchy with its inflexible hierarchy, dualism, and exclusivity, our quest for answers has necessarily turned inward. Seeking knowledge of the infinitely small, we have rediscovered the infinite variety of the God/dess. As the story of our social moment, the novel too must pursue its quest inward, to the rest of the world within its geographical borders, to the voices of the American Other.

7

Orbiting Home:
Toni Cade Bambara

In this section, we will meet some people who have not forgotten the romance or the realities of life, whose medial positions offer them a wider perspective by necessity rather than choice. Where are the margins when one belongs to two cultures? Boundaries must become thresholds to those born *Between Worlds* (as Amy Ling calls her study of women writers of Chinese ancestry); who can "walk the line" or "sit on the fence" forever? Each of these writers is American; each also enjoys another cultural perspective on what that means. Embodying the meronymic perspective, each offers a healing pattern, the child of that intermarriage, which could reorder our priorities.

Toni Cade Bambara will add to the African American dialogue with our dualistic black-and-white ideology in *The Salt Eaters*. This meronymic blend of myth and history offers the fable of a community that allows its members to orbit as far away as they require to pursue their own quests and waits to welcome them back when they need healing. Such a community exists only in the imagination today, but its perspective reverses our social conviction that mental breakdown is an individual phenomenon. Ann Folwell Stanford has observed that this novel, Naylor's *Women*, and Paule Marshall's *Praisesong for the Widow* "foreground the connections between an individual's physical body and her private as well as collective history. In these stories, living human bodies pay the price for and carry within them the symptoms of a sick world" (29).

Claybourne, Georgia, is located between the healing salt marshes and a threatening nuclear power plant. Balancing these two extremes is the infirmary, in which we will observe the healing of Velma Henry, a worker in the plant and a central figure in the community. After trying too hard to balance the world on her own shoulders, Velma attempted suicide. The plot and present of the novel last only the time it takes for Minnie Ransom to initiate Velma's self-healing, but time and space expand concentrically as the fable of Claybourne revises and updates that of the Garden of Eden. Claybourne reminds us that Adam's name means "clay," which is a marriage of earth and water.

Velma is surrounded by modern doctors, but it is Minnie Ransom, with her gift of healing and the aid of the larger circle of African loa and other spirits, who conducts the healing ceremony. To guide her among the spirits, Minnie in turn can enlist the ghost of Karen Wilder, or Old Wife, who holds a firm Christian conviction that there are no ghosts. Having survived a demanding "spiritual adolescence"—similar to the Transition Butler's Patternists survive to realize their gifts—Minnie has earned understanding. She can now judge "justly" which of the Old Wife tales is true for her. "Ain't you omniscient yet, Old Wife?" she asks. "Don't frown up. All knowing. Ain't you all knowing? What's the point of being in all-when and all-where if you not going to take advantage of the situation and become all-knowing? And all the wisdom of the ages is available to you, isn't that so?" Bambara's rich human comedy and gift for oral discourse lightens and enlightens the reader.

Minnie was able to heal patients because she "could dance their dance and match their beat and echo their pitch and know their frequency as if it were her own." So too does Bambara offer in her healing story what Eleanor W. Traylor has called "a rite of transformation quite like a jam session. The familiar tune is played, reviewed, and then restated in a new form" (69).

Minnie is assisted as well by a supporting chorus of twelve community members who represent another wheel of life, defined by astrological signs. Since each sign governs a part of the body, its importance to healing goes beyond the supportive communal love it images. The novel itself comprises twelve chapters, completing a cycle with Velma's near-suicide and her rebirth. Scorpio, however, removes herself from the circle. Velma's god(dess)mother, Sophie "M'Dear" Heywood, breaks the Master's Mind, reminding us that all rituals and ceremonies must remain flexible. M'Dear needs to separate herself and sit still in a quiet office near Velma—to recenter herself and become the medium through which Velma can be recentered in their African goddess traditions. Velma had seen these Mud Mothers as she tried to climb back into the cave of death, into her gas oven. Simultaneously, she had slit her wrists, the forced opening of her body and loss of her blood that symbolized patriarchal violation and Christian self-crucifixion.

Bambara takes us back to the Mud Mothers because there our clay is still enriched with the water of life; only then are we ready for the potter's wheel. Transforming nadir into M'Dear turns that wheel of life into a circle of love; this is the language of empowerment, imaging the communal balance achieved in Claybourne that makes healing possible. With Velma as well is a young couple who represent the future. Buster and Nadeen have come because "Even Cousin Dorcas, who had gone to specialists as far away as Boston, said this was the real place and Miss Ransom was the real thing." Nadeen's name tells us that she is the Virgin face of the Goddess—she is already pregnant—and promises that the nadir of darkness will again re-turn us to new life. Nadeen must not become another Maideen, the maiden who sacrifices herself to suicide in Welty's community and whose name is an expanded form of maiden. Nadeen needs to be present at the healing not only to prepare herself for the weight she will be gaining with the duties of bearing life but also to show Velma as she penetrates the veil of her darkness that life is beginning again. As the youth implied by his name indicates, Buster too needs to learn his job; his Uncle Thurston has thus ordered him to take the "father classes" at the infirmary. The community, our extended family, concerns itself with each other's welfare.

The salt water of tears can hold our "dust" together and provide clay for the "Potter's wheel," the unifying symbol of the novel. Claybourne itself is the potter's wheel that remolds and recenters individual lives, a united African American community dissolving differences in the shared grief and hopes of its "salt of the earth" members. Although Susan Willis worries that "the novel approximates a postmodern narrative, whose profuse array of disconnected detail denies interpretation and suggests a world where meaning no longer pertains" (139), Bambara's language actually allows us entrance to the other realities below the surface of our society, the otherness behind the mask of difference that, when recognized as our mirror image, promises an integrated whole. Like postmodernism, the meronymic novel offers fragmented, multiple perspectives; unlike postmodernism, it posits a greater whole in which those fragments fit together. That the greater whole is beyond human comprehension does not negate its promise of unity. A multimythic perspective on Claybourne reveals a culture that embraces African myth, spiritualism, Christian fellowship, ecological feminism, and political consciousness. As Margot Anne Kelley argues, "Bambara presents these various spiritual and analytical approaches, so often considered antithetical to one another, as not only complementary, but as radically related" (486).

To center us in this community, Bambara provides a plethora of circles, as Gloria T. Hull and Bambara herself have explained: "Its design is concomitantly determined by the deliberate way that 'everything becomes a kind of metaphor for the whole.' Bambara herself explains it this way: 'We have to put it all together. . . . The masseur, in my mind is the other half of the potter, in the sense that to raise the clay you've got to get the clay centered. The potter's wheel is part of the whole discussion of circles'" (223).

Hull maps in her article the community centers in which the people of Claybourne meet and are served. Unlike Naylor's patriarchal wheel with its resisting goddess circle, Claybourne encompasses several circles, turning in different directions but meshing together like the gears of a watch to keep the potter's wheel revolving in/on time. On this potter's wheel, they can be recentered when their own orbits become eccentric, elongated into ellipses that try to take in too much in their efforts to rebalance an eccentric world or shrunk to dark, dense dots when they retreat from the demanding effort. Centers unite otherwise divided citizens in healing confrontations that reveal their essential fellowship. The infirmary offers both modern medicine and spiritual healing. While our larger society favors practical sciences, The Academy of the Seven Arts teaches only arts—performance, martial, medical, scientific, spiritual, fine, and human—reminding us that learning is the art of living. It is attended by ordinary people, who earn no credit but become "change agents" who can transform our world. The art of life is the real work of a community, this symbol would suggest; art provides the pattern that the communal potter can offer the clay.

The opposing viewpoints within and among the centers balance each other. The masseuse Ahiro balances the education of the mind with that of the body. The Academy's political Brotherhood is balanced by The Seven Sisters, who represent the nurturing gifts of Nature. Theirs is the sisterhood of nature and of the various colors of the people of the world. Currently the seven sisters are Inez, Nilda, Chezia, Cecile, Iris, Mai, and Velma's sister Palma. Not only do their given names come from nature, but they are also identified by the natural nutrient of their respective cultures. Palma is the Sister of the Yam.

In the Avocado Pit Cafe the Sisters balance the table of six nuclear plant engineers, while the communal activists Jan and Ruby are balanced by the outside observers Donaldson and Campbell. Yet who is really an outsider? Anyone who lacks balance benefits from wandering through Claybourne. Fred, the overburdened bus driver, finds his own way to the infirmary; Dr. Meadows leaves it to rediscover his "country" self in this city, following the biblical directive of "Physician, heal thyself."

This seemingly chaotic journey through time and space is centered by Velma's healing and Claybourne's spring festival, a communal healing that draws on African and Christian tradition and reminds us of rebirth and resurrection. Velma's eccentric circle elongates as it is expressed in her others—in family, community, and by extension the larger "off-centered" families of our society. Historically, she relives the civil protests of the sixties, noting gender inequities and betrayals within and of the black community. Her personal past is recalled in all its violence and pain by the wise elder Sophie, whose dead son Smitty was Velma's first love, to place the past in the larger contexts that give it meaning and make the pain bearable.

Because her job, family, and community responsibilities and disappointments have become too much to bear, Velma must be healed by communal support and put back in touch with her own spiritual strengths, as symbolized by the African Mud Mothers. Bambara stretches and shapes her story, finding the fragment of "white plaster"—the inflexible piece of white ideology in the rich terra-cotta of her people's clay—which has thrown them off center. Undetected, these fragments defeat the potter's art, and the result may very well be a "crackpot." The conflicts of yesterdays must be resolved in the necessities of today so that healthy choices can be made for possible tomorrows.

Thrust out of their Garden by our gods, African Americans yet comprise a definable community planted in contemporary America. Here the spirit is accessible, and suffering can be balanced with communal love. If we are in danger of turning into pillars of salt from too much looking backward, we are also the salt of the earth and have already survived and transformed that past. When the rains come to Claybourne, we cannot be sure it isn't acid rain, or nuclear fallout. Clouds are gray tricksters, and the world outside has been dumping its garbage on its devalued members for centuries. Water brings life, however, and Claybourne's artists will take the wet mud after the storm and its healers will draw on whatever powers make themselves available because its people still want to live. The balance of hope over fear is essential for survival.

As she circles back through time and space, as she teaches us to sit still and be centered in our own traditions, Bambara reveals the pattern of the circles, spiraling from the common center from which we all originated. If on the surface the circles conflict and shatter, a wider perspective promises the turning of the wheel, which reestablishes balance. A community centered in its own traditions and balancing the diversity of its members can provide healing for those members who are suffering from the violence of the moment, from the unbalancing influence of fragmented values.

Bambara's language empowers us by giving equal weight to spiritual and visible realities and allows us to wander freely though time and space because the human mind is not buried in the present moment. Her linguistic humor includes multileveled puns that reveal the incongruity of appearances. We are always conscious, for instance, of the immodesty of Velma's hospital gown and the unprofessional attire of Minnie Ransom. The name of the cafe reminds us of Nature's own incongruities: the avocado pit is just too big. Sometimes the story itself seems too big.

Can our minds stretch as far as Necessity demands without breaking? While Ruth Rosenburg argues that Campbell is named in honor of the black poet, James Edwin Campbell, the name also puns on this alphabet soup we find ourselves in. This "spy"/trickster has taken up residence in the cafe to learn from watching—and to profit from what he learns. Spying the unity in apparently contradictory realities, he "[k]new in a glowing moment that all the systems were the same at base—voodoo, thermodynamics, I Ching, astrology, numerology, alchemy, metaphysics, everybody's ancient myths—they were interchangeable, not at all separate much less conflicting. They were the same, to the extent that their origins survived detractors and perverters. How simple universal knowledge is after all, he grinned."

Bambara's history as an activist is reflected in the gender inequities and political activism threatening to fragment even Claybourne. Her ecofeminist consciousness draws our attention to the nuclear plant by positing a dystopic future of radioactive mutants. But she has chosen to write a fable of hope rather than fear. Thus she empowers the perspective of the Mothers: we are parts of a community responsible for its members. We survive by healing each other and by tending the garden given us by nature. We perform our tasks by using our minds, but associative thinking proves more useful than rational counting of things. While we may re-count our trials, this telling is only part of the tale. Write it down and pin it to the skirts or float of the Goddess; then begin again and write a better story.

Life is our story, as Bambara re-minds us. We are the dancer and the dance, as Tina/Khufu, or ancient mother, will remind the dancers of Claybourne in all their diversity in her dance studio, whispering into their ears, "Remember." If that life must be seized from patriarchy's in-between places, between salt marshes and nuclear plants, then so be it.

In *Origins*, Charles Doria and Harris Lenowitz divide the stories of creation into "word" and "elemental" processes; what we say is just as important as what we do to keep the world going. The "ancients" believe that our job lies in maintaining that balance: "The will here is human. There is nothing in the nature of things that wants us to make this apprehension. People make connections and predictions and are empowered to keep things going" (xx). Society is created to help us "keep things going." Ibo culture embraces this need for balance, as Achebe reveals in *Things Fall Apart*. The individual can "belong to his fatherland when things are good and life is sweet." In difficult times, however, "he finds refuge in his motherland" (124). The circles of family and community support us: "We are better than animals because we have kinsmen," Uchendo explains (154).

We can accept change, even such disruptive ideological change as the Ibo are facing in Achebe's moment, because we are artists; we can expand our story to fit any growing, changing reality without losing its pattern. "'There is no story that is not true,' said Uchendo. 'The world has no end, and what is good among one people is an abomination with others'" (130). We all must be artists, reshaping our lives as needed. No face our brother or sister wears, no ritual or ceremony that seems strange, is excluded from the whole story. When we have to live in the same place with people who practice "abominations," we must see through appearances to understand, to accept their apparent differences while rejecting the inflexible, ideological fragment of plaster that would throw us off balance.

The whole story is simple; it is also true and beautiful and maybe even humorous. We can recognize its different faces if it has managed to survive "detractors and perverters"; if it has been buried among the "ancients" who precede our version of the story, then we may have to dig it out. Too bad we cannot go home to our mothers' villages, as still can happen in Africa, but we can go home to our mothers' stories. Because they know we need them, our mothers are spinning those stories out to us, releasing us to wander but hoping to bring us back to safe circles before we spin out of control, reminding us that the road can curve back to the community that supports us through the darkness. Bambara is such a talespinner, and the spiraling circles of this novel carry us far enough back to recapture the hope of beginnings that promise to carry us forward from this, the "Last Quarter," into a future both diverse and unified, both centered and open.

In *The Salt Eaters* we find the salt of the earth, refusing to be turned into pillars by always looking back, healing the painful bites of the snake in their paradise with the salt of their tears. Tears are salty, but they are just another form of the water of life. Minnie Ransom has paid her ransom; now she can quest(ion) even Old Wife: "Don't they know we is on the rise? That our time is now? Here we are in the last quarter, and how we gonna pull it all together and claim the new age in our name? How we gonna rescue this planet from them radioactive mutants? No wonder Noah tried to bar them from the Ark."

8

Unwinding the K(Not): Maxine Hong Kingston

If Bambara's story offers a healing community that can reshape and empower the individual, Maxine Hong Kingston in *The Woman Warrior* will choose a more narrow focus. Even the Chinese American family is too divided by its inherited gender construct to be embraced holistically. Not only American society but also the China of her ancestors devalue women so much that Kingston feels constrained to discuss her maternal and paternal heritages in separate works. Within those constraints, she creates a healing pattern in *The Woman Warrior* by balancing her historical and mythic mothers and aunts, shadows and doubles.

Within the enclosure of the patriarchy, Chinese American women might seem to be even more trapped than other Americans in a series of Chinese boxes, the outer one housing progressively smaller ones. We ignore, however, the evolving culture that produced the China we think we know. The ideas and stories of that culture that were brought to the new world in which today's children, like Kingston herself, were born have themselves been affected by that journey and by later American experiences. Kingston "recognizes that the power of myth resides in its capacity to be recontextualized and inscribed with new meanings," Robert G. Lee has argued (59). She says herself in "Cultural Mis-Readings by American Reviewers" that "Chinese myths have been transmuted by America" (58); elsewhere she has added that "myths have to change, be useful or be forgotten. . . . The Myths I write are new, American" ("Personal" 18). Born an American, Kingston's story is already our story as well.

Immigrants are not invaders; nor are they the spoils of an invasion. Choices have been made, and our ideology, our new world, is the otherness they have chosen to embrace. Kingston's family has already decided that she will confront rather than avoid otherness, that she will learn not only the language of that Other along with Chinese but also the language of nature in another geography from that which is described in her mother's stories. Therefore, her quest must be couched in the story of the family that made those choices. Bringing autobiography into the novel is recognizing yet another boundary as a threshold, for what can be more "realistic" than our own lives? Once we realize that the story of life is the story of the novel, such boundaries become difficult to discern. While this blurring of literary borders may bother the compartmentalizing mind that our ideology has produced in us, it helps to unify our fragmented perspective.

By incorporating her autobiography, Kingston suggests how we also can question the choices our family has already made for us as an essential step in understanding who we are. Expanding the self through the generations and the myths that culminate in us and in the present moment reveals the imagination as our house of the spirits. The past only really lives there, because we are the center of our own lives. Centering ourselves in our own traditions does not mean hanging our grandmother's quilt on the walls of a New York apartment; as Alice Walker reminds us, re-membering our heritage is for "Everyday Use." Rather than being obsessed with the past, we must bring the past into the present moment and translate it through our own experiences and beliefs.

"The contribution of mythology," Clyde Kluckhohn has explained, "is that of providing a logical model capable of overcoming contradictions in a people's view of the world and what they have deduced from experience" (58). Usually we interpret this concept to mean that myths provide human explanations for natural phenomena, but it seems equally applicable to overcoming social contradictions. Perceiving contemporary reality within the greater context of their inherited myths and legends enables some contemporary American novelists of non-European ethnicities to overcome the contradictory ways in which their "people" are seen both within the ethnic community and within the larger American society. As a native-born Chinese American, Kingston will never be either "Chinese" or "American"; she is both by definition. Within her self social contradictions must be overcome and encompassed.

The novel is the literary genre precisely designed to explore social definitions of the individual. Exposed to quite different myths than are most of her fellow citizens, Kingston will seek self-definition by discovering the cumulative stories of her kindred and from them, not unlike Allende's Alba, compiling her own story. Rejecting the parameters of reality drawn by the dominant discourse, she will give the same weight to myth and "imagined life" as she does to the "real world" of family and history in order to recreate the whole story. Overcoming the artificial boundaries that marginalize her in order to center herself in her own traditions, however, she still finds herself bounded by gender constructs. Since she is female and her mother was the storyteller of the family, it is within her maternal heritage that Kingston has the greatest access to the cultural myths that provide the other parts of her story.

Because the novel is an artifact as well as a language art, it can be shaped by the author artist into the form that best expresses the story being told. Only when we read the words and connect them in the pattern provided do we understand what stands under, what orders, the actions of Kingston's story. Therefore, while *The Woman Warrior* has a beginning, middle, and end, which allows us to read its linear progression from silence to song through the conflict between mother and daughter at its center, it offers simultaneously a cyclical pattern. Its mythic and artistic "knotmaking" expands our appreciation both of the individual self in which the mother finds expression through her daughter and of this moment of time in which our place has become the planet and our community the human family.

Although Kingston's book won nonfiction awards, it can only be fully appreciated and understood as a novel, depending more heavily on "imagined life" than on its historically precise information about individuals. Balancing the personal, historic, and mythic throughout, Kingston the writer condenses time and place into the mind of Kingston the character, who learns to follow the twists and loops of the many stories that together define her life. The storytelling process itself creates the "outlawed knot" that Kingston offers us as a "novel" pattern.

Art, of which the novel is but one form, always offers its unified vision of the human condition that transforms seemingly contradictory realities by encompassing them in an ordered whole. In *The Woman Warrior*, Kingston creates a novel order as well as incorporating allusions to both Chinese and family history and myth in her exploration of her female self. As Shirley K. Rose has argued, "The particulars of the story are less interesting than her telling of that story, for Kingston's narrative brings together 'reality' and 'myth' from the perspectives of both the Chinese culture and American culture" (12). Nor should we separate either reality or myth from Kingston's unique perspective on both; as she explains in the novel, she must come to her own understanding of her inherited myths because "How can Chinese keep any traditions at all? They don't even make you pay attention, slipping in a ceremony and clearing the table before the children notice special-ness." Frustrated by the silences, she complains, "I don't see how they kept up a continuous culture for five thousand years," concluding that "maybe everyone makes it up as they go along."

Nor does Kingston want to confront Chinese culture in its historical accuracy, or even in China. Her Chinese culture consists of her family stories of the home-land she had never visited and the lifestyle of Chinese Americans. "I was de-scribing the place that we Americans imagine to be China. The mythic China has its own history, smells, flowers, one hundred birds, long-lived people, dialects, music," she explains in "Imagined Life." "If I had gotten on a plane and flown to the China that's over there, I might have lost the imagined land" (140). Thus the process Kingston uses to create her novel involves realistic details of a myth-ic China and mythic training for an autobiographical narrator raised in contem-porary America.

True to her traditions, Kingston must encompass the linear story within the cyclical pattern, eschewing the linear tightrope of chronology to order her story. The story balances and blends memories of the personal, historical, and mythic past with direct observation and rational analysis to place the reader in the landscape of the writer's imagination. The artistic pattern of that landscape takes shape as Kingston crafts an intricate twisting of five knots from her own story-line, her own life, each one curling in on itself to form a section of the book.

The narrator explains her artistic process at the beginning of the final section, "A Song for a Barbarian Reed Pipe." She has taken her brother's brief and already second-hand version of her aunt's story as the basis for the previous chapter and has transformed it. She admires the "bareness" of his account, "not twisted into designs" as hers will be, and she compares herself with an outlawed Chinese knot-maker as she follows the twistings of her female heritage and traces how it ties into her own life. Her intricately interwoven frog knot images her own upbringing as a Chinese American daughter. Paternal aunt, mythic woman warrior, mother, maternal aunt, and an historical exiled Chinese poetess respectively reveal themselves to be part of the possibilities that shape the narrator, as is her shadow and double, the young playmate she abuses in the final section whose silence elicits a violent attack. We might be reminded of Virgie Rainey's hatred of Maideen, who failed to tell her story and instead killed herself; the silences of our other selves threaten to negate us as well. Because of this, Kingston opens the novel by filling in the silences of No Name Woman, her paternal aunt.

However, each character's story is limited by the narrator's use of it, for only inasmuch as she can imagine these women in her own mind, her own life, and conversely imagine herself in their lives are they important to her story. The present rather than the past determines the life Kingston chooses to imagine for each woman. Thus, the narrator refuses to believe that No Name Woman might have committed adultery because she was sexually promiscuous: "Imagining her free with sex doesn't fit, though. I don't know any women like that, or men either. Unless I see her life branching into mine, she gives me no ancestral help."

As Kingston's narrator discovers and constructs her female multiple identity, she creates anew the inherited culture hero myths of the first woman warrior and of the poetess Ts'ai Yen by seeing herself as their contemporary expression. She too is a "[s]wordswoman" motivated by, carrying "on her back," the words of her people; she too must sing her song among "barbarians." Simultaneously she recognizes that she is the culmination of the female line from which she comes, which helps her to realize fully the shared stories of her father's disowned sister, her mother's earlier life as a medical student and doctor in China, and the "madness" that comes over her culturally uprooted maternal aunt, Moon Orchid, when she cannot adjust to American expectations. Stanford's comments on African American women writers, "that individual disease is inextricably bound up with broader social ills—sexism, racism, classism, and heterosexism, to mention but a few" (28), fit Kingston as well.

The center loop of this complex knot of relationships that Kingston must unwind—must imagine and write about to open the stories of her female ancestry —is the story of her mother, which she calls Shaman. While her mother is also Kingston's source and model for her gift for "talk-story," Shaman imagines her role as a doctor in China, which is denied her in America. Brave Orchid is able to face ghosts as well as medical emergencies, for the women medical students are trained in both science and magic spells that heal body and spirit. In America, Brave Orchid must work in a laundry and heal with talk-story. Differences between mother and daughter, China and America, past and present, are acknowledged and encompassed rather than resolved as the narrator accepts her own role as storyteller and transforms that role to fit the present moment. She will give the explanations that are never given and write down the stories that were preserved only in her mother's oral discourse to offer a contemporary version of the myth to a world that desperately needs explanations, needs to know the words, and needs a more encompassing pattern. The "[s]wordswoman" that she has become is as well a "woman warrior":

The swordswoman and I are not so dissimilar. May my people understand the resemblance soon so that I can return to them. What we have in common are the words at our backs. The ideographs for *revenge* are "report a crime" and "report to five families." The reporting is the vengeance, not the beheading, not the gutting, but the words. And I have so many words—"chink" words and "gook" words too—that they do not fit on my skin.

The narrator's ethnic heritage is continuously re-experienced as coterminous with the American context in which she has matured, and her individuality is mirrored in communal faces. Kingston's intricate knot-making enables the reader to realize that history is myth and myth is history, that the personal is communal and vice versa. As we return to a mythic China to discover her real aunt being ostracized in a historic village ceremony condemning her adultery, we also remain with the narrator in contemporary America who must imagine plausible reasons why a woman who shares her ethnic heritage would give up her social status by getting pregnant and then kill herself and her child. Each twist of the knot is imaginative but rooted in human history. We cannot know what actually motivated this personal act, but we do know that each reason is validated and could have motivated it, or a similar act by a similar woman.

Linking myth and reality, Kingston can identify the words at our backs—the words that motivate our actions—and the very telling of her version of our story offers us other choices, other patterns. She provides the words particular to her family as a definition of self, those particular to her ethnic heritage as the inescapable other demands of community, the plot incidents particular to her gender as the social impact of belonging to two patriarchal societies, and the seemingly contradictory demands of her American context and Chinese community. To escape madness, her narrator must unwind each twist in the cord to know what stories have nurtured her and to reshape the whole story of who she is.

"'The difference between mad people and sane people,' Brave Orchid explained to her children, 'is that sane people have variety when they talk-story. Mad people have only one story that they talk over and over.'" As a meronymic story-teller, Kingston offers us the variety that keeps us sane, freeing us from a dominant discourse that convincingly describes the inevitable tragedy of our death but fails to remind us of the simultaneous richness of our lives.

With her complex knot-making ability, Kingston reveals that we too must follow the twists of our own story through family, community, and social versions and know in our own selves the order we can achieve, the work of art we can create by reconstructing our own story from its many components. Denying any of the components means sacrificing parts of the self, which is why she turns to her paternal heritage in *China Men*. Neither Chinese nor American society, however, can house these gender-divided members of the same family/self comfortably together.

"There is only the eternal present, and biology," Kingston's narrator explains to her mother as she takes on the role of storyteller. "We belong to the planet now, Mama. Does it make sense to you that if we're no longer attached to one piece of land, we belong to the planet? Wherever we happen to be standing, why, that spot belongs to us as much as any other spot." Telling the whole story from a meronymic perspective, an encompassing vision that expands our definitions of self, family, community, and society, is essential in our contemporary world village in which we too "belong to the planet."

We approach the Other to find ourselves. Their otherness is their own, although we can learn to appreciate its unique beauty and truth. We must not assume that we know them in the linear particulars when we have discovered the cyclical wave/patterns we share with them. Their lives are as unique as ours; their society offers its own rituals and ceremonies, although it may share ideological foundations, hidden or otherwise, with our own society. Simply to accept their personal or social definitions is to become an actor in their script. Literature lets us learn from cumulative scripts the whole story so that we feel able to write our own script, shaping our common future by our choices.

When we unwind the knot of Kingston's novel and follow its single cord, we discover a maturation pattern that continuously acknowledges the communal as well as the individual self. As Michael Young argues, "We do not wholly reinvent ourselves in each new present" (11). With each step of that maturation, however, Kingston the storyteller questions the particulars of the pattern, asserting her own judgments on the social process.

When we are young and innocent, we accept the social ideology into which we are born as the absolute, objective truth. Kingston offers that story in the first loop of her frog knot through her father's sister in "No Name Woman." The very telling of the story challenges her mother's version, rejecting the silent acceptance of Chinese society's judgment that led to the suicide of her aunt and her infanticide.

When we grow to question our training, we are likely to oppose it, to fight for our own ideas. Kingston must turn to myth to find this pattern of opposition for a Chinese woman, which she does in "White Tigers." In that myth, however, she discovers a woman warrior rather than a slave, a (s)wordswoman role model. Nature is her foremost teacher, the dragon that is this world and whose truths dwarf any social ideology.

Next, if we have not succeeded in changing the world by opposing it, then we may appear to accept social constraints and silently live our lives in the white spaces, or as a negative "magic" version of the picture. Christabel LaMotte makes such a choice, ending as a "witch in a turret." Kingston too offers a fairy tale, another mother unrecognizable and fantastic to her own daughter. In Shaman, however, Kingston imagines that mother fully as a doctor in China challenging Sitting Ghosts and chanting medical texts, reclaiming her from myth and uncovering their common story, for they too are both dragons.

The implicit danger of her mother's willingness to leave part of her own story in the past, however, warns Kingston of the dangers of silent, apparent acceptance of social definitions. The strong may lead double lives, their mythic selves surviving in the in-between spaces of that society as does Brave Orchid's in her talk-story; they may even pass their stories on to their daughters. Others, however, may become sacrificial victims, as did Welty's Maideen and Naylor's Lorraine. Moon Orchid cannot unwind the k(not) in At the Western Palace; cultural clashes are too much for her to bear. Her husband's new marriage reduces her to one story, another diminished goddess narrowed to the moment, offered asylum in yet another patriarchal house.

Finally, however, the quest for knowledge might introduce us to alternatives, even to an understanding that encompasses self and all otherness—here in the family and out there in the barbarian society in which we must live and tell our stories, sing our songs. We reach this possibility by internalizing our past—memory and myth—in our present moment. Kingston will offer that understanding in A Song for a Barbarian Reed Pipe, telling a story she has learned from her mother, now that she realizes that "[t]he beginning is hers, the ending mine."

The vision we can have is in our moment—not the climax of one day in one place that would prove our tragic heroism, but the fullness of understanding which can be achieved in the twists and turns of our own complexly knotted brain in one moment. "There is only the eternal present, and biology," Kingston reminds us. We are not simply preparing for life or moving toward our climactic goal from which we must fall away and accept linear decay until death resolves our story; we are writing our lives right now, and we can enjoy each happy ending that comes along. This moment is when we need to love and understand each other; where we are is where we need to call home.

Like Lessing's Zones, we might compare Kingston's five-part frog knot with the five-pointed star and love knot of medieval perfection drawn as one continuous line that seems to have no beginning or end. Whether that star is the astral map of the human being or an imaginative frog only a kiss away from being a prince, in relating our myths we can rediscover the patterns they share in a language less laden with ideological baggage.

Kingston has two cultural languages to draw from as well. The pictographic Chinese language still acknowledges its many simultaneous meanings; every "letter" is both story and image. Because of this, Gary Zukav chooses to use the Chinese term for quantum physics in *The Dancing Wu Li Masters* even though translation into English really demands, as he admits, "both a poet and a linguist": "For example, 'Wu' can mean either 'matter' or 'energy.' 'Li' is a richly poetic word. It means 'universal order' or 'universal law.' It also means 'organic patterns'. . . . In short, 'Wu Li,' the Chinese word for physics, means 'patterns of organic energy'" (5). There are over eighty different meanings for "Wu" in Chinese, depending upon how it is pronounced, keeping cultural secrets within the untranslatable variations of oral discourse. Zukav has to combine five meanings of "Wu Li" to name the new physics to his own satisfaction.

Language will be Kingston's work, as her mother seems to have known from the moment she was born. She has been treated differently by her mother because she will be the storyteller of her generation, just as Brave Orchid has preserved and passed on the stories of hers. Kingston accepts her role as storyteller, but she knows that she must transform the story to make it new, to make it hers, because the story we tell is the story we live.

In "White Tigers," Kingston revisions myth to offer a *yin yang* image of the old couple who train her, which in its dynamic dance promises a world without the gender construct that divides her family's stories. The language of growth and change has revealed the brevity of appearances: the man and the woman grow and change and brighten until she must look away; when she looks back they are simply the old couple again. Although she has come to the mountain to be taught warrior skills, she is also taught the love and beauty and wonder of the world.

The myths of the East keep the cyclical story alive, as does the following expression of that myth from the *Bhagavad Gita*:

> Never the Spirit was Born
> The spirit shall cease to be never
> Never was time it was not
> End and beginning are dreams
> Birthless and deathless and changeless
> Remaineth the spirit for ever
> Death hath not touched it at all
> Dead though the house of it seems

Kingston's story in its realistic details, however, reminds us that the house of the body is a major concern. A cyclical bias can be quite as destructive to the people in a society as can a linear bias. Nature may be the enemy to a linear society because she seems to promise only death, but to a cyclical society she is irrelevant; only the spirit need be considered. Either imbalance establishes an hierarchy that devalues women inasmuch as they are the biological expression of nature in the human family. Her healing pattern embraces both body and spirit, both self and familial others, both myth and history—but it falls short of including both male and female except in mythic shapeshifting.

9

Weaving the Web: Leslie Marmon Silko

Committing the spirit of her maternal heritage to the body of a novel, to a written text, Kingston reaffirms the marriage of mind and body that communicates our living ideas and creates our art. While the novel is complete, however, her story is only half told until she adds *China Men*. If mothers and fathers must live in separate texts, in many ways the novels offer mirror images: the gender-defying woman warrior is reversed into the china/fragile man in the Land of Women episode. Neither novel, however, escapes the gender construct; as Qing-yun Wu observes:

Due to the double oppression of patriarchy and racial discrimination, Chinese-American women have been fragmented, diminished, and excluded from history. If they wish to enter history, they have to smuggle themselves in under a male guise and acquire a manly endurance for pain. However, in the frame of Kingston's American society, China men, alienated, fragmented, and muted as they are, nevertheless appear as complete human beings when compared to Chinese-American women. (92)

Bambara stretches her text to embrace the intracultural oppositions of African Americans and incompatible Euro American myths that have married into the community. If she must invent Claybourne, still she plants it in the in-between spaces of contemporary America. Tayo in Leslie Marmon Silko's *Ceremony* need only return to his Laguna reservation to find such a community. He need only turn to his New Mexico landscape to find nature and imagination compatibly married and ready to offer him rebirth. That larger house is big enough to hold the whole human family. Turning and returning, however, can seem almost impossible when the air is polluted with white smoke and we have lost our way.

If Kingston's family confronts and unites East and West in the Western Palace of a barbarian land, and Bambara ends the civil war between North and South in a healing community, then their combined texts can center us in our shared American traditions. For a three-dimensional location, however, six coordinates are required; we need to turn to the traditions of the Laguna Indian, who has always belonged to this land, to locate that center.

Descendants of the even more ancient tribes of the Anasazi and the Mogollon cultures, the Zunis of New Mexico are neighbors of the Laguna tribe of which Silko writes. These mythically active cultures have not separated out from the universal community of which the human family is only a part. The meronymic consciousness of a greater whole finds expression in their immediate relationship to nature. Myth and history are both seen in the light of the individual moment and the individual member of their society. In the Zuni origin and emergence narrative, "Talk Concerning the First Beginning," their search for a home is completed only when "their grandchild, water bug" finds the middle, the place of balance for them: "He sat down. To all directions he stretched out his arms. Everywhere it was the same. 'Right here is the middle.' Thus he said. There his fathers, his mothers, . . . and all their children came to rest" (Zuni 41). Important to this narrative is the dependence on the contemporary generation for guidance, which reverses our common expectation that experience teaches best. Nor is the grandchild a human member of the family; bugs know the landscape intimately. While our fables have held nature up as a mirror to our foibles and vanities, this Zuni fable dissolves both sides of the mirror to discover thresholds in every direction.

To speak with the powers that surround us, the Zuni shaman puts on a kachina mask, puts on the face of the appropriate spirit, and is thus transformed into the spokesperson for the community. The ritual performed and the words chanted constitute the ceremony in which the spirit will answer the questions asked for the community. The shaman will then communicate that answer, that vision, to the community. Although American Indian traditions are many and varied (over 350 tribes once shared the geography of the United States), a common ecological ideology extends their sense of community beyond the human family. Seldom have we sought out their stories, but their awareness that we are all part of the whole story has led them to us. Silko centers her novel in the Laguna version of that story and lets it radiate outward to encompass us all. She puts on the mask of Tayo to perform the ritual and chant the words of her healing ceremony; the novel *Ceremony* communicates that vision to us.

"Here we are in the last quarter, and how we gonna pull it all together and claim the new age in our name?" Minnie Ransom asks her spiritual guide in Bambara's novel. "How we gonna rescue this planet from them radioactive mutants?" Unless we want to become "them radioactive mutants," we should be asking these questions of our spiritual guides. Tayo will ask the same questions of Thought Woman, who makes herself available in his traditional stories of Spider Woman. Imagination and nature, *theoria* and *praxis*, come together in this Laguna creatrix: "Thought Woman's name is reserved for use only in sacred ceremonies. In secular discussions and teachings, Tse che nako is often referred to as Old Spider Woman or Spider Woman" (Purley 31). Clearly, then, Silko is completing a sacred ceremony as her title promises us, because she invokes the sacred name.

It is uncomfortable to see ourselves in the mirror of the Other perspective, to recognize that "radioactive mutants" refers to us. If that perception is just, we too must remove those hardened fragments of our ideology that make us the crackpots that defy the art of the potter. The Puritan ideology that inspires Atwood's dystopic vision once established itself and one book, the Bible, as the answer to all questions in order to make the good, the just, choice. This monomythic theocracy initiated our Euro American story and religiously exterminated many of the Northeastern American Indian tribes. Even before we freed ourselves from England, however, we began to free church from state, to open some centers to multimythic perspectives, as Thomas Jefferson explains: "Our sister states of Pennsylvania and New York . . . have long subsisted without any [religious] establishment at all. . . . They flourish infinitely. Religion is well supported; of various kinds, indeed, but all good enough; all sufficient to preserve peace and order. . . . Their harmony is unparalleled, and can be ascribed to nothing but their unbounded tolerance" (907). Have we lost that willingness to embrace diverse beliefs in our community centers? While we have successfully silenced many American voices, our need to "preserve peace and order" may yet teach us to read/listen to the others.

If we do not "pull it all together," our society and our world seem likely to fall apart. If we do not "claim the new age," then it may go to some other species that will do the job we have been assigned in the Chain of Being. "People are going to have to learn to be intercultural if our species, and many of our sister species, are to survive," argues Richard Schechner. "Clearly nationalism, and its rivalries, armaments, boundaries—culminating in the nuclear catastrophe of mass extinction—is something we humans are going to have to learn to get rid of" (3). Schechner offers different definitions for nationalism, that ideological drawing of borders between people, and culture: "If nations jealously defended their boundaries, cultures have always been promiscuous, and happily so" (3).

Silko's Laguna culture is promiscuously inclusive, embracing Christian and Laguna myth and intercultural children, maintaining its faith in our ability to choose between good and evil. It is a realistic society as well; it has lived with poor choices and been subjected to the poor choices of larger societies who have invaded its home and inevitably changed its people. Such realities send Tayo on his quest to seek the advice of Spider Woman. Silko's choice of a male mask/persona reminds us that the imagination, at least, need not be gender defined.

Silko is of mixed heritage herself, Mexican and Laguna and Euro American. Through her chanting of Thought Woman's story and Tayo's direct experience of that story within the chant, she completes a ceremony that can recenter us in our common American home and offer an intercultural pattern of possibility to our human family. To appreciate the whole story, however, we must look in the mirror of our otherness, diagnose our illness, and recognize why she has chosen—not the renewal ceremony, but the healing ceremony—to communicate her story.

Ceremony opens with the invocation of a mythic storyteller centered on the page of Silko's text, as shown here:

> Thought-Woman, the spider,
> named things and
> as she named them
> they appeared.
> She is sitting in her room
> thinking of a story now
> I'm telling you the story
> she is thinking.

This mythic framework establishes the form of both the story and the text. Thought Woman, the spider, spins a web of connections between East and West and North and South, jungle and desert and mountains and rivers. In the spaces between those natural connections we find the boundaries that divide the human family today: war and peace, white people and people of color, male and female, body and spirit. All stories come together in the personal journey of the Laguna World War II veteran Tayo as he tries to recover his mental and physical health.

Eschewing the linear plotline that might make us see Tayo as a tragic hero, Silko tangles her human and mythic realities by interrupting the prose with poetic retellings of traditional tales that parallel or explain the human experience being related. The structure is reminiscent of storytelling patterns of the Southwestern Mohave tribe, as Alfred Kroeber observes: "A myth might be characterized as a web loaded with a heavy embroidery of songs which carry an emotional stimulus of their own, and at the same time endow the plot with a peculiar decorative quality and charge it with a feeling tone which renders of secondary importance the sort of consistency of character, motivation, and action which we expect in a narrative" (1). As Silko similarly weaves her web, the prose itself is interrupted with white spaces as Tayo's path of memory and/or action changes direction to reveal a simultaneous truth and to help create the intricacies of the web. Only by working through these tangles can Tayo recover from his war trauma and discover the healing pattern, the ceremony, which will enable both himself and his community to understand their contemporary reality: "He could get no rest as long as the memories were tangled with the present, tangled up like colored threads from old Grandma's wicker sewing basket. . . . He could feel it inside his skull—the tension of little threads being pulled and how it was with tangled things, things tied together, and as he tried to pull them apart and rewind them into their places, they snagged and tangled even more."

Our linear plot will not encompass all the realities of which Tayo has become aware; the web that Silko and Thought Woman weave maps the connections that help Tayo understand the whole story and begin to heal. Healing can never happen, however, cut off from the worlds in which we live. Tayo cannot be healed in the spaces in-between, or in the whiteness of veteran hospitals, where he is lost in the "white smoke," which obscure his vision but which, if he were out in nature again, might be read as smoke signals. In that closed box he can only choose to sleep or die. He must come home to his family before the healing can begin.

As Minnie Ransom initiates Velma's self-healing, Tayo too must find a community healer to assist him. The Laguna priest Ku'oosh knows himself to be unequal to the task because this illness involves intercultural influences beyond his experience. "There are some things we can't cure like we used to do," he admits, so Tayo is referred to a Navajo medicine man, Betonie. As in the Claybourne infirmary, inclusive approaches offer the patient the best possible chance for healing. Himself of mixed heritage and unconventional in his healing methods, Betonie is therefore best suited to share and clarify Tayo's perspective. Betonie's interpretation can help Tayo identify what is of the spirits in his haunting dream and what is witchery.

First, however, Tayo must act to save himself. The other veterans who have come back to the reservation remain "crazy," although their bodies have healed; they are still trapped in the witchery of despair, which manifests itself in destruction and hatred. A witch, Paula Gunn Allen explains in her discussion of the Hopi, is "a person who uses powers of the universe in a perverse or inharmonious way—as a two-hearts, one who is not whole but split in two at the center of being" (61). It is not enough simply to have a home to come to; we must heal the split "at the center of [our] being." If we dwell on what we perceive as our failures, we can become pillars of salt or, even worse, part of the witchery that destroys its own.

Tayo's despair is similar to Velma's; he too is trying to carry the world on his shoulders. He blames himself for his Uncle Josiah's death: because he was away from home, therefore not lending his loving support to keep Josiah alive, and because he was killing Japanese soldiers, members of the family, since, to Tayo, each wore the face of his uncle. From the Laguna perspective, he is not wrong, inasmuch as the universe is interdependent. Not deceived by apparent differences, he suffers from being a part of such destruction. He needs a ceremony to heal that personal split; we need his ceremony to heal our communal split.

Tayo also feels culpable for the death of his half-brother Rocky, although he literally carried the injured Rocky through the wet jungles of the Pacific island on which they had fought and been captured. Tayo's awareness of the connections, of the interdependency of all members, not only of the human family but of nature's larger family, forces him to bring that guilt home. In the jungles he had cursed the rain, which seemed to fight his attempts to save Rocky. At home, his people are suffering a drought. He can make the connection. He knows now that he has to find the healing ceremony not only for himself but for his community. All the violence and suffering he sees there he must take responsibility for, attribute to his present inaction.

Tayo is clearly out of balance, and those who love him are all aware of this. Tangling his personal and communal selves are multicultural threads that increase his problem and threaten to prevent him from untangling the web and discovering its healing pattern. He cannot even begin to heal until he can penetrate his own silences. Sitting still can be death if we do not at least chant the words, or dance the dance, or dare the journey that is the quest for knowledge. Idea must finally be expressed in act, but to do so Tayo must see things clearly enough to choose from his multicultural possibilities. He is experiencing what Young Yun Kim describes as the "stress-adaptation-growth" of the intercultural person, which can render him "capable of creatively conciliating and reconciliating seemingly contradictory characteristics of peoples and events by transforming them into complementary, interacting parts of an integral whole" (145).

Some of the threads tangling Tayo's story can be traced to his communal self, to the war in which he participated and the devaluation he and all of his tribe suffer within Euro American society. Others are of individual origin: he is a "half-breed" mestizo and illegitimate. His mother is dead—a sacrificial victim, too, of the conflicting ideologies in which she lived. He lives with his maternal aunt, whose grief for her son Rocky reinforces Tayo's guilt. His aunt is also caught between—a Christian Laguna. The inclusive Laguna community makes room for Tayo, but to the extent that it too has been transformed by Euro American ideology, the behavior of individual members varies. Only Uncle Josiah loved him unconditionally, and he is dead.

Not only mestizos like Tayo need to balance their Laguna and Euro American communal realities internally as well as externally. Rocky, a full-blooded Laguna, chose to empower his Euro American ideological education by becoming a heroic—and dead—soldier. Tayo's loyalty has always been to Laguna values, and only in this more inclusive myth can he find the strength to go on. Being a mythically active culture means remaining flexible, adapting to the Necessity while performing the ceremonies that link all life and allow us to communicate. Silko will image that adaptability, for instance, in the Mexican cattle that Tayo must reclaim from white thieves. They can survive better than cows from the east in the geographical realities of New Mexico. Tayo's hazel eyes—a mix of the earth colors brown and green—image the balance of his multiculturalism and will relate him to the mestizo shaman Betonie and the two women, Night Swan and Ts'eh, who will help him heal by marrying him to nature. Hazel eyes also seem to indicate, as their colors suggest, a mythic link between nature and humanity. Turning and returning to our natural selves might be imaged in the Spanish love song Tayo associates with Night Swan, "Y volvere," and the seasonal return of nature realized in Tayo's faith that Ts'eh "had always loved him, she had never left him; she had always been there." Thought Woman in her Spider Woman manifestation as nature is there to assure us of life's ongoing possibilities for renewal and healing.

The linear component, the journey outward, of Tayo's healing ceremony, comes from a series of Spider Woman stories involving the culture hero/trickster Tiyo. These episodic tales provide a flexible order of connections that must be made on the journey with different aspects of nature, with the different directions. Since the healing journey must involve facing our own darknesses, these are not just the four directions outward from the center. One story in G. M. Mullet's version is titled "Tiyo Travels Through the Underworld," reminding us that Southwestern Indians believe that human life has been a process of emergences, as was imaged in their original homes, an image preserved in the sacred kiva with its door on the top. This womb, or grave, image, opening upward toward the sun, expresses hope of enlightenment.

Carrying Spider Woman's map in the memory of her stories—which Silko assumes are in the memories of her readers as well—and seeking the images dreamed by him and interpreted by Betonie, Tayo is ready to transform *theoria* into *praxis*, not just to wander. He purposes to find the healing ceremony to relate to his community, but the purpose of Silko's larger story in which his story is told is to create an image and a narrative of Thought/Spider Woman's web of communication, to spread out the tangled threads that Tayo discerns but could not order. Tayo expands our perception through his journey, while Silko orders our web of communication through her story. *Theoria* and *praxis* are coterminous, opened by the invocation of Thought Woman and closed by a dedication to the rising sun:

Sunrise,
accept this offering,
Sunrise.

I have also centered this dedication because, in the artifact that is Silko's novel, this is how it appears, alone on the final page. Tayo's story opens with the single word "Sunrise" centered on an otherwise blank page. Symbolically then, the novel takes place between two sunrises, in the present moment, with Thought Woman offering us yet another beginning. Each of the chants given in the novel are similarly centered, reminding us of the mythic purpose of Silko's ceremony. There are no chapters, separating out parts of the story, although the narrative might be interrupted by chants, tales, and memories that reveal connections and help untangle the web.

Silko offers to center us in her traditions because, as she informs us in the chant of witchery in the middle of her story, we belong to those traditions. Kingston has learned that her past and present heritage doesn't own her; rather, its imagined lives are recreated by her imagination and become therefore a part of her. Silko chants the songs of the shamans to locate the center of her web, when each tries to scare the other as the healing ceremony of facing the darkness until one shaman tells the story that invents the white man and initiates his invasion of America. Euro America doesn't own the American Indian. We have been recreated by their imagination and are instead a part of their culture, of their community, which stretches beyond the human family. The power of storytelling is the power of creation.

From our perspective, we think that we have pushed the American Indians off their lands. From a linear perspective, that is the history of America. We consider ourselves the larger society of which they are a part, albeit kept safely in the boxes of their reservations and under our control. From the Laguna perspective, the land of this America belongs to the Great Spirit and was given to the Indian; this is their garden, not ours. Since we are in their garden, however, they must name us and keep us in order. The tale of the shaman names us; it also predicts our actions. Silko's tale achieves what Kim calls a "third-culture perspective" by creating an "integral whole" (145). It is as members of the same family that we sadden the Indian; it is our healing that is sought just as it is our sickness that the Indian must share. Most of all, it is the sickness of the garden that is the responsibility of all of us who share it.

We see the edges of the reservation as boundaries that separate us, but the Indian knows that the land laughs at our feeble fences, our superimposed grid that claims ownership of what we can never own. The Indian hope that our boundaries can become thresholds of communication, however, has empowered Silko to be a mediatrix, to spread out our rigid plotline and reveal it to be a delicate web of connection stretched so tightly that we cannot see our in-between spaces, so tautly that it threatens to snap if we do not spread it out and "pull it all together," if we do not heal ourselves and begin to heal the land that loves us. Only the pattern of the spider's web is flexible enough to span the gap that seems to be between us without ignoring the many threads. Silko traces the weaving of the web with her symbolic language and offers the reader the larger skeleton of the poetic retellings. In the center of the novel's web, Silko warns us that once a story is told "it will begin to happen" and "it can't be called back," an affirmation of the power of the storyteller. Silko's collection *Storyteller* shares with us our common story; her later work, however, a complex cautionary tale called *Almanac of the Dead*, reveals the dark power of our expectations.

As deeply rooted as *Ceremony* clearly is in American Indian traditions, Silko continuously opens it up to the wider community of America and of the contemporary world. She sends Tayo to fight the Japanese on a Pacific island, where the "enemies" resemble his Uncle Josiah. The web of connection in the human community East and West is thus established on a personal level, just as the witchery tale has reaffirmed the connection between the American Indian and Euro Americans on the mythic level. Place is also linked, as the jungles of the Pacific force Tayo to curse the rain and "cause" the drought on the New Mexico reservation. That thread tangles within the larger American society when he realizes that the atomic bombs that destroyed the Japanese were tested near his reservation and that their destructive power still haunts this land with nuclear waste that increases his sickness and vomiting. Does this mirror again show us creating "radioactive mutants" in Tayo's physical symptoms?

Thus grows the web; the novel forces the reader to include everyone and each place as well in the truths that are explored. But it is the pattern and language of American Indian traditions that clarifies, orders, and reveals those truths; it is from these traditions that the novel can offer a new ordering of experience. Linear chronology is simply the web pulled tautly and hides its intricate pattern; Silko acknowledges the web and spreads it out, untangles the threads to reveal the human and natural connections that unite this world. While Tayo seems isolated, his is a communal quest, and we are all linked to his success or failure; we all need his healing ceremony.

Silko's novel web of connection and communication arises from an ideological respect for all life and an awareness of interdependency. This ideology necessitates an egalitarian existence, because we are dependent on each other for health and balance. If we do not assist the work of the garden, we are assisting its destruction. The witchery is the story we have told that cannot be taken back; it cannot be healed in the past or denied in the present. Yet Nature always turns and returns to share her secret mysteries; we merely have to ask the questions in the respectful ways in which they should be asked. Earth's imbalance is our sickness, just as ours is hers.

Allen, in *The Sacred Hoop*, yet another image of the circle that embraces us all, describes the American Indian ideology as gynocratic, a society based on the feminine principle of respect for all life and the balance essential to a harmonious existence. This, Yeats might say, is a center that can "hold." While Silko traces the web of connection, the elemental story of creation, through Tayo's journey, she also traces the process of thought, the creation by word, the pattern of human consciousness. Spider Woman and Thought Woman are simultaneously one and not-one, individual and communal, as are we. Silko's web is echoed in Butler's Pattern of communication, but for Butler there is no center, no place on earth, that her uprooted web can take hold. To know, even to tell, the story is not enough; humanity must act on this idea to reshape our social realities. While appearances tell us that Nature created us, our consciousness reminds us that we create, or destroy, Nature by the way we live our story.

Our present society has shaped Nature as red of tooth and claw and inconsiderate of individual life in its blind desire for reproduction. This is the Spider Woman who would kill her mate once reproduction is achieved; this is the darkness that would smother its own children if there is no door at the top to let in the sun and from which they can emerge. This goddess of the dark must be faced; otherwise, it is her face that our society will wear. It is an *Almanac of the Dead* that will tell this story—witchery of daily destructions that Silko will find easily in today's history. Are we wearing the wrong masks in our stories, asking the wrong questions of our spiritual guides? Thought Woman is waiting as well; her web of connection is open.

None of these writers could confine their insights to the linear patterns of chronology, but each could find in her ethnic traditions a pattern of possibility that was more inclusive. As each views contemporary American experience from her meronymic perspective, she offers a fresh hope for American, world, and universal unity. The individual who achieves identity through these personal, historic, and mythic insights need not be in conflict with the Other, society, or the universe. Rather, similarities trace a web of connection; family and communal commitments form intricate knots that must be opened through imagined lives; and such a centering in one's own traditions can provide the support and healing that enable us to expand our perspective until we recognize that our truths are "not at all separate much less conflicting." As the title of Alice Walker's article on Zora Neale Hurston reminds us, "Anything we love can be saved." This love is both individual and communal, acknowledging our interdependence as members of the human family. "It takes only one person to injure this fragile world," Ku'oosh tells Tayo; "I'm afraid of what happens to all of us if you and the others don't get well."

Velma, Kingston, and Tayo all need healing because they embody in themselves our society's illness—its hierarchical and dualistic exclusivity that denies parts of its own body the loving care they must have if the whole body is to survive. As Allen warns us, "only a cosmic ceremony can simultaneously heal a wounded man, a stricken landscape, and a disorganized, discouraged society" (123). Not by the shapeshifting survival tactics of the individual but by a shapeshifting society, a Pattern that speaks the language of growth and change, can we realize our intercultural selves and reinvent our world.

Order can be dynamic; balance and reciprocity can constitute a rational social order when individuals recognize our human and universal interdependency. Two is not the magic number here, however much romance and marriage promise a heroic husband who can carry us over thresholds. Three is not a crowd, but a hope for the future, the child of that union who teaches us familial and by extension communal responsibility. How can children heal themselves when they are expressing our sickness?

Other choices are open to us than simply to belong or not to belong to our current society. In our multicultural, multimythic moment, culture too is a construct. Every moment is a new world, nature tells us, and every world in which humans live is shaped by their ideologies. It may be time to have new ideas, to learn new languages, to discern other patterns that order our common story. Meronymic novelists help us see our world freshly within that world we know is reborn seasonally; a new social order may save both us and the world we shape with our ideologies. Not only societies are twisted and divided by eccentric ideology; Nature herself falls victim to the destructive power of the human animal. Yet Nature could as easily be enriched by our gifts, our contribution to the idea of a universal order. The Renaissance faith in a Great Chain of Being led to the greatest quest for knowledge the Western world has ever known. Yet during that quest we lost touch with its *mythos*, with the romance of the quest, and with its myth, the universal order both art and Nature find culminating in the potentials of human consciousness.

Who better than women to reinvent our world in their art? With its denigration of women patriarchy devalues the Goddess. Ecofeminism is a contemporary consciousness expressed in and out of women's literature that is concerned with the themes of balance, interconnectedness, harmony, egalitarian existence, cyclical time, reverence for nature, and healing patriarchal alienation. Silko's Tayo is surely an ecofeminist, which negates the gender construct of patriarchy when it is applied to human consciousness. Healing must begin; the story needs to be told as part of that healing ceremony. These writers remind us that as we tell the story, we order the world, and a fragmented story without the promise of a greater whole fragments the world.

Conclusion

None of these novelists has failed us in her quest for knowledge; each has tried to tell our story justly from where she is. A story provides answers only inasmuch as that story *is* the answer, the human response. The novel begins dialogues; hopefully those can become conversations. When read as part of each other, its metonymic and metaphoric images create a symbolic language that can embrace all of the meanings we have invested in our languages and our patterns. It can identify for us the languages and patterns that empower us in our moment. It can diagnose those that weaken us and our ability to communicate with each other, among ourselves and among our social groups. It offers us fresh perspectives to facilitate growth and change.

Encompassing human experience requires addressing the mind, body, and spirit equally in mythic, historic, and personal terms. To do this, I have discussed ten novelists in nine chapters, a neat "nine-person goddess" pattern divided into three parts. The writers in Part I address the American mind, both in its ideological restraints and its imaginative creativity, as its story shapes the communal constructs of white Southern Morgana and black Northern Brewster Place, the patriarchal enclosure of Gileadean history and the cry of its daughters, and the individual balance of personal and social consciousness on Shikasta, our broken planet.

Part II offers its own quest for the spirit of love, which could make possible the correspondences and conversations that can transform fragmentation and dialogues into an integrated whole. Such a quest must explore the greater whole in which the American mind and body must live together. Housing that spirit stretches our geographical boundaries to Africa, Europe, and Latin America, since Atwood has already dissolved the boundary between Canada and the United States for us. But our writers warn us in their cautionary tales that gender, race, class, and religious constructs keep us living in separate houses and sleeping in separate beds even after marriages of mind and body promise otherwise. Only in an imaginative future can Butler construct a Pattern of honest communication and interdependence for a community simply defined by its humanity; even that future depends on individual sacrifice of a Patternmaster, trapped at the center of the very web we hope to create. Allende faces the history of the patriarchal family in her own Chile through generations of women and their art to build a house for that spirit, but she must share the world with other houses in which the disempowered Other and Nature are oppressed and abused and love itself is perverted. Byatt recaptures the power of romance and art, letting each of us name our world and shape our quest in hopes of balancing a metronomic society whose ideology has become fixed in an exclusivity of hierarchy and dualism. Her conversations and correspondences attest to the connections that shape our (un)common English language, transforming her own text into the house flexible enough to embrace our diversity; but even that text needs an omniscient, intrusive Romancer to tell the whole story, while its lovers meet briefly and then retreat to solitary beds in a continuously shrinking historical moment.

To see our story embodied in our moment, we must heal ourselves from our contemporary malaise of despair. Part III turns inward, penetrating the Shadow that hides the beauty of the American Other within us. The African American woman has had to imagine for us a healing community in which the mind can be taught the arts of balance and harmony and the body can be massaged and reshaped to survive its historical moment and reach its mythic promise. In a world she never chose she can yet make choices; her story challenges each of us to rid ourselves of the re-counting of our pains and reclaim our lives. Asian Americans have chosen this barbarian land, but their children must make that choice their own; in doing so, they can teach us how to achieve cultural and personal balance within our smallest social unit, the family. Because the men prefer to be silent while the women talk-story, they also make us aware of the gender construct that permeates East and West, which traps our moment in the enclosure of the patriarchy and makes it necessary for Kingston to write two novels and for me to limit this study to women writers. Only if we center ourselves in this geography that each of us shares with the Laguna tribe and with each other—only if we become oblivious to the boundaries drawn on its surface, can we heal the individual expression of a cosmic malaise. Whether or not we can see all the colors of the rainbow, we know that they are there, blending into each other where they touch and brightly individual in their own centers but interdependently existing in the same wave of light, made visible to us by the marriage of that light to the water of life. The boundaries between us are equally permeable; the covenant between us and the universe imaged by that rainbow is still intact.

In today's fragmented society, each way of perceiving our world, of telling our story, has become separated from the other; in the meronymic novel, however, they are reunited in the story of love as it happens, then and now. Our individual and communal vision may be clouded by inflexible social ideologies, but our artists can see and say the world so that we can rediscover the universe that surrounds us with shapeshifting possibilities, that acknowledges us as its own imaginary animals and reminds us in the languages of trees and flowers of its neverending story. Rooted in that story, ours can once again make sense.

Each writer has opened our story to offer novel patterns and neglected languages to help us understand each other. Since it is the same story, we can best conclude by allowing their characters to converse and their written texts to correspond. As Toni Morrison reminds us, "A conversation—well now—that's something. Rare and getting more so. . . . Not one but two people present on the scene, talking the kind of talk in which something of consequence is willing to be revealed; some step forward is taken; some moment or phrase flares like a lightning bug and both of us see it at the same time and will remember it the same way" (Naylor, "A Conversation" 591). A conversation provides the meronymic perspective that expands our consciousness: "It was a conversation. I can tell, because I said something I didn't know I knew" (593). While I have tried to be Fuller's apprehensive critic thus far by entering into the novel perspective of each writer, to achieve her comprehensive goal the writers must now converse with each other to uncover their correspondences.

From their explorations of the constructs of the American mind, the novelists in Part I offer us the purest of human languages, that of mathematics, with which to begin our exploration of correspondences. While their novels do not "lapse . . . anywhere from the picture to the diagram," as Eliot warns, those skeletal patterns can be discerned most clearly in their constructs. The communal wheel of life, that potential circle of love that in itself is concentric with the greater circle of Nature, emerges in the seven ages and seven women of Welty's and Naylor's community. Even the number seven is echoed in Lessing's Shikastan version of our planet with its six surrounding zones that block its reception of the Substance of We Feeling. Such circles will be seen in the humanly imperfect attempts at community imaged in Butler's Pattern, in Bambara's potter's wheel and community centers as well as her Master's Mind, and finally in Silko's sharing with us of Thought Woman's/ Spider Woman's web of connections. Such a circle embraces us all as it spirals onward.

However, even Welty's Morgana is boxed in, bordered by Moon Lake and the Big Black River beyond which we cannot follow our wanderers. The story of "the silver apples of the moon" lies beyond the patriarchal enclosure, which is imaged as well in the walls that enclose Gilead and Brewster Place, keeping mothers and daughters, nature and humanity, apart. In these ideological grids, which Lessing attributes to "the mind of the Northwest Fringes," Nature and the human Others are diminished and denigrated, while the cyclical promise of resurrection seems to lie beyond this life. In similar boxes can be found Butler's slaves; only Anyanwu, who can leave her humanity behind, can leap to freedom as a dolphin. Not even the Patternists can reach the stars. Allende builds as many rooms as she can within the boxes in which the patriarchy houses her spirits, but separate houses hold other members of the family, although Nature's earthquake levels the enclosure that would entrap her story of Tres Marías. Their solitary beds enclose even the contemporary lovers in Byatt's romance, nor can Kingston's maternal and paternal heritage share the same novel, boxed as they are within gender constructs. Even Bambara's Fred Holt, whose name suggests two boxes and whose two marriages—one black and one white wife—reflect his obsession with the black and white boxes of crossword puzzles, can find love only in memories of a dead past until his dead friend, Porter, is resurrected in the stormy streets and healing infirmary of Claybourne.

In such boxes, it is not surprising that woman has kept her story secret and separate in the three diminished goddesses of Virgin, Mother, and Elder (read witch from the patriarchal perspective, while Atwood's dystopia also dismisses the Virgin as Jezebel to box in the handmaid alone for motherhood). Meanwhile, man's story of antagonism has taken its own dominant shape as Freytag's pyramid, a story narrowed to the tragic rise and fall of our heroic but individual lives disconnected from each other and from the communal circle. We must turn away from history and socially defined families to discover in the individual, as in Lessing's five ideological zones, the unending love knot of the five-pointed star, the astral self known to the Age of Faith but forgotten as our Renaissance gave way to the Age of Reason and its rational clockwork. Revealing our interdependence, this inclusive image embraces the individual and communal self, delineates our personal and social consciousness. In its dynamic realization alone do we find the balance possible in this life.

That realization, however, must happen within ourselves. Naylor knows the pointlessness of attaching ourselves to a "black star" when, as Butler names in Doro and Anyanwu, each of us is a sun—that star so close to us we sometimes forget its astral beauty. Bambara appreciates that individual diversity among her Seven Sisters, an earth-bound Pleiades rooted in and nurturing this life. Kingston must reconstruct her own star, balancing paternal and maternal aunts and Chinese myth and Barbarian history to reconnect with her own mother in both myth and history, and she must disguise it as a frog to protect its regal heritage. Only love can transform this frog into the princess/swordswoman who serves her people best by becoming her complete self. In this balancing love knot, oppositions can be overcome by love, as imaged in the Castor and Pollux myth that Welty alludes to in her hopes for Ran and Scooter MacLain. In the myth, as in Morgana, however, they can only be reunited after death; only then does the star pattern of their individual possibilities become apparent to a discerning reader as it already was to Mattie Will Sojourner in her fond memories.

The patterns of the circle, the box, the pyramid, and the five-pointed star diagram our story. The beauty of these geometric forms is only enhanced by the art of the novelist who admits the imperfections of our perspective and transforms the circle into a wheel of life, a web of connections, a Pattern of communication and mutual support, the meshing of communal circles, and a rainbow of consciousness. Quite as lovely as the rainbow blending its colors is the winding of the intricate frog knot of the self; even boxes can be made as attractive as possible when the hacienda expands to embrace the whole family.

The art that enhances the diagram depends upon language, and the writers of Part II reveal that Nature is waiting to answer that need when we know the quest(ions) to ask Her. In white America this means diving into the moonlight of Moon Lake or the dark of the Big Black River, for it is there that the orphans of our society hold the key to our other self. *Playing in the Dark: Whiteness and the Literary Imagination* is the title of Toni Morrison's perspective on our American story, and it is in the dark silence of the night that Atwood's handmaid is able to gain consciousness of her oppression and try to imagine another future. Dreams hold the hope of community for Naylor's women, while daily life reflects the nightmare of sexism, classism, racism, and homophobia. Lessing's "language of growth and change" will only be revealed when we listen to the nature that still shares our walled garden with us; even within that enclosure, she can share our tears with life-giving rain, washing the smoke out of our eyes and revealing our common blood seeping from the blocks that blind us to loving sisters and shrink our children's hopes to the six-foot turf of a buried life.

Butler will hear that language of nature within both Anyanwu and Doro, but he will use this scent to track and abuse his seed, good or wild, while Anyanwu will take within herself the pattern of the Other and recognize their differences as mere appearance. Her love will even reach within Doro, risking the heat of his star structure, until he learns to let go before he destroys what he loves with his appetite for sharing its life. So too did Mattie Michael have to learn from Butch to spit out the sugar cane before it became bitter in her mouth, and Byatt's lovers learn to leave the relics of love and blossoming for nature to reclaim in order to be transformed themselves by its "enduring beauty" in their memories. Allende's Clara knows with clarity that understanding takes time—generations of women clarifying the same small part of our story—and art—preserving the "living ideas" of that story through time and place to balance the "lifeless barbarisms" of its known history. Nature gives us the time with each new child, whatever its genetic heritage, whatever ideological scars it may bear that shape-shift us into seemingly unrecognizable imaginary animals. Still, in the center is the crèche and the virgin; giving birth to the Pattern is Mary, the contemporary child of Doro's and Anyanwu's love.

That still center from which life begins again is located for us by the writers of Part III in the stories and histories they add to our recorded American story from the ethnic Other cultures to which they also belong. Bambara centers us on the potter's wheel of Claybourne to dialogue with Christian and African myth only as a beginning point in the garden of Adam and Eve and the cave of the Mud Mothers. In the Apocryphal New Testament, interestingly enough, in versions of Christian myth known to the medieval serfs of the Age of Faith but rejected by the Church Fathers for final inclusion in our Bible, Adam and Eve live in caves and have both daughters and sons. Kingston's Chinese myths come from the other side of our global village, but they too have separated the daughters from the sons, the caves from the gardens. She will still find in them the marriage of lover and warrior in the swordswoman who can fight for the other and the self, as she finds in Chinese history the poet who can learn to sing in a barbarian land and be understood by both cultures because the song goes deeper than the words to root itself in human nature and that soiled world in which we live. Finally, Silko offers the ceremony that marries our expanded ideas to Tayo's individual acts to transform our mutual reality through conversations with Thought Woman herself. Once these stories have been told, re-member, they cannot be taken back.

The contemporary world is more fragmented than the past of our metronomic society, with Centers popping up everywhere. It narrows rather than expands the vision of those adhering to their "crumb" of a crumbling ideology, of that "bread of life" that sustains our spirit. The meronymic novelist reminds us that it is the human gardener, the imaginary animal, who tells the story that orders our world. If often only the past seems clear, we have detected a linear imbalance in our thinking. On the other hand, if the present overwhelms us, the bias is cyclical. Home offers healing rest and love only to prepare us for the outward quest, which curves to become the journey home again to tell the story. The dream reveals the images of our imagination, and the quest fills them with the wisdom of the God/dess; living and telling that story centers us in the world of the God/dess.

Every history has its heroes; every myth has its riddling sphinx. Every language reflects its social priorities; every plot or *mythos* reflects how those priorities shape the members of the human family and the part of the world garden dominated by that social ideology. The language our artists of the meronymic novel have sought to rediscover is nature's language of growth and change. Within the social constructs of our ideology, that language is hidden. To solve the riddle, they have dialogued with all the baggage that the letters and words carry of past versions of the human story. In the language of Romance, these have been preserved in myth and literature, imaged metaphorically in art and life, then dismissed as fantasy and hearsay. In the language of Realism, these carry our scientific and historical evidence of human events, are imaged metonymically in the things of this world, and are empowered socially as objective truth. Embracing but balancing both languages and all sources, our writers place humanity in its universal setting and speak with forked tongues, out of both sides of their mouths, revealing secrets and risking blame to tell the whole story.

That there can be knowledge of the past is a romantic idea; even if the past has some linear reality, what we can know of it is a construct of our perspective on it. The meronymic novel tries to achieve balance in the literary present of both the cyclical and linear versions of our past. It also realizes, however, that stylistic corners are meant to be turned, because they are themselves social constructs. Literature in English, Frye argues in "The Nature of Satire," "has never taken kindly to strict forms" (15). It re-turns, therefore, to the poetry of language itself to find the *mot juste*. The languages of trees and flowers are preserved in human stories and earlier alphabets; the shifting names of places reflect the various societies that have called them home. The emblematic language of art and artifacts, even the language of the stones, may provide the "just word," the word that penetrates the bias of its own social construct to balance the inequities of that society. If one word cannot accomplish this in its own poetry, then the novelist assists by ephemeralizing the advantaged words and concretizing those abstracted or devalued, by combining and even inventing words, by defamiliarizing or estranging the reader from the expected word through distancing or irony—and, when necessary, by naming the world anew.

Words are not enough for the novelist, however, who must be concerned with the "betterment of the world." This social and developing genre, like the mythic *undine*, must take the shape of its container, must shapeshift to catch the contemporary moment of its time and place. The novel is itself a social artifact; it must reflect in its "novel" structure the story it tells just as its characters must have lives imaginable in this world, in that society, at our moment if the whole is to be recognizable to the reader. The artifact itself may be transformed into a wheel of life, a walled enclosure, an archive of documents, concentric circles, a shapeshifting Pattern, a rambling house of the spirit, a text of poems and correspondences, the meshing gears of a potter's wheel, a twisted five-looped knot, and an ever-expanding web of connections. The plotline may echo that appearance, or it may metamorphose, shapeshift itself from the romance to the mystery to the quest to the chase to the race on its way back to the romance *ad infinitum*. The cycle of life might pause at each age, each ceremony, as characters chase around in circles looking for the golden apples at the ends of the earth, or it may be re-turned by internal resistance. Other stories, however, may teach us to sit still, lending the circles surrounding us Clara-ty, joining past and present and future, here and there in the present everywhere, so that we can center ourselves and learn from the greater whole that embraces us. If the plotline tries to simplify itself, it may be confined in someone else's story, a narrowed definition of what is reality. Or it may find that Necessity jerks the characters loose from time and place to serve the ends—and the simultaneous beginnings—of the human family.

The old stories can often offer their patterns, help us recognize the recurrences so that we can better see the uniqueness of the particulars. The only end of the story may be the last page, and that may echo the first page. "Closure, if not finality," Byatt reminds us in *Possession*, lets the novelist share the vision, not trying to answer unanswerable questions or promising happy endings beyond the fragmented moment it captures. The meronymic novelist knows as well, however, that the unshared dream can become a nightmare, that burying and burning the story or never trying to tell it does not halt the growth and change of nature; instead, it hides the unique beauty of an individual blossoming in a glass coffin, a closed box, a silent house. Humanity is lessened by that loss, lessened by every silenced story, lessened by the physical death of any member of its body.

Blatantly artificial, the artifact does not try to mislead us that the truth it tells is either absolute or objective. It reminds us, however, that the empowered story, the ideology which shapes society, can limit us all with its witchery. Mythically active cultures know that stories must be continuously made new, which is why the novel exists. "The novel is the expression of a Galilean perception of language, one that denies the absolutism of a single and unitary language—that is, that refuses to acknowledge its own language as the sole verbal and semantic center of the ideological world," Mikhail Bakhtin explains in *The Dialogic Imagination* (366). In "Epic and Novel," he adds that "the novel is the only developing genre and therefore it reflects more deeply, more essentially, more sensitively and rapidly, reality itself in the process of its unfolding. Only that which is itself developing can comprehend development as a process" (53). A meronymic perspective—which always acknowledges its parts and itself as a part of a greater whole, then centers itself in the human Middle—must continually turn and return to take in and turn out its story. Conversely, "A sealed-off interest group, caste or class, existing within an internally unitary and unchanging core of its own, cannot serve as socially productive soil for the development of the novel unless it becomes riddled with decay or shifted somehow from its state of internal balance and self-sufficiency" (Bakhtin, *Dialogic* 368).

Nature tells its own continuing story of change, evolution, and recurrence; if our stories are too much in conflict, one or the other—or even both—might very well come to an end. The content of these stories, then, is their least original aspect. They have returned to the old stories, rediscovered the old story made new in our moment, and anticipate with love the future versions of that story. However, inasmuch as the undulating, living story must take the shape of its society, each offers a diagnosis and a warning of that social order that has forgotten to re-member the stories, which devalues or ignores both its members and its own membership in a larger order. In such a society, the old stories might themselves be fragmented; hierarchical devaluation of some members might place undue hardship and responsibility on each member one way or another; fear of nature's changes might blind us to all but death and destruction, facilitating that prophecy by its half-truth.

Even such a dark "November tale" can inspire us, as does Greek tragedy, with the human potential of the characters caught in its unraveling. If we are, as we think, the resident consciousness of this planet, then we need to expand our perspective to see justly from where we are. We must balance seemingly oxymoronic perspectives within our own human community. This is too big a job for any individual; consequently, the society that narrows its plotline to the story of one group, one individual, will become overwhelmed by the responsibility. Conversely, however, the society that offers no story, depending expediently on nature with her slow but sure order of chaos and randomicity, may well find itself superfluous. Together we can share the work, which is why we invent societies. A dynamic social structure that empowers each of us to do our part and seeks to balance priorities can be seen as a reflection of the Integrated Self, each balancing the other and striving to balance Purpose and Necessity with love.

While Nature creates, we imagine the world, shaping what shapes us, living in "the eternal Present, and biology." The meronymic novel houses that story.

To tell the story of love today when we have such difficulty even saying the word demands that these writers reinvent language as well as revision reality. The alternative myths and social history of "doubly marginal" American women writers provide them with the multicultural perspective necessary to do both— and more. Margins are the border between worlds; one need only to look around, feel with, and listen to the surrounding story in each direction to perceive a new world; shaping that vision into a novel offers a new world order. The "hyphen-ated American" is already both a part, however marginalized, of mainstream society and a part of her ethnic culture. More importantly, each is the cumulative total of her own parts. She especially embodies the meronymic perspective; Silko in particular with her cultural link to the landscape of America, can help us see that Thought Woman is Spider Woman. To be doubly marginal is to realize culture itself as a construct, which allows us to choose consciously our cultural selves. We can center ourselves within the more inclusive culture of which we are already a part; we can shift our cultural perspective to meet the current necessity; we can even marry perspectives in our imagination to create yet an-other alternative action. Peter S. Adler describes such a multicultural person as "1) psychoculturally adaptive, . . . 2) ever undergoing personal transitions . . . always in a state of becoming, and 3) maintaining indefinite boundaries of the self" (29). Such a balancing act achieves Emerson's "valor" of "self-recovery" as it expands the world in which each of us lives.

A mestizo herself, Silko reminds us that such a balance is possible in both our "eternal present and biology." In our minds, however, where art is created and *theoria* chosen, we are all capable of achieving a multicultural perspective. While we cannot understand all the particulars of a culture that is not our own, we can share their stories and expand our own possibilities. The more we have to choose from and the more information we have to draw on, the better choices we are all likely to make if we can discern an order that can encompass the alternatives. The meronymic perspective assumes such an order and turns to find evidence of it in nature and our own lives.

Bibliography

Abel, Betty. "Quarterly Fiction Review [A. S. Byatt]." *Contemporary Review* 256:1492 (May 1990): 273–74.

Abrams, M. H. *A Glossary of Literary Terms*. 5th ed. New York: Holt, Rinehart & Winston, 1988.

Achebe, Chinua. *Things Fall Apart*. Greenwich, CT: Fawcett, 1959.

Adler, Margot. *Drawing Down the Moon: Witches, Druids, Goddess-Worshippers, and Other Pagans in America Today*. Boston: Beacon, 1979.

Adler, Peter S. "Beyond Cultural Identity: Reflections on Cultural and Multicultural Man." In *Topics in Culture Learning*. Ed. Richard W. Brislin. Vol. 2. Honolulu, HI: East-West Culture Learning Institute, 1974: 23–40.

Agosín, Marjorie. "Chile: Women of Smoke." In *Sisterhood Is Global*. Ed. Robin Morgan. New York: Doubleday, 1984: 138–42.

Alexander, Flora. *Contemporary Women Novelists*. London: Edward Arnold, 1989.

Allen, Paula Gunn. *The Sacred Hoop: Recovering the Feminine in American Indian Traditions*. Boston: Beacon, 1986.

Allende, Isabel. *Eva Luna*. New York: Alfred A. Knopf, 1988.

———. *The House of the Spirits*. New York: Bantam, 1985.

Allison, Dorothy. "The Future of Female: Octavia Butler's Mother Lode." In *Reading Black, Reading Feminist*. Ed. Henry Louis Gates, Jr. New York: Oxford University Press, 1990.

Andersen, Hans Christian. *Fairy Tales*. New York: Orion, 1958.

Anderson, Linda. "The Re-Imagining of History in Contemporary Women's Fiction." In *Plotting Change: Contemporary Women's Fiction*. Ed. Linda Anderson. London: Edward Arnold, 1990: 129–41.

Andrews, Larry R. "Black Sisterhood in Naylor's Novels." In Gates & Appiah: 285–302.

Aristotle. *Rhetoric and Poetics*. The Modern Library. New York: Random House, 1954.

Atwood, Margaret. *The Handmaid's Tale*. New York: Fawcett, 1985.

Augustine, St. *Confessions*. Tr. R. S. Pine-Coffin. London: Penguin, 1961.

Awkward, Michael. "Authorial Dreams of Wholeness: (Dis)Unity, (Literary) Parentage, and *The Women of Brewster Place.*" In Gates & Appiah: 37–70.

——. *Inspiriting Influences: Tradition, Revision and Afro-American Women's Novels.* New York: Columbia University Press, 1989.

Bakhtin, Mikhail M. *The Dialogic Imagination.* Tr. and ed. Caryl Emerson and Michael Holquist. Austin: University of Texas Press, 1981.

——. "Epic and Novel." In *Essentials of the Theory of Fiction.* Ed. Michael J. Hoffman and Patrick D. Murphy. Durham, NC: Duke University Press, 1988: 48–69.

Baldwin, James. *Another Country.* New York: Dell, 1988.

Bambara, Toni Cade. *The Salt Eaters.* Vintage ed. New York: Random House, 1981.

Bande, Usha. "Murder as Social Revenge in *The Street* and *The Women of Brewster Place.*" *Notes on Contemporary Literature* 23:1 (January 1993): 4–5.

Barr, Marlene S. *Alien to Femininity: Speculative Fiction and Feminist Theory.* Westport, CT: Greenwood, 1986.

—— (ed.). *Future Females: A Critical Anthology.* Bowling Green, OH: Popular Press, 1982.

Barreca, Regina. *They Used to Call Me Snow White . . . But I Drifted: Women's Strategic Use of Humor.* New York: Viking, 1991.

Barthes, Roland. *A Barthes Reader.* Ed. and intro. Susan Sontag. London: Cape, 1985.

——. *Mythologies.* London: Cape, 1972.

——. *The Pleasure of the Text.* New York: Hill & Wang, 1975.

Bascom, William. *African Folktales in the New World.* Bloomington: Indiana University Press, 1992.

Bassard, Katherine Clay. "Gender and Genre: Black Women's Autobiography and the Ideology of Literacy." *African American Review* 26:1 (Spring 1992): 119–30.

Battiscombe, Georgina. *Christina Rossetti: A Divided Life.* New York: Holt, Rinehart & Winston, 1981.

Bauer, Dale M., and S. Jaret McKinstry (eds.). *Feminism, Bakhtin, and the Dialogic.* Albany: State University of New York Press, 1991.

Bhabha, Homi K. "Articulating the Archaic: Notes on Colonial Nonsense." In *Literary Theory Today.* Ed. Peter Collier and Helga Geyer-Ryan. Ithaca, NY: Cornell University Press, 1990: 203–19.

Borges, Jorge Luis. *The Book of Imaginary Beings.* New York: Avon, 1969.

Bradbury, Malcolm. "On from Murdoch." *Encounter* 31:1 (July 1968): 72–74.

Bradbury, Malcolm, and David Palmer (eds.). Preface to *The Contemporary English Novel.* Stratford-Upon-Avon Studies 18. New York: Holmes & Meier, 1980.

Brooke-Rose, Christine. "Illiterations." In *Breaking the Sequence: Women's Experimental Fiction.* Ed. Ellen G. Friedman and Miriam Fuchs. Princeton: Princeton University Press, 1989: 55–72.

Brookner, Anita. "Eminent Victorians and Others." *The Spectator* 264:8434 (3 March 1990): 35.

Butler, Octavia E. *Clay's Ark.* New York: St. Martin's Press, 1984.

——. *Kindred.* Garden City, NY: Doubleday, 1979.

——. *Mind of My Mind.* New York: Avon, 1977.

——. *Parable of the Sower.* New York: Four Walls Eight Windows, 1993.

——. *Patternmaster.* New York: Avon, 1976.

——. *Survivor.* New York: New American Library, 1978.

——. *Wild Seed.* New York: Pocket Books, 1981.

Byatt, A[ntonia] S[usan]. Introduction to *George Eliot: Selected Essays, Poems and Other Writings*. Ed. A. S. Byatt and Nicholas Warren. London: Penguin, 1990: ix–xxxiv.

———. *Passions of the Mind: Selected Writings*. London: Chatto & Windus, 1991.

———. *Possession: A Romance*. New York: Vintage, 1990.

Calvino, Italo. "Myth in the Narrative." In *Surfiction*. Ed. Raymond Federman. 2nd ed. enlarged. Chicago: Swallow Press, 1981: 44–56.

Campbell, Jane. "The Hunger of the Imagination in A. S. Byatt's *The Game*." *Critique* 29:3 (Spring 1988): 147–62.

———. "'The Somehow May be Thishow': Fact, Fiction, and Intertextuality in Antonia Byatt's 'Precipice-Encurled.'" *Studies in Short Fiction* 28:2 (Spring 1991): 115–23.

Campbell, Joseph. *The Hero with a Thousand Faces*. Princeton: Princeton University Press, 1968.

———. "The Historical Development of Mythology." In *Myth and Mythmaking*. Ed. Henry A. Murray. Boston: Beacon, 1968: 19–45.

———. *The Masks of God*. 4 vols. New York: Penguin, 1976.

Cederstrom, Lorelei. *Fine-Tuning the Feminine Psyche: Jungian Patterns in the Novels of Doris Lessing*. New York: Peter Lang, 1990.

Chown, Linda E. *Narrative Authority and Homeostasis in the Novels of Doris Lessing and Carmen Martin Gaite*. New York: Garland, 1990.

Christ, Carol. *Diving Deep and Surfacing: Woman Writers on Spiritual Quest*. Boston: Beacon, 1980.

Christian, Barbara. *Black Women Novelists: The Development of a Tradition 1892–1976*. Westport, CT: Greenwood, 1980.

———. *Black Feminist Criticism*. New York: Pergamon, 1985.

———. "Naylor's Geography: Community, Class and Patriarchy in *The Women of Brewster Place* and *Linden Hills*." In Gates & Appiah: 106–25.

Cixous, Hélène, and Catherine Clément. *The Newly Born Woman*. Tr. Betsy Wing. Intro. Sandra M. Gilbert. Minneapolis: University of Minnesota Press, 1986.

Clark, Kenneth B. *Dark Ghetto: Dilemmas of Social Power*. New York: Harper, 1965.

Crane, Hart. "General Aims and Theories." In *The Complete Poems and Selected Letters and Prose of Hart Crane*. Ed. Brom Weber. Garden City, NY: Doubleday, 1966: 217–23.

Crowley, John. *Little, Big*. London: Methuen, 1981.

Cunningham, Valentine. "The Greedy Reader: A. S. Byatt in the Post-Christian Labyrinth." *Times Literary Supplement* (16 August 1991): 6.

Dale, Peter Allen. *In Pursuit of a Scientific Culture: Science, Art, and Society in the Victorian Age*. Madison: University of Wisconsin Press, 1989.

David, Dierdre. *Intellectual Women and Victorian Patriarchy*. Houndsmills, Basingstoke: Macmillan, 1987.

De Lauretis, Teresa. *Technologies of Gender*. Bloomington: University of Indiana Press, 1987.

De Weaver, Jacqueline. *Mythmaking and Metaphor in Black Women's Fiction*. New York: St. Martin's Press, 1991.

Dexter, Miriam Robbins. *Whence the Goddesses: A Source Book*. New York: Pergamon, 1990.

Doria, Charles, and Harris Lenowitz (eds.). *Origins: Creation Texts from the Ancient Mediterranean*. Garden City, NY: Anchor/Doubleday, 1976.

Drachler, Jacob (ed). *African Heritage*. London: Collier, 1969.

DuCille, Ann. *The Coupling Convention.* New York: Oxford University Press, 1993.

Eagleton, Mary (ed.). *Feminist Literary Criticism.* New York: Longman, Inc., 1991.

Eagleton, Terry. *Literary Theory: An Introduction.* Minneapolis: University of Minnesota Press, 1983.

Eliade, Mircea. Quoted in *A Dictionary of Symbols.* Ed. J. E. Cirlot. 2nd ed. New York: Philosophical Library, 1971: xiv.

———. *Myths, Dreams and Mysteries.* New York: Harper & Row, 1957.

———. *Myths, Rites, Symbols.* Vol. 1. Ed. Wendell C. Beane and William G. Doty. New York: Harper & Row, 1975.

Eliot, George [Mary Ann Evans]. *Selected Essays, Poems, and other Writings.* Ed. A. S. Byatt and Nicholas Warren. Intro. A. S. Byatt. London: Penguin, 1990.

Emerson, Ralph Waldo. "The American Scholar" and "Circles." In *The Heath Anthology of American Literature.* Vol. 1. 2nd. ed. Ed. Paul Lauter et al. New York: Heath, 1994: 1529–66.

———. "Art." In *Society and Solitude.* Boston: Fields, Osgood & Co., 1870.

Epel, Naomi. *Writers Dreaming.* New York: Carol Southern Books, 1993.

Fetterley, Judith. *The Resisting Reader: A Feminist Approach to American Fiction.* Bloomington: Indiana University Press, 1978.

Fishburn, Katherine. *The Unexpected Universe of Doris Lessing: A Study in Narrative Technique.* Westport, CT: Greenwood, 1985.

———. "Wor[l]ds Within Words: Doris Lessing as Meta-Fictionist and Meta-Physician." *Studies in the Novel* 20 (Summer 1988): 186–205.

Fraser, Celeste. "Stealing B(l)ack Voices: The Myth of the Black Matriarchy and *The Women of Brewster Place.*" In Gates & Appiah: 90–105.

Frazer, Sir James George. *The Golden Bough.* Abridged ed. Theodor H. Gaster. New York: Criterion, 1959.

Friedman, Ellen G., and Miriam Fuchs (eds.). Introduction to *Breaking the Sequence: Women's Experimental Fiction.* Princeton: Princeton University Press, 1989: 3–55.

Frye, Northrop. *Anatomy of Criticism.* Princeton: Princeton University Press, 1957.

———. "New Directions from Old." In *Myth and Mythmaking.* Ed. Henry A. Murray. Boston: Beacon, 1960: 115–31.

———. "The Nature of Satire." In *Satire: Theory and Practice.* Ed. Charles A. Allen and George D. Stephens. Belmont, CA: Wadsworth, 1964: 15–30.

———. *Spiritus Mundi: Essays on Literature.* Bloomington: Indiana University Press, 1976.

———. *Words With Power.* San Diego: Harcourt Brace Jovanovich, 1990.

Fuller, Margaret. "A Short Essay on Critics." In *The Heath Anthology of American Literature.* Vol. 1. 2nd ed. Ed. Paul Lauter et al. Lexington, MA: Heath, 1994: 1616–20.

Fuss, Diana. *Essentially Speaking.* New York: Routledge, 1989.

Gates, Henry Louis, Jr. *Figures in Black: Words, Signs & the "Racial Self."* New York: Oxford University Press, 1987.

——— (ed.). *"Race," Writing and Difference.* Chicago: University of Chicago Press, 1986.

——— (ed.). *Reading Black, Reading Feminist.* New York: Meridian, 1990.

———. *The Signifying Monkey: A Theory of Afro-American Literature.* New York: Oxford University Press, 1988.

Gates, Henry Louis, Jr., and K. A. Appiah (eds.). Preface to *Gloria Naylor: Critical Perspectives Past and Present.* New York: Amistad, 1993.

Gilbert, Sandra M., and Susan Gubar. *The Madwoman in the Attic: The Woman Writer and the Nineteenth-Century Imagination*. New Haven: Yale University Press, 1979.

Gilligan, Carol. *In a Different Voice*. Cambridge: Harvard University Press, 1982.

Giobbi, Giuliana. "Sisters Beware of Sisters: Sisterhood as a Literary Motif in Jane Austen, A. S. Byatt and I. Bossi Fedrigotti." *Journal of European Studies* 22/3:87 (September 1992): 251–59.

Gottlieb, Anne. "Women Together." *New York Times Book Review* (22 August 1982): 11, 25.

Gould, Eric. *Mythical Intentions in Modern Literature*. Princeton: Princeton University Press, 1981.

Govan, Sandra U. "Connections, Links, and Extended Networks: Patterns in Octavia Butler's Science Fiction." *Black American Literary Forum* (Summer 1984): 82–87.

———. "Homage to Tradition: Octavia Butler Renovates the Historical Novel." *MELUS* (Spring/Summer 1986): 79–96.

Graves, Robert. *The White Goddess*. New York: Farrar, Straus & Giroux, 1948.

———. *The Greek Myths*. 2 vols. New York: Penguin, 1960.

Griffin, Susan. *Woman and Nature: The Roaring Inside Her*. New York: Harper & Row, 1978.

Hall, Nor. *The Moon & The Virgin: Reflections on the Archetypal Feminine*. New York: Harper & Row, 1980.

Hamilton, Edith. *Mythology*. New York: New American Library, 1969.

Hassan, Ihab H. *Radical Innocence*. Princeton: Princeton University Press, 1961.

———. *The Postmodern Turn: Essays in Postmodern Theory and Culture*. Columbus: Ohio State University Press, 1987.

Hawthorne, Nathaniel. "The Custom House" and *The Scarlet Letter: A Romance*. In *The Heath Anthology of American Literature*. Vol. 1. 2nd ed. Ed. Paul Lauter et al. Lexington, MA: Heath, 1994: 2178–315.

Heilbrun, Carolyn G. *Reinventing Womanhood*. New York: Norton, 1979.

Hine, Darlene Clark. *Black Women in America: An Historical Encyclopedia*. Brooklyn: Carlson, 1993.

Hite, Molly. "Romance, Marginality, and Matrilineage: *The Color Purple* and *Their Eyes Were Watching God*." In *Reading Black, Reading Feminist*. Ed. Henry Louis Gates, Jr. New York: Oxford University Press, 1990: 431–54.

Holloway, Karla F. C. "Revision & (Re)membrance: A Theory of Literary Structures in Literature by African American Women Writers." *Black American Literary Forum* 24:4 (Winter 1990): 617–31.

Houghton, Walter E. *The Victorian Frame of Mind, 1830 to 1870*. New Haven: Yale University Press, 1957.

Hulbert, Ann. "The Great Ventriloquist." Rev. of *Possession*. *The New Republic* 204:1 & 2 (7 & 14 January 1991): 47–49.

Hull, Gloria T. "What It Is I Think She's Doing Anyhow." In *Conjuring*. Ed. Marjorie Pryse and Hortense Spillers. Bloomington: Indiana University Press, 1985: 216–31.

Humm, Maggie. *Border Traffic: Strategies of Contemporary Women Writers*. Manchester: Manchester University Press, 1991.

Isaacs, Neil. *Eudora Welty*. Southern Writers Series 8. Austin, TX: Steck-Vaughn, 1969.

Jackson, Jerome. "Question & Answer: Sci-Fi Tales from Octavia E. Butler." *Crisis* 1:3 (1 April 1994): 4–6.

Jacobs, Harriet [Linda Brent]. *Incidents in the Life of a Slave Girl*. Ed. L. Maria Child. 1861; Ed. and intro. Jean Fagan Yellin. Cambridge, MA: Harvard University Press, 1987.

James, Henry. *The Art of the Novel*. New York: Scribner, 1962.

Jefferson, Thomas. From "Query XVII: Religion" in *Notes on the State of Virginia*. In *The Heath Anthology of American Literature*. Vol. 1. 2nd ed. Ed. Paul Lauter et al. Lexington, MA: Heath, 1994: 906–8.

Jenkyns, Richard. "Disinterring Buried Lives." *Times Literary Supplement* (2 March 1990): 213–14.

Johnson, Charles. *Being & Race: Black Writing Since 1970*. Bloomington: Indiana University Press, 1988.

Jones, Gayl. *Liberating Voices: Oral Tradition in African American Literature*. Cambridge: Harvard University Press, 1991.

Jung, C. J. *The Archetypes and the Collective Unconscious*. 2nd ed. Tr. R. F. C. Hull. Princeton, NJ: Princeton University Press, 1969.

———. "On the Psychology of the Trickster Figure." In Paul Radin, *The Trickster: A Study in American Indian Mythology*. New York: Schocken, 1972: 195–211.

———. *The Undiscovered Self*. Tr. R. F. C. Hull. New York: New American Library, 1957, 1958.

Kane, Sean. *Wisdom of the Mythtellers*. Peterborough, Ontario: Broadview Press, 1994.

Kaplan, Carey, and Ellen Cronan Rose. Introduction to *Doris Lessing: The Alchemy of Survival*. Ed. Carey Kaplan and Ellen Cronan Rose. Athens: Ohio University Press, 1988: 3–41.

Kaplan, Sydney Janet. "Passionate Portrayal of Things to Come: Doris Lessing's Recent Fiction." In *Twentieth-Century Women Novelists*. Ed. Thomas F. Staley. Totowa, NJ: Barnes & Noble, 1982: 1–16.

Kelley, Margot Anne. "'Damballah is the First Law of Thermodynamics': Modes of Access to Toni Cade Bambara's *The Salt Eaters*." *African American Review* 27 (1993): 479–93.

Kenan, Randall. "An Interview with Octavia E. Butler." *Callaloo* 142 (1991): 495–504.

Kenyon, Olga. *Writing Women: Contemporary Women Novelists*. London: Pluto Press, 1991.

———. *Women Novelists Today*. Brighton: Harvester, 1988.

Kim, Young Yun. *Communication and Cross-cultural Adaptation: An Integrative Theory*. Philadelphia: Multilingual Matters, Ltd., 1988.

Kingston, Maxine Hong. "Cultural Mis-Readings by American Reviewers." In *Asian and Western Writers in Dialogue: New Cultural Identities*. Ed. Guy Amirthanayagam. London: Macmillan, 1982: 57.

———. "Imagined Life." In *Women's Voices: Visions and Perspectives*. Ed. Pat C. Hoy II, Esther H. Schor, and Robert DiYanni. New York: McGraw-Hill, 1990: 137–44.

———. "Personal Statement." In *Approaches to Teaching Kingston's* The Woman Warrior. Ed. Shirley Geok-lin. New York: Modern Language Association, 1991: 24.

———. *The Woman Warrior*. Vintage ed. New York: Random House, 1977.

Kluckhohn, Clyde. "Recurrent Themes in Myth and Mythmaking." In *Myth and Mythmaking*. Ed. Henry A. Murray. Boston: Beacon, 1968: 46–60.

Kolbenschlag, Madonna. *Kiss Sleeping Beauty Good-Bye: Breaking the Spell of Feminine Myths and Models*. New York: Doubleday, 1979.

Kraditor, Aileen S., ed. *Up From the Pedestal: Selected Writings in the History of American Feminism.* New York: Quadrangle Books/New York Times Books, 1968.

Kroeber, A[lfred] L[ouis]. *More Mohave Myths.* Berkeley: University of California Press, 1972.

Lauter, Estella. *Women as Mythmakers: Poetry and Visual Art by 20th Century Women.* Bloomington: Indiana University Press, 1984.

Lavoisier, Antoine. *Traité Elémentaire de Chimie.* Tr. Robert Kerr. 5th Edinburgh ed. Vol. 1 [Microfiche]. 1789; New York: D. & G. Bruce, 1806.

Lee, Robert G. "*The Woman Warrior* as an Invention in Asian American Historiography." In *Approaches to Teaching Kingston's* The Woman Warrior. Ed. Shirley Geok-lin Lim. New York: Modern Language Association, 1991: 59.

LeGuin, Ursula K. "American SF and the Other." In *The Language of the Night.* Ed. Susan Wood. New York: G. P. Putnam's Sons, 1979: 97–100.

———. *The Left Hand of Darkness.* New York: Walker, 1969.

Lessing, Doris. *Documents Relating to the Sentimental Agents in the Volyen Empire. Canopus in Argos* series. New York: Alfred A. Knopf, 1983.

———. *The Making of the Representative of Planet 8. Canopus in Argos* series. New York: Alfred A. Knopf, 1982.

———. *The Marriages Between Zones Three, Four and Five. Canopus in Argos* series. New York: Random Vintage, 1980.

———. *Re: Colonized Planet 5, Shikasta. Canopus in Argos* series. New York: Random Vintage, 1979.

———. *The Sirian Experiments. Canopus in Argos* series. New York: Alfred A. Knopf, 1980.

———. *A Small Personal Voice.* Ed. Paul Schlueter. New York, Alfred A. Knopf, 1974.

Levy, Helen F. "Lead On With Light." In Gates & Appiah: 263–84.

Ling, Amy. *Between Worlds: Women Writers of Chinese Ancestry.* New York: Pergamon Press, 1990.

Louis, Frances D. "Sci-fi Writer Goes Where Few Have Gone Before." *Emerge* (June 1994): 65–66.

Lurie, Alison. "Bad Housekeeping." *New York Review of Books* 32:20 (19 December 1985): 8–10.

Maitree, Doreen. *Literature and Possible Worlds.* London: Middlesex Polytechnic/Pembridge Press, 1983.

Matus, Jill L. "Dreams, Deferral and Closure in *The Women of Brewster Place.*" In Gates & Appiah: 126–39.

McHale, Brian. *Postmodernist Fiction.* New York: Methuen, 1987.

Mellard, James M. *Doing Tropology: Analysis of Narrative Discourse.* Urbana: University of Illinois Press, 1980.

———. *The Exploded Form: The Modernist Novel in America.* Urbana: University of Illinois Press, 1980.

Merchant, Carolyn. *The Death of Nature: Women, Ecology, and the Scientific Revolution.* San Francisco: Harper & Row, 1979.

Merleau-Ponty, Maurice. *Sense and Non-Sense.* Tr. Hubert L. and Patricia Allen Dreyfus. Evanston, IL: Northwestern University Press, 1964.

Miles, Rosalind. *The Female Form: Women Writers and the Conquest of the Novel.* London: Routledge & Kegan Paul, 1987.

Moers, Ellen. *Literary Women.* Garden City, NY: Doubleday, 1976.

Monaghan, Patricia. *The Book of Goddesses and Heroines*. New York: Dutton, 1981.

Morgan, Robin. "Chile: Preface." In *Sisterhood Is Global*. Ed. Robin Morgan. New York: Doubleday, 1984: 135–38.

Morrison, Toni. *Beloved*. New York: Alfred A. Knopf, 1987.

———. *Playing in the Dark: Whiteness and the Literary Imagination*. New York: Random House, 1992.

Mullett, G. M. *Spider Woman Stories*. Tucson: University of Arizona Press, 1979.

Murray, Henry A. (ed.). Introduction to *Myth and Mythmaking*. Boston: Beacon, 1960: 9–17.

Murray, Janet Horowitz. *Strong-Minded Women and Other Lost Voices from Nineteenth-Century England*. New York: Pantheon, 1982.

Musil, Caryn McTighe. "A. S. Byatt." *British Novelists Since 1960. Dictionary of Literary Biography*. Vol. 14. Detroit: Gale, 1983: 194–205.

Nash, Christopher. *World-Games: The Tradition of Anti-Realist Revolt*. London: Methuen, 1987.

Naylor, Gloria. *The Women of Brewster Place*. New York: Penguin, 1983.

———. "The Women of Brewster Place." *Ebony* 41 (March 1989): 123.

Naylor, Gloria, and Toni Morrison. "A Conversation." *The Southern Review* 21:3–4 (1985): 567–92.

Nin, Anais. *The Novel of the Future*. New York: Collier, 1968.

Oakleaf, Zoe D. "Ozark Mountain and European White Witches." In *Black Folk Medicine: The Therapeutic Significance of Faith and Trust*. Ed. Wilbur H. Watson. New Brunswick, NJ: Transaction Books, 1984: 71–86.

Page, Philip. "Circularity in Toni Morrison's *Beloved*." *African American Review* 26:1 (Spring 1992): 31–39.

Pagels, Heinz R. *The Cosmic Code: Quantum Physics as the Language of Nature*. New York: Simon & Schuster, 1982.

Parini, Jay. "Unearthing the Secret Lover." *New York Times Book Review* (21 October 1990): 9, 11.

Patai, Raphael. *The Hebrew Goddess*. New York: KTAV, 1967.

Pearlman, Mickey (ed.). *American Women Writing Fiction: Memory, Identity, Family, Space*. Lexington: University Press of Kentucky, 1989.

Pearson, Carol, and Katherine Pope. *The Female Hero in American and British Literature*. New York: R. R. Bowker, 1981.

Perrakis, Phyllis Sternberg. "The Marriage of Inner and Outer Space in Doris Lessing's *Shikasta*." *Science-Fiction Studies* 17:2 (July 1990): 221–38.

———. "Sufism, Jung and the Myth of Kore: Revisionist Politics in Lessing's *Marriages*." *Mosaic* 25:3 (1992): 99–120.

Petry, Ann. *The Street*. 1946; reprinted Boston: Houghton Mifflin, 1991.

Pickering, Jean. *Understanding Doris Lessing*. Columbia, SC: University of South Carolina Press, 1986.

Piercy, Marge. *Woman on the Edge of Time*. New York: Fawcett, 1976.

Plant, Judith (ed.). *Healing the Wounds: The Promise of Ecofeminism*. Philadelphia: New Society, 1989.

Postlethwaite, Diana. *Making It Whole: A Victorian Circle and the Shape of Their World*. Columbus: Ohio State University Press, 1984.

Pratt, Annis, et al. *Archetypal Patterns in Women's Fiction*. Bloomington: Indiana University Press, 1981.

Pryse, Marjorie, and Hortense Spillers (eds.). *Conjuring: Black Women, Fiction, and Literary Tradition.* Bloomington: Indiana University Press, 1985.

Purley, Anthony F. "Keres Pueblo Concepts of Deity." *American Culture and Research Journal* 1 (1974): 29–32.

Radhakrishnan, S. (ed.). *The Bhagavadgita.* New York: Harper & Row, 1973.

Radin, Paul. *The Trickster: A Study in American Indian Mythology.* 1956. New York: Schocken, 1972.

Rank, Otto. *The Myth of the Birth of the Hero and Other Writings.* Ed. Philip Freund. New York: Vintage, 1964.

Reckley, Ralph, Jr. *20th Century Black American Women in Print.* Ed. Lola E. Jones. Acton, MA: Copley, 1991.

Rifkind, Donna. "Victorians' Secrets." Rev. of *Possession. The New Criterion* 9:6 (February 1991): 77–80.

Rigney, Barbara Hill. *Lilith's Daughters: Women and Religion in Contemporary Fiction.* Madison: University of Wisconsin Press, 1982.

————. *Madness and Sexual Politics in the Feminist Novel.* Madison: University of Wisconsin Press, 1978.

Roberts, Robin. "The Paradigm of *Frankenstein*: Reading *Canopus in Argos* in the Context of Science Fiction by Women." *Extrapolation* 26:1 (Spring 1985): 16–23.

Rohrlich, Ruby, and Elaine Hoffmann Baruch (eds.). Introduction to *Women in Search of Utopia.* New York: Schocken, 1984.

Rose, Shirley K. "Metaphors and Myths of Cross-Cultural Literacy." *MELUS* 4:1 (Spring 1987): 5–16.

Rosenburg, Ruth. "'You Took a Name That Made You Amiable to the Music': Toni Cade Bambara's *The Salt Eaters.*" *Literary Onomastics Studies* 12 (1985): 165–94.

Rosinsky, Natalie M. *Feminist Futures: Contemporary Women's Speculative Fiction.* Ann Arbor: University of Michigan Research Press, 1984.

Rossetti, Christine. Poetry collected in *The New Oxford Book of Victorian Verse.* Ed. Christopher Richs. Oxford: Oxford University Press, 1987.

Rubin, Louis D., Jr. *The Comic Imagination in American Literature.* New Brunswick, NJ: Rutgers University Press, 1973.

Rubenstein, Roberta. "*The Marriages Between Zones Three, Four, and Five*: Doris Lessing's Alchemical Allegory." In *Critical Essays on Doris Lessing.* Ed. Claire Sprague and Virginia Tiger. Boston: G. K. Hall & Co., 1986: 60–69.

Russell, Sandi. *Render Me My Story: African American Women Writers from Slavery to the Present.* New York: St. Martin's Press, 1990.

Sale, Maggie. "Call and Response as Critical Method: African-American Oral Traditions and *Beloved.*" *African American Review* 26:1 (Spring 1992): 41–51.

Salvaggio, Ruth. "Octavia Butler and the Black S-F Heroine." *Black American Literary Forum* 18:2 (Summer 1984): 78–81.

Saunders, James R. "The Ornamentation of Old Ideas: Naylor's First Three Novels." In Gates & Appiah: 249–62.

Schechner, Richard. "Intercultural Performance." *The Drama Review* 26 (1982): 3–4.

Schlueter, Paul. "Doris Lessing." *British Novelists, 1930–1959. Dictionary of Literary Biography.* Vol. 15. Detroit: Gale, 1983: 274–97.

Shange, Ntozake. *for colored girls who have considered suicide, when the rainbow is enuf.* New York: Macmillan, 1977.

Shinn, Thelma J. "The Fable of Reality: Mythoptics in John Crowley's *Little, Big*." *Extrapolation* 31:1 (Spring 1990): 5–14.

———. "A Fearful Power: Hawthorne's Views on Art and the Artist as Expressed in His Sketches and Short Stories." In *Nathaniel Hawthorne Journal 1978*. Ed. C. E. Frazer Clark, Jr. Detroit: Gale, 1984: 121–136.

———. *Radiant Daughters: Fictional American Women*. Westport, CT: Greenwood, 1986.

———. "The Wise Witches: Black Women Mentors in the Fiction of Octavia E. Butler." In *Conjuring*. Ed. Marjorie Pryse and Hortense Spillers. Bloomington: Indiana University Press, 1985: 203–15.

———. *Worlds Within Women: Myth and Mythmaking in Speculative Fiction by Women*. Westport, CT: Greenwood, 1986.

Showalter, Elaine. "Feminism and Literature." In *Literary Theory Today*. Ed. Peter Collier and Helga Geyer-Ryan. Ithaca, NY: Cornell University Press, 1990: 179–202.

Silko, Leslie Marmon. *Ceremony*. New York: New American Library, 1977.

———. *Storyteller*. New York: Grove Press, 1981.

———. *Almanac of the Dead*. New York: Simon & Schuster, 1991.

Spacks, Patricia M. (ed.). *Contemporary Women Novelists*. Englewood Cliffs, NJ: Prentice-Hall, 1977.

———. *The Female Imagination*. New York: Avon, 1976.

Spencer, Sharon. *Space, Time and Structure in the Modern Novel*. Chicago: Swallow Press, 1971.

Sprague, Claire. *Rereading Doris Lessing: Narrative Patterns of Doubling and Repetition*. Chapel Hill: University of North Carolina Press, 1987.

Sprague, Claire, and Virginia Tiger. *Critical Essays on Doris Lessing*. Boston: G. K. Hall & Co., 1986.

Spretnak, Charlene. *Lost Goddesses of Early Greece*. Boston: Beacon, 1978.

Springer, Christina. "Whose Goddesses Are They?" *New Directions for Women* (July/August 1990): 4.

Stableford, Brian. "Is There No Balm in Gilead? The Woeful Prophecies of *The Handmaid's Tale*." *Foundation* 39 (Spring 1987): 97–100.

Stanford, Ann Folwell. "Mechanisms of Disease: African-American Women Writers, Social Pathologies, and the Limits of Medicine." *NWSA Journal* 6:1 (Spring 1994): 28–47.

Starhawk. *Dreaming the Dark*. Boston: Beacon, 1982.

Stewart, R. J. *Celtic Gods, Celtic Goddesses*. London: Blandford, 1990.

Stone, Merlin. *Ancient Mirrors of Womanhood*. Boston: Beacon, 1978.

———. *When God Was a Woman*. New York: Dial Press, 1976.

Suvin, Darko. *Metamorphoses of Science Fiction*. New Haven: Yale University Press, 1979.

Swan, Edith. "Laguna Symbolic Geography and Silko's *Ceremony*." *American Indian Quarterly* 12:3 (Summer 1988): 229–49.

Swinburne, Algernon. Poetry collected in *The New Oxford Book of Victorian Verse*. Ed. Christopher Richs. Oxford: Oxford University Press, 1987.

Talley, Thomas W. *The Negro Traditions*. Knoxville: University of Tennessee Press, 1993.

Tate, Claudia (ed.). *Black Women Writers at Work*. New York: Continuum, 1983.

Thrall, William Flint, and Addison Hibbard. *A Handbook to Literature*. Revised and enlarged by C. Hugh Holman. New York: Odyssey Press, 1960.

Tiger, Virginia. "Candid Shot: Lessing in New York City, April 1 and 2, 1984." In *Critical Essays on Doris Lessing*. Ed. Claire Sprague and Virginia Tiger. Boston: G. K. Hall & Co., 1986: 221–23.

Toomer, Jean. *Cane*. Intro. Arna Bontemps. 1923. New York: Harper & Row, 1969.

Traylor, Eleanor W. "Music as Theme: The Jazz Mode in the Works of Toni Cade Bambara." In *Black Women Writers (1950–1980): A Critical Evaluation*. Ed. Mari Evans. New York: Anchor Press, 1984: 58–70.

Truth, Sojourner. "Reminiscences by Frances D. Gage of Sojourner Truth, for May 28–29, 1851." In *The Heath Anthology of American Literature*. Vol. 1. 2nd ed. Ed. Paul Lauter et al. Lexington, MA: Heath, 1994: 1959–61.

Vickery, John B. (ed.). *Myth and Literature: Contemporary Theory and Practice*. Lincoln: University of Nebraska Press, 1966.

———. *Myths and Texts: Strategies of Incorporation and Displacement*. Baton Rouge: Louisiana State University Press, 1966.

Wagenknecht, Edward. "The Novel." *Collier's Encyclopedia*. New York: Macmillan, 1974: 697–709.

Walford, George. *Angles on Anarchism*. London: Calabria Press, 1991.

———. *Beyond Politics: An Outline of Systematic Ideology*. London: Calabria Press, 1990.

———. "Meet S. I." *Ideological Commentary* 54 (Winter 1991): 2.

Walker, Alice. "Anything We Love Can Be Saved." In *Zora! Zora Neale Hurston, A Woman and Her Community*. Ed. N. Y. Nathiri. Orlando, FL: Sentinel Communication, Co., 1991.

———. "Everyday Use." *In Love and Trouble: Stories of Black Women*. New York: Harcourt Brace Jovanovich, 1973.

———. *The Color Purple*. New York: Harcourt Brace Jovanovich, 1982.

———. *The Temple of My Familiar*. New York: Harcourt Brace Jovanovich, 1989.

Walker, Barbara G. *The Woman's Encyclopedia of Myths and Secrets*. San Francisco: Harper & Row, 1983.

Warrick, Patricia, et al. (eds.). *Science Fiction: Contemporary Mythology*. New York: Harper & Row, 1978.

Watson, Wilbur H. (ed.) *Black Folk Medicine: The Therapeutic Significance of Faith and Trust*. New Brunswick, NJ: Transaction Books, 1984.

Weigle, Marta. *Spiders and Spinsters: Women and Mythology*. Albuquerque: University of New Mexico Press, 1982.

Welty, Eudora. *The Golden Apples*. New York: Harcourt, Brace & World, 1949.

———. *One Writer's Beginnings*. Cambridge: Harvard University Press, 1984.

Whittaker, Ruth. *Doris Lessing*. London: Macmillan, 1988.

Willard, Nancy. *Things Invisible to See*. New York: Bantam, 1986.

Williams, Peter Morton. "An Outline of the Cosmology and Cult Organization of the Oyo Yoruba." In *Peoples and Cultures of Africa*. Ed. Elliott P. Skinner. Garden City, NY: Doubleday/Natural History Press, 1973: 654 ff.

Willis, Susan. "Problematizing the Individual: Toni Cade Bambara's Stories for the Revolution." In *Specifying: Black Women Writing the American Experience*. Madison: University of Wisconsin Press, 1987.

Wittig, Monique. *The Straight Mind and Other Essays*. New York: Harvester Wheat Sheaf, 1992.

Wu, Qing-yun. "A Chinese Reader's Response to Maxine Hong Kingston's *China Men*." *MELUS* 17:3 (Fall 1991–92): 85–94.

Yeager, Patricia S. "'Because a Fire Was in My Head': Eudora Welty and the Dialogic Imagination." *PMLA* 99:5 (October 1984): 955–74.

Yeats, William Butler. *The Collected Poems*. New York: Macmillan, 1968.

———. *A Vision*. New York: Collier Books, 1966.

Young, David, and Keith Hollaman (eds.). *Magical Realist Fiction*. New York: Longman, 1984.

Young, Michael. *The Metronomic Society*. London: Thames & Hudson, 1988.

Zukav, Gary. *The Dancing Wu Li Masters: An Overview of the New Physics*. New York: William Morrow, 1979.

Zuni. "Talk Concerning the First Beginning." In *The Heath Anthology of American Literature*. Vol. 1. 2nd ed. Ed. Paul Lauter et al. Lexington, MA: Heath, 1994: 27–41.

Index

virgin, 22, 23, 25, 121, 152; within,
74, 117; in Allende, 93–94; in
Atwood, 43–44; in Bambara, 120,
121; in Butler, 77–84; in Lessing,
61, 62, 65, 68; in Naylor, 17; in
Silko, 139–45; in Welty, 20–23,
25–26, 30, 32, 74. *See also* Myth;
Nature, as Goddess
The Golden Apples. See Welty, Eudora
The Golden Bough. See Frazer, Sir
James George
Gottlieb, Anne, 20
Govan, Sandra U., 74, 79
Graves, Robert, 23, 24, 111, 113
The Greek Myths, 23

The Handmaid's Tale. See Atwood,
Margaret
Hassan, Ihab H., 25
Hawthorne, Nathaniel, 4, 5, 6, 81, 102,
104
Hellman, Lillian, 42
The House of the Spirits. See Allende,
Isabel
Hull, Gloria T., 121

Ideological Commentary, 60
Ideology, 17, 71, 82, 90, 98, 117, 151;
British, 15; Christian, 47; conflicting, 142; crumbling, 154; cultural/
social, 60, 132, 133, 154; dominant,
87–88; dualistic, 38, 65, 74, 89, 119,
146, 150; eccentric, 146; ecological,
138, 145; Euro American, 142;
gynocratic, 145; hierarchical, 38, 65,
146, 150; of oppression, 84;
patriarchal, 34, 37–38, 47, 55, 89,
94–95, 98; systematic, 60–68;
universal, 65, 92; Western, 66, 96,
122. *See also* Domination; Expediency; Precision; *Theoria*
Isaacs, Neil, 20, 25

Jacobs, Harriet, 43, 83
James, Henry, 6, 74
Jefferson, Thomas, 139
Jenkyns, Richard, 105
Jung, C. J., 59–62, 64, 67, 68; on
trickster, 75–76, 78, 84, 85

Kane, Sean, 16
Kelley, Margot Anne, 121
Kim, Young Yun, 142, 144
Kindred, 39, 128; female, 73, 78, 84; in
Butler, 73, 76–84
Kindred. See Butler, Octavia E.
Kingston, Maxine Hong, 127–35, 137,
138, 143, 146; "Cultural Mis-
Readings by American Reviewers,"
127; "Imagined Life," 103, 128, 129;
The Woman Warrior, 11, 12, 16,
103, 129–35, 153, 154
Kluckhohn, Clyde, 128
Kraditor, Aileen S., 50
Kroeber, A[lfred] L[ouis], 140

Lee, Robert G., 127
The Left Hand of Darkness, 37, 114
LeGuin, Ursula K., 10, 37, 114
Lessing, Doris, 11, 53–70, 71, 78, 87,
151; *Documents Relating to the
Sentimental Agents of the Volyen
Empire*, 58; *The Making of the
Representative for Planet 8*, 67; *The
Marriages Between Zones Three,
Four, and Five*, 56–70, 133, 152;
Re: Colonized Planet 5, Shikasta,
54–56, 61–62, 65–66, 69–70, 153;
The Sirian Experiments, 54, 55, 57,
58, 66; *A Small Personal Voice*, 53,
58. *See also* Canopus; *Canopus in
Argos* series; Necessity; Purpose;
Sirius
Ling, Amy, 119
Loa, 120. *See also* Ghost; Spirit
Louis, Frances D., 83
Love, 71, 72, 114, 117, 146, 149, 152,
154; communal, 73, 78, 120, 123,
146; in Allende, 90, 93, 97, 98; in
Butler, 76–84; in Byatt, 103, 106–8,
110–12; in Lessing, 44, 50, 54–56

The Man of La Mancha, 5
Marginality, 3, 10, 11, 15, 109, 111,
128; double, 10, 11, 30, 31, 73, 75,
82, 156
Marshall, Paule, 119
Matriarchy, 34
Matus, Jill L., 37

About the Author

THELMA J. SHINN is Professor of English and Women's Studies at Arizona State University. She has published in such journals as *Contemporary Literature, Explorations in Ethnic Studies, Nathaniel Hawthorne Journal, Literature and Psychology,* and *Modern Drama.* She is the author of *Radiant Daughters: Fictional American Women* (Greenwood, 1986) and *Worlds Within Women: Myth and Mythmaking in Fantastic Literature by Women* (Greenwood, 1986).

ISBN 0-313-29676-6

90000>

EAN

9 780313 296765

HARDCOVER BAR CODE